EX AUDITU

An International Journal for the Theological Interpretation of Scripture

Volume 23   2007

Ex Auditu is published annually by Wipf & Stock Publishers, 199 West 8th Avenue, Eugene, Oregon 97401, U.S.A.

Subscriptions

    Individuals:
        U.S.A. and all other countries (in U.S. funds) - $20.00
        Students - $12.00

    Institutions:
        U.S.A. and all other countries (in U.S. funds) - $30.00

This periodical is indexed in the ATLA Religion Database, published by the American Theological Library Association, 300 S. Wacker Dr., Suite 2100, Chicago, IL 60606, Email: atla@atla.com, WWW: http://www.atla.com/; *Internationale Zeitschriftenshau für Bibelwissenschaft*; *Religious and Theological Abstracts*; and *Old Testament Abstracts*.

Please address all subscription correspondence and change of address information to *Wipf & Stock Publishers*.

©2007 by Wipf & Stock Publishers
ISSN 0883-0053

EX AUDITU

An International Journal for the Theological Interpretation of Scripture

Klyne R. Snodgrass, *Editor*
Stephen Chester, *Associate Editor*
D. Christopher Spinks, *Associate Editor*

North Park Theological Seminary
3225 West Foster Avenue
Chicago, Illinois 60625-4987
USA

Tel. (773) 244-6243
Fax: (773) 244-6244
email: ksnodgrass@northpark.edu
Web site: http://wipfandstock.com/journals/ex_auditu

EDITORIAL BOARD

Terence E. Fretheim, *Luther Seminary, St. Paul, MN*
Richard B. Hays, *The Divinity School, Duke University, Durham, NC*
John E. Phelan, Jr., *President of North Park Theological Seminary, Chicago, IL*
Jon R. Stock, *Wipf & Stock Publishers, Eugene, OR*
Miroslav Volf, *Yale Divinity School, New Haven, CT*
John Wipf, *Wipf & Stock Publishers, Eugene, OR*

ADVERTISING: If you are interested in advertising in Ex Auditu, please contact James Stock (james@wipfandstock.com).

THE EDITORIAL BOARD MEMBERS AND CONSULTANTS represent various disciplines and denominations. Theological Interpretation of Scripture is a task to be taken seriously by scholars who are committed to the Christian faith and tradition. However, as one editorial consultant stated: "let people gradually get used to the idea that a sane hermeneutics is both oriented in advance toward agreement/consent and is simultaneously exigent, discriminating, critical."

EDITORIAL CONSULTANTS

RICHARD BAUCKHAM
University of St. Andrews
St. Andrews, Scotland

M. DANIEL CARROLL R.
Denver Seminary
Denver, Colorado

JAN DU RAND
Rand Afrikaans University Johannesburg,
South Africa

WILLIE JENNINGS
The Divinity School
Duke University
Durham, N. Carolina

ROBERT JOHNSTON
Fuller Theological Seminary
Pasadena, California

R. WALTER L. MOBERLY
University of Durham
Durham, England

KATHLEEN M. O'CONNOR
Columbia Theological Seminary
Decatur, Georgia

IAIN PROVAN
Regent College
Vancouver, B.C.

GRAHAM STANTON
University of Cambridge
Cambridge, England

ANTHONY THISELTON
University of Nottingham
Nottingham, England

AUGUSTINE THOMPSON
University of Virginia
Charlottesville, Virginia

MARIANNE MEYE THOMPSON
Fuller Theological Seminary
Pasadena, California

KEVIN J. VANHOOZER
Trinity Evangelical Divinity School
Deerfield, Illinois

GEOFFREY WAINWRIGHT
The Divinity School
Duke University
Durham, N. Carolina

SONDRA WHEELER
Wesley Theological Seminary
Washington, D.C.

WILLIAM H. WILLIMON
Bishop the North Alabama Conference
The United Methodist Church
Birmingham, Alabama

N. T. WRIGHT
Bishop of Durham
Durham, England

TRIBUTE TO
DIKRAN HADIDIAN

The picture on the following page is of Dikran Hadidian. If not for his efforts, the journal *Ex Auditu* would not exist. Dikran loved books, theology, the academic life, and the concerns of the church. He was born in Turkey into a pastor's family and then was raised in Lebanon. His educational journey included the American University of Beirut and the Near East School of Theology, Hartford Seminary Foundation, Harvard University, and Columbia University School of Library Service. Later he served as librarian at Hartford Seminary Foundation and at Pittsburgh Theological Seminary. He was a member of both Studiorum Novi Testamenti Societas and the American Theological Library Association.

Dikran and his wife Jean established Pickwick Press and over the years published a significant number of academic theological works. In his capacity as publisher Dikran brought to reality his dream of a symposium focused on the theological interpretation of Scripture and a journal to publish the papers from the symposium. The symposium and *Ex Auditu* originally were associated with Princeton Theological Seminary but after two years moved to North Park Theological Seminary. Dikran attended all the symposia, and he and Jean personally worked each year to bring out the journal. After many years Pickwick Press and the journal *Ex Auditu* were acquired by the present publishers, Wipf and Stock. The theological community owes a great deal to Dikran and Jean for their foresight and their work. Thanks be to God for the work of Dikran Hadidian.

EX AUDITU

Volume 23 2007

In Memoriam

Dikran Hadidian

CONTENTS

Announcement of the 2008 Symposium	vi
Abbreviations	vii
Introduction *Klyne Snodgrass*	viii
Interpreting the Times *David Tiede*	1
Response to Tiede *Osvaldo Padilla*	18
Christ, Culture, and the Sermon on the Mount Community *Paul Louis Metzger*	22
Response to Metzger *G. Sujin Pak*	47
Discerning the Spirit in Culture: Observations Arising from Reflections on General Revelation *Robert K. Johnston*	52

Response to Johnston
Jim Dekker   70

Propriety and Trespass: The Drama of Eating
Ellen F. Davis   74

Response to Davis
Frank M. Yamada   87

Christian *Communitas* in the *Missio Dei*: Living Faithfully in
the Tension Between Cultural Osmosis and Alienation
Paul De Neui   92

Response to De Neui
Luis R. Rivera   108

The Biblical Theological Contribution of Pandita Ramabai:
A Neglected Pioneer Indian Christian Feminist Theologian
Rajkumar Boaz Johnson   111

Response to Johnson
Amanda Beckenstein Mbuvi   137

Missionary Acts, Things Fall Apart: Modeling Mission in Acts 17:15–34
and a Concern for Dialogue in Chinua Achebe's *Things Fall Apart*
Andrew M. Mbuvi   140

Response to Mbuvi
Velda Love   157

Global Cultural Traffic, Christian Mission, and Biblical Interpretation:
Rereading Luke 10:1–12 Through the Eyes of
an Indian Mission Recipient
Sathianathan Clarke   162

Response to Clarke
Soong-Chan Rah   179

The Reason for Our Engagement with Culture
Osvaldo Padilla   184

Annotated Bibliography on Christianity's Engagement with Culture	188
Presenters and Respondents	203
Ex Auditu – Volumes Available	205

ANNOUNCEMENT OF THE 2008 SYMPOSIUM

North Park Theological Seminary in Chicago, Illinois, is pleased to announce that the twenty-fourth Symposium on the Theological Interpretation of Scripture will take place September 25–27, 2008. The symposium will start at 7:00 p.m. on September 25 in Nyvall Hall and will extend through a Saturday afternoon worship service on September 27. The theme in 2008 will be the Idolatry of Security. The following persons have agreed to make presentations:

Scott Bader-Saye, University of Scranton, Theological Ethics
John Barclay, University of Durham, New Testament
M. Daniel Carroll R., Denver Seminary, Old Testament
Jill Carlson Colwell, Yale University Ph.D. Candidate, Theology
C. Andrew Johnson, Nazarene Theological Seminary, New Testament
Walter Moberly, University of Durham, Old Testament
G. Sujin Pak, Duke Divinity School, History
Ben Witherington III, Asbury Seminary, New Testament
Randall C. Zachman, University of Notre Dame, History

Persons interested in attending the sessions should write before September 1 to:

Ms. Guylla Brown
North Park Theological Seminary
3225 W. Foster Avenue
Chicago, Illinois 60625

Meals may be taken at North Park and assistance can be provided in finding nearby lodging.

ABBREVIATIONS

AB	Anchor Bible
ABD	*Anchor Bible Dictionary*
BBR	*Bulletin for Biblical Research*
Bib	*Biblica*
CBQ	*Catholic Biblical Quarterly*
DJG	*Dictionary of Jesus and the Gospels*
HBT	*Horizons in Biblical Theology*
Int	*Interpretation*
JBL	*Journal of Biblical Literature*
JSNT	*Journal for the Study of the New Testament*
JSNTSup	Journal for the Study of the New Testament: Supplement Series
LW	*Luther's Works*
NIV	New International Version
NRSV	New Revised Standard Version
NTS	*New Testament Studies*
SBL	Society of Biblical Literature
SBLDS	Society of Biblical Literature Dissertation Series
SNTSMS	Society for New Testament Studies Monograph Series
WA	D. Martin Luthers Werke, Kritische Gesamtausgabe. 65 vols. Weimar: Verlag Hermann Böhlausn Nochfolger, 1883-1966.

INTRODUCTION

Søren Kierkegaard presents a parable about a fortress that raises some of the issues involved in Christianity's engagement with culture:

> Imagine a fortress, absolutely impregnable, supplied with provisions for an eternity. Then a new commandant comes. He gets the idea that the right thing to do is to build bridges over the ditches—in order to be able to attack the besiegers. Charming! He transformed the fortress into a village—and the enemy captured it, naturally. So it is with Christianity. They changed the method—and the world conquered, naturally. (*Søren Kierkegaard's Journals and Papers* [7 vols.; ed. and trans. Howard V. Hong and Edna H. Hong; Bloomington, Ind.: Indiana University Press, 1967–1978], 1.227)

Chrisitianity was never an impregnable fortress, and the analogy works only partly, as is always the case with parables. Still, Kierkegaard is correct. Chrisitianity does not have a good record of engaging culture. Some Christians know how to isolate themselves from culture, but that is not a reasonable route. For those of us who seek to engage culture, we are more likely to be taken over by culture than to have the kind of impact we should. The problem of our time is that the church is more likely to mirror the culture perfectly than to transform it.

The degree to which this symposium on Christianity's engagement with culture ended up being about missions was rather surprising. It was also striking how much about culture was merely assumed in the discussion. Admittedly it is difficult for one to see his or her own culture; we just assume our own culture is reality. Furthermore, it became clear in Boaz Johnson's paper that we do not even have clean language with which to carry on the discourse, for our language is already "infected" with a culture that, at least at points, is unbiblical. The problems with Hindu culture and language in Boaz's paper are obvious to us, but our own language has its blind spots and distorts just as easily.

We have the responsibility to evaluate our culture(s), and we cannot abdicate the responsibililty to critique culture, both our own and that of others. Culture is not an adiaphora; at times it may be a help and at times innocuous, but other times it is antithetical to the gospel. In order to evaluate and engage culture, one must to some degree disengage, but what guides reengaging? How does one avoid syncretism when trying to engage? How much does our engagement with culture challenge the scandal of particularity? In engaging culture do we only make Jesus look like us, just as the Old Questers for the historical Jesus did long ago? It is one thing to be transformed into the image of Jesus; it is quite another for Jesus to be transformed into our image.

Thanks is expressed once again to all the presenters and respondents who made a significant investment in the life of North Park. The friendship of these people is a privilege. The authors of papers were given a chance to edit their contributions after the symposium, but the responses are essentially as they were presented. As is obvious, the views expressed are those of the authors and not necessarily those of the journal or of North Park. We also thank all those in attendance for their interest and contribution to the discussions.

A change in the management and production of the journal takes place with this issue. Two associate editors have been appointed: Stephen Chester, who teaches New Testament at North Park Theological Seminary, and Chris Spinks, whose training is in hermeneutics and who will be the primary point person for the journal with his employers at Wipf and Stock. The work of the journal will be significantly enhanced by these two men, and gratitude is expressed to both of them for their willingness to be involved.

As has been the case in recent years, this journal was typeset using the word processor *NotaBene*, and gratitude is expressed to the good people at *NotaBene* for their continued, generous help. Special thanks is expressed to Rebekah Eklund, who proofread the journal, to Chris Nelson and Nathanael Putnam, who among other things prepared the bibliography, and to Guylla Brown from North Park's staff, without whom the symposium would not be possible.

Klyne Snodgrass
The Editor

NEW FROM BRAZOS PRESS

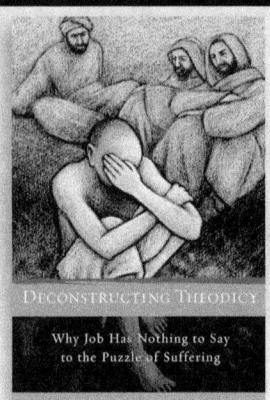
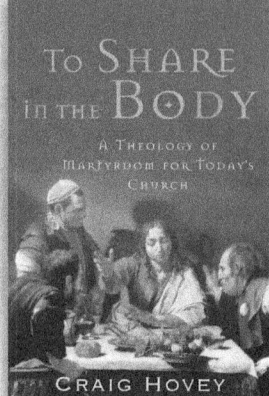

Deconstructing Theodicy
WHY JOB HAS NOTHING TO SAY TO THE PUZZLE OF SUFFERING
David B. Burrell
9781587432224
144 pp. • $19.99p

An ancient commentator called Job a "strange and wonderful book." For many readers, "strange" might do. Though Job has been characterized as an answer to the problem of suffering, for many the book fails to satisfy the longing for answers it supposedly contains. Perhaps that, in fact, is the point of Job—there are no satisfactory arguments for why people suffer. In this compact yet substantial volume, David B. Burrell argues that this is the message of Job. Burrell engages major movements of the book in theological and philosophical reflection. The book also contains an interfaith perspective with the inclusion of a chapter by Islamic scholar A. H. Johns on the reading of the Job figure in the Koran.

To Share in the Body
A THEOLOGY OF MARTYRDOM FOR TODAY'S CHURCH
Craig Hovey
9781587432170
160 pp. • $21.99p

"Hovey's *To Share in the Body* is a profound reflection on Mark's Gospel. These timely and poignant words encourage Christians to think about what it means to be a martyred church. The extraordinary and simple truth of martyrdom is actually a refusal 'to play the martyr' in order to turn the axis of history in your favor. Hovey offers a biblical vision of a non-instrumental martyrdom, which can point, witness, and testify to the truth of Jesus Christ, but can never be used as a tool for social or political change in the church or in the world.... I recommend this remarkable book to any person interested in what it really means to live and to die in the body of Christ."—**C. C. Pecknold**, University of Cambridge

Solomon among the Postmoderns
Peter J. Leithart
9781587432040
176 pp. • $19.99p

"Here is a vivacious account of postmodern culture from a true Renaissance man. With characteristic verve, Leithart deftly narrates the postmodern critique of modernity—without the typical fixation on epistemology and questions of knowledge. But the story doesn't end on the postmodern bandwagon; rather, Leithart pushes further to show that the postmodern critique of idolatry still fails to yield wisdom. In the wake of Derrida and Foucault, we still find ourselves waiting not for Godot or St. Benedict, but Solomon. Amidst the ruins of modernity, this book is an invitation to feast in the temple."—**James K.A. Smith**, Calvin College

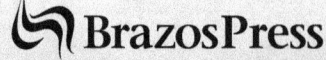

Available at your local bookstore, www.brazospress.com, or by calling 1-800-877-2665
Subscribe to *Border Crossings*, the Brazos monthly electronic newsletter, at www.brazospress.com

INTERPRETING THE TIMES: THE VOCATION OF SCRIPTURE

DAVID L. TIEDE

HEAT AND LIGHT: SUBJECT AND OBJECT

Four decades ago a young African American friend began his remarkable scholarly career at Harvard University. As the teaching fellow in New Testament, I helped induct him into the arcane mysteries of the program, especially as he prepared his first papers for the exhilarating and fearsome doctoral seminar. His lament over the bloodless, analytic method of the seminar stays with me.

"Listen," he declared, "when my Mama makes stew, she peels the potatoes, cuts up the vegetables and the meat, measures in the spices, and puts it all in a pot of water. But that's not stew! This seminar is cutting up all the pieces and thinking it's stew. No, that's just a pot of cold vegetables. You don't get stew until you put the fire in it!"

This is the first time I have been privileged to attend North Park Seminary's Symposium on the Theological Interpretation of Scripture, but I have watched, cheered, and read many of the papers from this venture for years. You were one of the forums that reopened the question of the theological interpretation of Scripture long before it again became fashionable, or even acceptable in some scholarly circles. The theological interpretation of Scripture is itself a venture with fire in it!

Fire is a good metaphor because it has both heat and light. You are right if you hear me welcoming the temperature at least of a living body in our interpretive work. Since North Park bears the mantle of the Evangelical Covenant tradition, we expect and respect the warmth of your piety, and your community is a living body of interpretation into which you have graciously welcomed those of us from other traditions. Sometimes the heat rises in disputes. None of us is dispassionate about our interpretations, especially if our traditions have enough theological vitality to embody an argument.[1] At our best we are contending for the gospel truth. Heat means some things are worthy of passion.

The light counts too! In the first instance, this means that all of us are like the Baptizer pointing to Christ Jesus: "He himself was not the light," declares the prologue to John's Gospel, "but he came to testify to the light. The true light, which enlightens everyone, was coming into the world" (John 1:8–9). In a well-centered Christian tradition like North Park's, the theological interpretation of Scripture is worthy of its claim when it is the light of Christ that illumines the discourse.

Since our topic is "Christianity's Engagement with Culture," we must also make decisions about how we will engage the dominant academic culture of biblical interpretation. It is melodramatic to lament a generation of exclusion of theological questions from the work of the Society of Biblical Literature. It is also immature to cheer that recently the theological camel's nose appears to have gotten under the SBL tent. This symposium displays the respect our faith communities have for academic standards of historical, literary, and social-cultural methods of interpretation. We claim our place in the academy, and we rely on the "light" of the western cultural "Enlightenment" to gain critical insights into the origins and purposes of our Scriptures and Christianity.

The fact that we are engaged together in this deliberation means we have already refused a dichotomy between faith and reason in our theological interpretation of Scripture. We are not preoccupied with fighting the old modernist wars about authority. We use the tool boxes of historical, literary, and social analysis in service of the illumination that has come into the world in the light of Christ Jesus. Sometimes the light of disciplined learning can cool overheated passions.

As we apply our efforts to the theological interpretation of Scripture, we find ourselves engaged in another dynamic, another vital tension. Yes, heat and light, heart and mind, but also subject and object, the witness of Scripture and our interpretation of it. The energy in this tension is compounded because we are dealing with our Scripture. We would have the subject/object dialectic with any text that says something. This is the common hermeneutical circle of approaching a text as the object of our inquiry and then making sense of its enduring witness. When the post-modern critic Stanley Fish asks, *Is there a Text in this Class?*,[2] we not only respond "Yes," but we add, "And the text is Scripture, the script of our faith!"

To say "the text is Scripture" is to identify the object of our study. Our task is the theological interpretation of Christian *Scripture*, not the lives of the saints, not the liturgy, not our faith stories, and not the *Chicago Tribune* or the artifacts of the ancient Near East. We are attending theologically to the collection of writings that became the Bible of the Christian community. Our theological interest is focused on a very distinctive object. We know the Bible deserves to be studied objectively for itself, as the sacred text of our faith communities and for its place in the world.

But when we engage in a symposium on the theological interpretation of Scripture, the Scriptures, individually and collectively as Scripture, are both the *object* and the *subject* of our interpretation. Christian communities read Scripture trusting in the living God. In our theological interpretation of Scripture we expect that the God of Scripture will have an agenda for us and for the world.

Every first year Greek student is tutored in the objective and subjective genitive in translating a phrase like *agapē Christou*. We may speak of the "love of Christ" in terms of our love for Christ Jesus or of the *pistis Christou* as our faith in Christ. But, the phrase "the love of Christ" also announces the evangelical promise of Christ's love for us, and the "faith of Christ" also means Christ's fidelity for us. The subjective genitive reveals we are not the measure of all things. The subject of the gospel verb is always God.

This symposium on the theological interpretation of Scripture is, therefore, alive with the expectation that Scripture will not be a passive object. The witness of Scripture also interprets the world, and we are ultimately intent on knowing the God to whom the Scriptures bear witness. Thus, if many of the terms of our engagement with various cultures are already set by the fact that *Scripture* is the *object* of our theological interpretation, the character of our engagement is even more profoundly marked by the fact that *Scripture* is also a *subject,* in that it is, or that it bears, the living word of God for us. We hope to hear the call of the living God in Christianity's engagement with culture.

THE APOSTOLIC INTERPRETATION OF SCRIPTURE

After eighteen years of administration I have been drawn back into study of the New Testament and Christian origins by two developments that at first seem disparate: the renewal of theological education and the recovery of Christianity's Jewish origins.

The renewal of theological education is both a necessity and a hope. Throughout the United States and Canada profound changes are occurring in the churches and communities of faith. Deeply engrained with the criteria establishing quality in European academic cultures, the seminaries and divinity schools of the Association of Theological Schools in North America are now regularly warned to quit preparing their graduates for churches that no longer exist. Maintaining the parishes of Christendom is no longer adequate to our calling from God. Theological education must prepare the graduates for a new time of God's mission in a world of many cultures and religions, and this mission lies at the front door of every Christian community as well. To provide the leaders the church needs for its twenty-first-century vocation, theological schools must be abbeys, academies, and apostolates. This also means our theological interpretation of Scripture must be alive to interpreting the times of God's work in the world.

The theological school as abbey is a place where novices are inducted into the beliefs and practices of a Christian tradition. Whether monastic, pietist, or social activist, every tradition needs times in a community of shared commitments to protect its treasures and inculcate its convictions. The culture of the abbey is infused with concern for spiritual formation, and the experience of interpretation is marked by dwelling in the tradition's profound resources to nurture its soul. All traditions need times apart, but some specialize in the seminary as abbey, especially when they sense peril.[3] Furthermore, theological interpretation of the Scriptures in the abbey means an exploration of the wisdom each Christian tradition brings to the reading of Scripture. The Bible is the church's book in the abbey, and learners are disciples, dwelling together in the Word of God, drawing from its wells of spiritual refreshment.

The theological school as academy has been the dominant pattern in North America, at least since World War II. The Association of Theological Schools' standards of accreditation were built largely on a shared vision of the good theological school.[4] A half century of raising the academic standards of all accredited ATS schools has yielded faculties that are deeply formed by their doctoral educations in the guilds of their disciplines, and the standards of quality have been consistently calibrated by the faculties' research capacities and critical academic productivity. Deeply influenced by the Academy of the University of Berlin, theological studies drew upon their historical, philosophical, and ethical disciplines to serve the churches of Christendom. The seminary as academy continues to bring historical, philological, and anthropological intelligence to the interpretation of the Christian Scriptures, first distancing these ancient texts from varied pieties, then inviting the reader to ask about the relevance of books written for significantly different times. In the academy the theological interpretation of Scripture is largely a descriptive task, resisting absorption in the enduring meaning of biblical texts to communities of faith.

The seminary as apostolate is shaped by a critical awareness that the NT offers an apostolic interpretation of the faith and Scriptures of Israel. Furthermore, in the twenty-first century when the establishment of Christendom is fading, the interpretive context of contemporary communities of faith needs the insight and inspiration of pre-Christendom Jesus communities. In the seminary as apostolate, the theological interpretation of Scripture is grounded in the conviction that God continues to be at work in the world. God has a mission, and the Scriptures both report how the early Christians lived into the script and require the interpreter to deal with the prophetic and apostolic vocation of the people of God.

Both the seminary as abbey and the seminary as academy can bring proven wisdom and critical understanding to the theological interpretation of Scripture, but this essay is written in the conviction that the interpretive culture of the seminary as apostolate is also necessary to authentic theological interpretation of

Scripture. The broader changes in theological education toward "leadership education" are producing a remarkable range of definitions of leadership, agency, and authority as varied theological traditions take up the educational challenge. Those that identify the leadership needed in terms of the apostolic callings of Christian communities are at the cutting edge of the renewal in theological education to which this essay is pointing.

A second development that has refreshed the theological interpretation of Scripture is the recovery of early Christianity's Jewish origins. Since the discovery of the Qumran library, the past sixty years have marked an era of rediscovery of the complexity of first-century Jewish history. This remarkable light on the past has opened many eyes to the profoundly Jewish character of the entire NT. Many Christian, Jewish, and secular scholars now share the historical judgment that neither "Christianity" nor "Judaism" existed in the first century, at least not in the normative forms they assumed in the second and third centuries of the common era when they increasingly defined one another as heretics.[5]

Put these two pieces together, and a deep question arises: How did the early apostolic movement with its irrepressible hope emerge into the Greco-Roman world of many cultures and religions as one of the two surviving forms of Israel's faith? It is a big question, even a dangerous one. It risks pitting the enclave strategy of the synagogues of Judaism against the boundary-crossing apostolic mission of the followers of Jesus, neglecting the influence both the synagogue and the church continued to have on each other. When the Christian movement eventually became dominantly non-Jewish or "gentile," the NT fell into the hands of people who understood little of the profound claim the early Jesus communities made on the theological interpretation of Israel's Scriptures. Sadly, history demonstrates that when the Christian movement loses Israel's scriptural soul, it becomes self-righteous, anti-Semitic, and violent.

But, how did the messianist form of Israel's faith become apostolic? And what can we learn from that profound adaptation as we again engage a world where Christianity has lost or is losing its standing as the legally or culturally established religion?

While teasing a friend who is an OT scholar, I once said, "It's a good thing someone bothers with the Hebrew Bible. What an intriguing collection of documents from the world of the ancient Near East. Somebody should attend to it." He came right back, "Well, yes, and someone should fuss with the New Testament. After all, it is one of the major commentaries on the Old Testament." We were amused by our silliness. Then I returned to my study and thought, "That's exactly what the New Testament is: the apostolic commentary or interpretation of the Scriptures of Israel in the light of the life, death, and resurrection of Jesus Christ."

So how does that work? Fifty years ago Krister Stendahl broke new ground with *The School of St. Matthew*,[6] recognizing the Matthean engagement in the intra-Jewish debates about the theological interpretation of Israel's Scriptures. Communities of interpretation emerged from the shadows of the past. When Jesus challenged the lawyer, "What is written in the law, how do you read?" in Luke 10:25, he was asking about what united and divided Israel. The Torah, prophets, and writings were the common ground and the battleground. Richard B. Hays and his students have filled in the picture of "the echoes of Scripture" in Paul.[7] And in contrast to previous assumptions about the gentile or even anti-Jewish character of Luke–Acts, the essays in the volume *Jesus and the Heritage of Israel*[8] explore Luke's narrative claim on Israel's scriptural legacy.

Remember, "Christianity" in the social reality we know did not yet exist. Even normative "Judaism" was still in formation. Thus it is anachronistic to mine Luke's narrative in its historical context for direct examples of "Christianity's Engagement with Culture."

Perhaps a more intriguing historical and theological quest is possible. Consider the likelihood that Luke–Acts was written in the time when the Romans had besieged Jerusalem and destroyed the temple. Looking back, the narrator we call the third evangelist is recounting the early history of Jesus and the apostles. How do the stories in the Acts of the Apostles disclose the formation within the Jesus community of Israel's fundamental terms of engagement both with Jewish communities and with the Roman empire?

Even the stories we select affect what we will see. Previous generations, often focused on the history of the ideas, turned to Paul's speech on the Areopagus in Acts 17. If our sense of "culture" has become more broadly aware of arenas of power, politics, and imperial economies, let me suggest we explore Luke's presentation of Paul's final self-defense before the Roman authorities and their Jewish client rulers in Acts 26.

In Luke's formal preface (Luke 1:1–4), the author adapts the conventions of Hellenistic historiography to purposes of writing a "narrative" (Greek: *diēgēsis*) in which the things that have happened mark the "fulfillment" (*peplērophorēmenōn*), probably of the scriptural promises, to make known the "truth" or "assurance" (*asphaleia*) about the things in which the reader has been instructed. Luke–Acts is, therefore, appropriately read 1) as a "narrative" or "story," 2) as a "commentary" or scriptural interpretation, and 3) as a testimony to the truth, indeed a witness to God's engagement in human history.

Acts 26 is lengthy, but its sweep provides a rich example of Luke's apostolic narrative, commentary, and testimony to God's work in human history. Listen to a well-told story, filled with scriptural claims and constructed to testify to the truth of God. Listen for how Luke's literary, scriptural, and social witness display pre-Christianity's engagements with Jewish and Roman culture.

¹Agrippa said to Paul, "You have permission to speak for yourself." Then Paul stretched out his hand and began to defend himself: ²"I consider myself fortunate that it is before you, King Agrippa, I am to make my defense today against all the accusations of the Jews, ³because you are especially familiar with all the customs and controversies of the Jews; therefore I beg of you to listen to me patiently.

⁴"All the Jews know my way of life from my youth, a life spent from the beginning among my own people and in Jerusalem. ⁵They have known for a long time, if they are willing to testify, that I have belonged to the strictest sect of our religion and lived as a Pharisee. ⁶And now I stand here on trial on account of my hope in the promise made by God to our ancestors, ⁷a promise that our twelve tribes hope to attain, as they earnestly worship day and night. It is for this hope, your Excellency, that I am accused by Jews! ⁸Why is it thought incredible by any of you that God raises the dead?

⁹"Indeed, I myself was convinced that I ought to do many things against the name of Jesus of Nazareth. ¹⁰And that is what I did in Jerusalem; with authority received from the chief priests, I not only locked up many of the saints in prison, but I also cast my vote against them when they were being condemned to death. ¹¹By punishing them often in all the synagogues I tried to force them to blaspheme; and since I was so furiously enraged at them, I pursued them even to foreign cities.

¹²"With this in mind, I was traveling to Damascus with the authority and commission of the chief priests, ¹³when at midday along the road, your Excellency, I saw a light from heaven, brighter than the sun, shining around me and my companions. ¹⁴When we had all fallen to the ground, I heard a voice saying to me in the Hebrew language, 'Saul, Saul, why are you persecuting me? It hurts you to kick against the goads.' ¹⁵I asked, 'Who are you, Lord?' The Lord answered, 'I am Jesus whom you are persecuting. ¹⁶But get up and stand on your feet; for I have appeared to you for this purpose, to appoint you to serve and testify to the things in which you have seen me and to those in which I will appear to you. ¹⁷I will rescue you from your people and from the Gentiles—to whom I am sending you ¹⁸to open their eyes so that they may turn from darkness to light and from the power of Satan to God, so that they may receive forgiveness of sins and a place among those who are sanctified by faith in me.'

¹⁹"After that, King Agrippa, I was not disobedient to the heavenly vision, ²⁰but declared first to those in Damascus, then in Jerusalem and throughout the countryside of Judea, and also to the Gentiles, that they should repent and turn to God and do deeds consistent with repentance. ²¹For this reason the Jews seized me in the temple and tried to kill me. ²²To this day I have had help from God, and so I stand here, testifying to both small and great, saying nothing but what the prophets and Moses said would take place: ²³that the Messiah must suffer, and that, by being the first to rise from the dead, he would proclaim light both to our people and to the Gentiles."

²⁴While he was making this defense, Festus exclaimed, "You are out of your mind, Paul! Too much learning is driving you insane!" ²⁵But

Paul said, "I am not out of my mind, most excellent Festus, but I am speaking the sober truth. ²⁶Indeed the king knows about these things, and to him I speak freely; for I am certain that none of these things has escaped his notice, for this was not done in a corner. ²⁷King Agrippa, do you believe the prophets? I know that you believe." ²⁸Agrippa said to Paul, "Are you so quickly persuading me to become a Christian?" ²⁹Paul replied, "Whether quickly or not, I pray to God that not only you but also all who are listening to me today might become such as I am—except for these chains."

³⁰Then the king got up, and with him the governor and Bernice and those who had been seated with them; ³¹and as they were leaving, they said to one another, "This man is doing nothing to deserve death or imprisonment." ³²Agrippa said to Festus, "This man could have been set free if he had not appealed to the emperor." (Acts 26:1–32)

THE STORY OF PAUL'S TRIAL

It is a great story. Let me make five observations on Luke's narrative strategies.

First, in the book of Acts, the author dealt more extensively with fewer episodes than in the Gospel according to Luke. The Cornelius story takes almost two full chapters (Acts 10–11), and Acts 26:9–18 includes the third account of Paul's call (see also 9:1–22; 22:3–21). Paul's arrest and trial scenes extend over six chapters (Acts 21–26). The very length of this story signals the confident public witness of the apostolic movement to Israel's Messiah in the midst of an oppressive and indifferent Roman order.

Second, Luke's formal prologues, especially in the Gospel (Luke 1:1–4) demonstrate his mastery of the rhetorical conventions of Hellenistic historiography. The speeches in Acts again exhibit the historian's art of constructing plausible speeches for leading figures at critical moments in the story. A previous generation worried whether Paul was quoted precisely. Now we are grateful Paul had such a good speechwriter. The address fits Luke's Paul and defines the context with theological wisdom.

Third, these court appearances are depicted as grandiose. A full trial scene was first staged in Acts 24 before the high priest Ananias, with an attorney named Tertullus bringing charges to the previous Roman procurator named Felix. That encounter ended without any clear judgment against Paul. It was followed by Paul's engagement with Felix's Jewish wife Drusilla, speaking about "justice, self-control, and the coming judgment." Luke reports that Felix was frightened by Paul's counsel and then gives two reasons for keeping Paul in confinement for two more years: Felix was looking for a bribe and he "wanted to grant the Jews a favor" (24:26–27). Acts 25:23 then reports that when Paul was summoned before Festus, King Agrippa II and his sister Bernice "came with great pomp, and they entered the audience hall with the military tribunes and the prominent men of the city."

Apart from the question of whether the historical Paul actually attracted such high level attention, the grandiosity fits with the court practices of the Roman occupation. The Jewish historian Josephus restages similar court scenes in his Jewish histories, providing gossipy details about who attended the affair and placing local personalities and intrigues on the grand imperial stage.[9] The trial and death of Jesus was also a lengthy narrative in Luke's Gospel, but Luke's Paul engages this occasion differently from Jesus, or even from Stephen in his prophetic martyrdom. Here the grand scene is the backdrop for the play, but the present is an occasion for scriptural interpretation. Luke's Paul is fulfilling the vocation he received from the risen Lord, "testifying to both small and great, saying nothing but what the prophets and Moses said would take place" (26:22).

Fourth, Luke depicts the Apostle as mastering the engagement with Roman rulers and Jewish kings who were culturally elite and politically complicated. When he earlier addressed the philosophers on Mars Hill in Acts 17, they called Paul a "babbler" or *spermologos* in an ironic insult compared to the true philosopher in whom the seminal reason or *spermatikos logos* dwells. Festus tells him he is "out of his mind" (*mainē*), which can also describe people in divine ecstasy, but Paul affirms he is speaking words of truth and philosophic wisdom (*aletheia kai sophrosunē*). The script being played out in the trial encounters was prophetically defined in Luke 21 by Jesus: "They will arrest you and persecute you, they will hand you over to synagogues and prisons, and you will be brought before kings and governors because of my name. This will give you an opportunity to testify" (Luke 21:12–13).

Fifth, the narrative staging of this episode ostensibly portrays Paul's encounter with the imperial powers. What is surprising, however, is how little difference the realities of Roman authority make to the outcome of the trial. Once again it all ends inconclusively. This time the charges of insurrection (see 21:31–38; 23:29; 24:5–6; 25:8, 18) are not even raised. The Romans are convinced that Paul is not a threat to the Empire (see 25:8), but now the procurator Festus needs to sort out the problem before Paul goes to Rome: "I have brought him before all of you, and especially before you, King Agrippa, so that, after we have examined him, I may have something to write—for it seems unreasonable to send a prisoner without indicating the charges against him" (25:26–27).

The plot is not being driven by Roman authority. The Sovereign Majesty to be feared in history is not *Lord Caesar* before whose court Paul has appealed to stand (see 25:10–12, 21, 25–26). The *Lord* who is writing the script is known to Paul, having stood near him by night in prison and said, "Keep up your courage! For just as you have testified for me in Jerusalem, so you *must* bear witness also in Rome" (23:11).[10] This is the Lord who gave Paul the apostolic commission that has produced such conflict, as he tells Agrippa and the entourage, "I was not disobedient to the heavenly vision" (26:19).

The terms of Paul's engagement with the apparently dominant culture are thus "theological" in the first order sense. Paul is an apostolic agent[11] in God's mission. In their pomp and grandiosity, the agents of the Roman order are befuddled, attempting to make sense of this trial according to the standards of Roman jurisprudence or control. Paul's witness will only be recognized as "true and sensible" when it is clear what God is up to in the story. Paul's argument turns on his theological interpretation of Scripture.

THE SCRIPTURAL SUBSTANCE OF PAUL'S TESTIMONY

If the Roman authorities who are the ostensible audience for this speech are evidently confused, Paul is scoring major points in the intra-Jewish discussion of the interpretation of the Scriptures and claiming the messianist identity of true Israel. Again let me name five.

First, the six-chapter account of Paul's arrest and trials in Acts 21–26 consistently sets the dispute in the context of "the customs and controversies of the Jews" (26:3). The well-known disagreements between the Sadducees and the Pharisees on "the hope of the resurrection of the dead" reflected their differing social locations and epitomized their distinctive interpretations of the law and the prophets.[12] "The sect of the Nazareans," as Paul's accusers call the followers of Jesus (24:5) or "the Way," as they identify themselves (see 24:14), stands clearly on the Pharisee side of the interpretive divide, particularly regarding the resurrection, but also as Luke's narrative shows in affirming the reality of angels and the Holy Spirit (see Acts 23:8). As the "oral Torah" of the Pharisees discloses their lively interpretive engagement with the written text, the heavenly visions to Paul (see 23:11; 26:12–19) cause him to read the Scriptures of Israel in a new light.

Second, Luke's Paul is emphatic about his Pharisaic identity (see also Paul himself in Phil 3:5). His mission is centered, as it apparently was before his vision of Jesus, in his "hope in the promise made by God to our ancestors, a promise that our twelve tribes hope to attain, as they earnestly worship day and night" (26:6–7). The Torah observance Luke's Paul practices in Acts has surprised many readers of Paul's own letters. The circumcision of Timothy (Acts 16:1–3), Paul's vow and shaving his head (18:18), and his paying for the vows of other pilgrims when he visited the temple to complete "the days of purification" (21:23–26) are depicted as efforts to establish solidarity with the "thousands of *believers* there are among the Jews" who have been wrongly told that Paul is teaching "all the Jews living among the Gentiles to forsake Moses, and that you tell them not to circumcise their children or observe the customs" (21:21). These Jews are followers of the

Way. Acts 15:5 also refers to "some *believers* who belonged to the sect of the Pharisees," and in Acts 23:6 Paul announces, "I am a Pharisee, the son of Pharisees."[13] Luke–Acts presents Paul as a Pharisee of the Way!

Third, the Pharisaic scriptural argument of Paul's speech is primarily an appeal to his fellow Jews, especially to those already belonging to the Way. The resurrection is not incredible for those who are Pharisees (26:9), but the resurrection of Jesus not only vindicates Pharisaic teaching. It also vindicates Jesus as "the one we had hoped would redeem Israel," as the disciples say on the road to Emmaus (Luke 24:21). The Pharisees would probably echo Paul's call "to those in Damascus, then in Jerusalem and throughout the countryside of Judea, and even to the Gentiles, that they should repent and turn to God and do deeds consistent with repentance" (Acts 26:20). But, what is the substance of this repentance? From what should the people turn? The Pharisaic "turn to God" and the "deeds consistent with repentance" meant Torah observance. For Luke's Paul, by contrast, the "turn from darkness to light and from the power of Satan to God" announced by the resurrected Jesus was to the "forgiveness of sins and a place among those who are sanctified by faith in me" (Acts 26:18). The content of repentance is the turn to faith in Jesus the Messiah who has suffered and become the first to rise from the dead to "proclaim light both to our people and to the Gentiles" (26:23). This is the "repentance and forgiveness of sins" God has given to Israel (Acts 5:31) through which the twelve tribes will attain the promise "God made to our ancestors" (26:6–7). Repentance is itself a gift, restoring God's promises to Israel and to the world (see Acts 5:31; 11:18).

Fourth, Paul is interpreting the Scriptures of Israel in the light of the appearance of the risen Messiah Jesus, but his argument in this context[14] is minimally based on appeals to particular passages. He is rather claiming to say "nothing but what the prophets and Moses said would take place" (26:22, see also v. 27). He is making a comprehensive reinterpretation, much as the risen Jesus did on the road to Emmaus when "beginning with Moses and all the prophets, he interpreted to them the things about himself in all the Scriptures" (Luke 24:27, see also v. 32). The risen Messiah defined the apostolic hermeneutic of all of Israel's Scriptures. Within the rich scriptural debates in Israel, Luke's Paul is a Pharisee of the Way, practicing an oral theological interpretation of the Scriptures, informed and inspired by the witness of the resurrected Messiah.

Fifth, the profound innovation Luke's Paul makes in the theological interpretation of Scripture is his reiteration of the theme of Luke–Acts that Israel's vocation is to be a light to the nations. God's call to Israel to be a light to the end of the earth in Isa 49:6[15] was the foundation for the risen Jesus' last words on earth, transforming the disciples' question about the timing of the restoration of the kingdom to Israel into true Israel's calling. Still earlier in the story, Isaiah's word filled Simeon's song with prophetic confidence that the light to the nations *is* the glory of God's people Israel (Luke 2:32). Isaiah's promise resounded again in Peter's sermon in Acts 13:47, both as a prophetic warning against unbelief in Israel and as a ratification of the mission to the Gentiles.[16]

In the Acts 26 setting of Paul's address to Israel in a Roman court, his theological interpretation of Scripture is fundamentally a declaration of promise: "that the Messiah must suffer, and that by being the first to rise from the dead, he would proclaim light to both our people and to the Gentiles" (26:23). The resurrection of Jesus means the restoration of the vocation of the people of God to be a light to the Gentiles beyond the fence of observant Israel. God's salvation does not stop with Israel. The peoples and cultures of the world are the object of God's desire.

THIS WAS NOT DONE IN A CORNER!

Our theme, Christianity's Engagement with Culture, is urgent because we and our institutions are called not to lives of comfort but to bear the light of Christ into the lives of people, communities, and nations. Our quest is for the theological interpretation of Scripture because through the Scriptures we have heard the promises and commands of the living God. Our methods are literary, historical, and social because the Scriptures are embedded in the complex and compromised human realities of the world God so loves.

Reading Luke–Acts as a narrative filled with commentary on Israel's Scriptures invites interest in the social, political, and economic realities surrounding the story. As Luke's Paul insists to the procurator Festus, King Agrippa II "knows about these things . . . for this was not done in a corner" (Acts 26:26).

Other historical sources locate Agrippa II as the client king in Judea from the era of Claudius in the mid-first century of the Common Era through the Roman siege and destruction of Jerusalem until his death in 93 CE. Felix was the Roman Procurator in Palestine from 52–60 CE, during the later years of the Emperor Claudius, and Festus was appointed Procurator by Nero from 60–62 CE. In his account of *The Jewish War*, the Jewish historian Josephus presents all of these players on the stage of the profound conflicts within Judea, the Roman mismanagement of the province, the carnage of the Jerusalem siege, and the fierce Roman annihilation of Jewish national hopes. The conquest was celebrated in Rome with a triumphal procession of the captives through the streets, the spoils of war "borne in promiscuous heaps" (most notably the treasures captured in the Jerusalem temple and a copy of the Jewish Torah), and the execution of the Jewish leader Simon, son of Gioras, at the temple of Jupiter Capitolinus (*The Jewish War* 7:148–157).

The Romans, of course, thought their victory again demonstrated their legitimacy and the blessings of their gods. The Jewish historian Josephus also acclaimed the triumph of Roman virtue and declared with regard to many of the Jewish insurgents that "each found a fitting end, God awarding due retribution to them all" (*Jewish War* 7:271). In the agony of disbelief at the Roman triumph, the Jewish author of *2 Baruch*, calling Israel to the repentance of Torah, refused the possibility that God's promises to Israel had failed:

> But you ought to know that our Creator will surely avenge us on all our brothers according to everything which they have done against us and among us; in particular that the end which the Most High prepared is near, and that his grace is coming, and that the fulfillment of his judgment is not far. For now we see the multitude of the happiness of the nations although they have acted wickedly; but they are like a vapor. (*2 Baruch* 82:1–4)[17]

The exact dates and provenance of the Luke–Acts narrative are not clear, nor can the identity of the author be precisely established. Since Festus is in the story, a date in the mid-sixties is the earliest possible. Most scholars place Luke's work in the eighties or nineties. Luke's version of Jesus' prophetic predictions about the fate of Jerusalem cause the reader to wonder if Jesus' words were altered or how they would have been heard when recited in the wake of the destruction. "When you see Jerusalem surrounded by armies, then know that its desolation has come near. . . . They will fall by the edge of the sword and be taken away as captives among all nations; and Jerusalem will be trampled on by the Gentiles, until the times of the Gentiles are fulfilled" (21:20–24).

Listening to the testimony of Luke's story within the struggles of the late first century removes the narrative from direct use in describing "Christianity's Engagement with Culture." This reading, however, also liberates Luke–Acts from the triumphal script of "how Christianity superseded Judaism." When "Christianity" became the religion of the Roman Empire, not only was the day dark for non-Christian Jews, but the self-righteous arrogance of conquerors tempted the faithful with dangerous illusions.

No, Acts 26 is the story of the engagement of Paul the Pharisee and Apostle of the Way with the cultures of his own people and in the midst of the Roman regime, with no delusions of political power. The theological interpretation of Scripture is at the center of this engagement, testifying to God's purposes in sharp contrast not only to the views of the Jewish and Roman officials in the story, but also filled with irrepressible hope in the promises of God.

This "hope in God" (see Acts 24:15) may even disclose lessons for later eras to learn from the terms of engagement of the Jesus community with both Israel and the Roman Empire. Let us risk naming three scandalous particularities from which "Christianity" dare not retreat in its engagement with any culture.

First, the promises of God to Israel are the ground of hope. Non-Jewish Christians have often been perplexed or even offended by the particularity of God's election of Israel, but historical honesty cannot evade the Jewish character of the NT as interpretation of the Scriptures of Israel. The theological interpretation of Scripture is always about the God of Abraham, Sarah, Elizabeth, Zechariah, Jesus, and Paul. Christianity cannot boast in its non-Jewish identity, but hopes in the God whose promises will not fail. In Rom 9–11 the Apostle Paul explicitly stated the terms of engagement. The scandal of Israel is never removed: "To them belong the adoption, the glory, the covenants, the giving of the law, the worship and the promises; to them belong the patriarchs, and from them, according to the flesh, comes the Messiah who is over all, God blessed forever, Amen" (Rom 9:4-5). These terms are again articulated by Paul in Luke–Acts: "I stand here on trial on account of my hope in the promise made by God to our ancestors" (26:6). God's election of Israel is not superseded.

Second, the repentance God has given to Israel and to all the peoples of the earth, what Luke calls the "repentance that leads to life," is the turn to trust in Jesus as the Messiah sent by God (see Acts 2:37–39; 3:19–26; 5:31; 11:18; 13:24; 20:21; 26:20). If the election of Israel is a scandal in Christianity's engagement with culture, Jesus of Nazareth, proclaiming good news to the poor, reaching out to the outcasts, crucified and vindicated in resurrection, is even more particular. Paul again states this sharply in affirming that he proclaimed Christ crucified, "a stumbling block to Jews and foolishness to Gentiles" (1 Cor 1:23). Acts 26 again zeros in on Jesus, historically and in his history transforming resurrection. Jesus' resurrection is not only an unparalleled event in history, prompting profound faith in the hope of life after death.[18] His resurrection, especially in Luke–Acts, is the vindication of Jesus as God's Messiah for Israel and the nations and leads to his authorization of the mission of God's people.

Third, the vocation of God's people to be a "light to the nations" is a stunningly specific and humbling third term of Christianity's engagement with culture. At times, "Christianity's" engagement with culture has been co-opted by the economic, political, and religious sensibilities of western Christendom, but at their best, God's "missionaries" have learned to distance themselves from colonializing systems.[19] God's mission of reconciliation needs servants, not masters (2 Cor 5:19–21). The risen Jesus' charge to "make disciples of all nations" (Matt 28:18–20) or to "be my witnesses . . . to the ends of the earth" (Acts 1:8) is the holy calling of God's people. In its scandalous engagement with a world of many cultures and religions, Christianity, hoping in the promises to Israel and bearing Jesus' name, has a vocation from Scripture and from God.

CONCLUDING POSTSCRIPT ON MODERNITY AND GLOBALIZATION

In 1997 Bishop Lesslie Newbigin was invited to Luther Seminary to address the Congress on the World Mission of the Church. I treasure the letter he wrote declining our invitation for both his humanity and his vision. He described how his wife's and his failing health would prevent the journey. "I am also increasingly blind," he added, "and quite unable to read a text, so any talk I give has to be from the memory bank. I can still type a letter but—as this letter probably shows—I am liable to hit the wrong key. In good Lutheran terms, I type by faith, but am not thereby justified!"

Then he offered a luminous comment on Christianity and culture. "I am sure that the most urgent missionary task for this time is the development of a genuinely missionary encounter with the culture of Europe and North America. . . . There is already plenty of evidence that among those Christians of the so-called third world who have been deeply influenced by modernization, the 'acids of modernity' are already having the destructive effects which have almost wiped out Christianity in Europe."

Many of us have been deeply aware of the reality Newbigin called "modernization." We have also learned from his critique of the "optimism" of modern technologies coupled in our time by the pessimism of artists and poets.[20] We have been blessed both by Newbigin's analysis of the realities facing Christianity and his astute grasp of the non-Western character of biblical culture. Our practices of the theological interpretation of Scripture will also be strengthened by listening carefully to the reading of Scripture in interpretative traditions less controlled by rationalistic reductionism.

The time has also come to face the realities Thomas L. Friedman, among many others, calls "globalization," with particular attention to the economic technologies of our ingenuity. In *The Lexus and the Olive Tree*, which was published before the destruction of the World Trade Center,[21] Friedman acknowledged the tensions between traditions of culture, geography, and religion, but he was hopeful an accommodation could be reached to the benefit of all. In *The World is Flat*,[22] his analysis has been compelling to many to the point that Francis Fukuyama declared that this volume "comes as close as anything we now have to a definition of the real character of the new world order."[23] This vision, however, also carries the capacities for arrogance in Alexander the Great's visions of a cosmopolitan world or the violence visited on many in Caesar's *pax Romana*.

It is beyond the purview of this brief essay to pursue how God's engagement with culture can best be addressed in this world of many cultures and religions. Suffice it for the moment to say that Luke's Paul, the Pharisee of the Way and Apostle of Hope extraordinaire, would not have been willing to accord ultimate reality to any economic or political vision. The theological interpretation of Scripture is an act of apostolic faith in the God who raised Jesus. This witness is not madness, as those in the seats of power may suppose (Acts 26:24–25), but the sober truth of hope in God for all who will hear.

ENDNOTES

1. See Alisdair MacIntyre, *After Virtue* (Notre Dame: University of Notre Dame Press, 1981).

2. See Stanley Fish, *Is there a Text in this Class? The Authority of Interpretive Communities* (Cambridge, Mass.: Harvard University Press, 1980).

3. For a delightful story see Thomas Cahill, *How the Irish Saved Civilization* (New York: Doubleday, 1995).

4. See H. Richard Niebuhr, Daniel Day Williams, and James M. Gustafson, *The Advancement of Theological Education* (New York: Harper and Row, 1957) and the discussion in David H. Kelsey, *To Understand God Truly: What's Theological about a Theological School* (Louisville: Westminster/John Knox, 1992).

5. See especially Daniel Boyarin, *Border Lines: The Partition of Judaeo–Christianity* (Philadelphia: University of Pennsylvania Press, 2004).

6. Krister Stendahl, *The School of St. Matthew and Its Use of the Old Testament* (Acta Seminarii Neotestamentici Upsaliensis 20; C. W. K. Gleerup, Lund, 1954; 2d ed.; Philadelphia: Fortress, 1968). See also O. Lamar Cope, *Matthew: A Scribe Trained for the Kingdom of Heaven* (CBQ Monograph Series 5; Catholic Biblical Association, 1976), and J. Andrew Overman, *Matthew's Gospel and Formative Judaism: The Social World of the Matthean Community* (Minneapolis: Augsburg Fortress, 1990).

7. See Richard B. Hays, *Echoes of Scripture in the Letters of Paul* (New Haven: Yale University Press, 1993).

8. David P. Moessner, ed., *Jesus and the Heritage of Israel: Luke's Narrative Claim Upon Israel's Legacy* (Luke the Interpreter of Israel 1; Harrisburg, Pa.: Trinity Press International, 1999); see the introduction by David P. Moessner and David L. Tiede, pp. 1–4.

9. See *The Jewish War* 1:620–640.

10. The theme of "necessity" in Luke–Acts is regularly signaled by the Greek word *dei*. The most fundamental "necessity" in Luke's historiography is not fate or invincible powers, but God's will and plan engaged in contention with human defiance of God's rule. See David L. Tiede, *Prophecy and History in Luke–Acts* (Philadelphia: Fortress, 1980), 70–78.

11. Luke's profound conviction that Israel's identity means Israel's mission is evident in his emphatic linkage between the twelve apostles and the twelve tribes (see Luke 22:28–30 and Acts 1 where Matthias was added to the eleven apostles to replace the betrayer who was "numbered among us" and "allotted his share in this ministry"). In Acts 14:4, 14, however, Paul and Barnabas are called "apostles" in Iconium and Lystra where the legitimacy of their ministries was again challenged by both Jews and Gentiles. Although the author does not identify Paul as an "apostle" in this speech, he is advocating and advancing the "promise that our twelve tribes hope to attain" (26:7).

12. See Luke 20:27–47; Josephus, *Antiquities of the Jews* 18:16 and *The Jewish War* 2:164–165. Linked closely with the temple and its priesthood, the Sadducees were identified by Josephus as belonging to an elite minority "of the highest standing," but he also judges the Sadducees to be politically ineffective because they are compelled to submit "to the formulas of the Pharisees, since otherwise the masses would not tolerate them" (*Antiquities* 18:17). "As for

the persistence of the soul after death, penalties in the underworld, and rewards," states Josephus, "they will have none of them" (*Jewish War* 2:185).

13. See also Paul's own claims as one of those "who are the circumcision, who worship in the Spirit of God" in Phil 3:3–6.

14. The narrative of Luke–Acts is, however, thoroughly infused with scriptural allusions, citations, and arguments, especially in Peter's Pentecost address in Acts 2. See Donald Juel, *Luke–Acts: The Promise of History* (Atlanta: John Knox, 1983).

15. "It is too light a thing that you should be my servant to raise up the tribes of Jacob, and to restore the survivors of Israel; I will give you as a light to the nations, that my salvation may reach to the end of the earth."

16. In the face of rejection Isaiah's prophetic warnings also resound through the narrative of Luke–Acts (see the use of Isa 6 in Luke 8:9; 19:42; with Hab 1:5 in Acts 13:40–41 and Acts 28:26–28).

17. James H. Charlesworth, *The Old Testament Pseudepigrapha*: Vol. I: *Apocalyptic Literature and Testaments* (New York: Doubleday, 1983), 649. See also Gwendolyn B. Sayler, *Have the Promises Failed? A Literary Analysis of 2 Baruch* (SBLDS 72; Chico, Calif.: Scholars Press, 1984).

18. See Rodney Stark's social analysis of factors in his *The Rise of Christianity* (San Francisco: Harper, 1993) and N. T. Wright's remarkable study of the consequence of Jesus' resurrection as a demonstration in history in his *Jesus and the Victory of God* (Minneapolis: Fortress, 1996).

19. See Roland Allen, *Missionary Methods: St. Paul's or Ours* (Grand Rapids: Eerdmans, 1962: reprinted with a forward by Lesslie Newbigin from the 1927 edition).

20. See *Foolishness to the Greeks: The Gospel and Western Culture* (Grand Rapids: Eerdmans, 1986), and *The Gospel in a Pluralist Society* (Grand Rapids: Eerdmans, 1989).

21. New York: Anchor Books, 2000.

22. New York: Farrar, Straus, and Giroux, 2005.

23. Publisher's blurb from *The New Statesman* on the cover of *The World is Flat*.

RESPONSE TO TIEDE

OSVALDO PADILLA

I appreciate this paper and value its contribution for several reasons. First, I admire Prof. Tiede's frank statement that the proper object of Christian theological study is Scripture. This is particularly refreshing in the context of contemporary theological education, where the scriptural text itself seems to be marginalized. Second, I resonate with his conviction of the "profoundly Jewish character of the entire NT." In my own studies of that Gospel writer held to be the most gentile, namely Luke, I have become more and more convinced of his Jewish roots in both his theology and historiography. I would not be surprised if the third evangelist turned out to be of Jewish birth after all. Third, I think it is a shrewd methodological move to focus on Paul's "trial" scenes in the latter chapters of Acts. This is a good location to glimpse the Christians' terms of engagement with Israel and the Empire. These apologetic scenarios provide us with rare glimpses into the defense and evangelism of the early followers of Jesus.

There is another reason for my enjoyment of this paper, perhaps a more selfish one: in my own dissertation I examined the speeches in Acts. It is a great delight to interact with a paper treating a topic close to one's own heart. It means, at least, that one was not insane in investigating the topic. There is even more delight when the author at least partly agrees with one's own conclusions: that means perhaps your research was not so off the wall after all. Regardless of one's enjoyment of a paper, there will still be differences of opinion, to which I now turn with hopes of strengthening the discussion.

Let me begin with a peripheral observation. The historiographic milieu within which we place an author has serious ramifications for our reading of his or her work. It will affect our understanding of purpose, rhetorical techniques, and historicity. Regarding this, in the context of the strategy of the speech in Acts 26, Prof. Tiede invokes Luke's apparent expertise in the conventions of *Hellenistic* historiography. He claims the prologues as proof for this. However, I think other scholars have made a strong case for viewing the prologues, not as examples of fine historiographic handling, but rather as showing the vocabulary and style of ancient scientific writers.[1] In addition, Luke lacks many of the distinctive marks of belletristic writers of the end of the first century—things such as Atticism, the copious quotations of the Greek classics, and in the matter of speeches, lengthy, side-by-side forensic discourses. I thus find it an overstatement to say that Luke demonstrates "mastery of the rhetorical conventions of Hellenistic historiography." I doubt that a Greek person reading Luke–Acts would have reached this conclusion. It may be better to say that while he does employ certain Hellenistic *topoi*, nevertheless his historiographic foundation is Jewish. I think this is significant for our understanding of the speech before Festus and its level of historicity.

Second, although Prof. Tiede is surely correct in observing that the Lord is the one who ultimately drives the plot of Acts, and *not* Lord Caesar, I think that he has underplayed the role of Rome. In my opinion it is more accurate to say that the Lord controls the plot *through* the Roman authorities. This is not to say that Rome is portrayed as a conscious, protecting benefactor of the Jesus movement. Rather, as we can see from characters like Gallio and Claudius Lysias, the Romans, while looking out for their own interests, end up helping in mobilizing the missionaries to their appointed ends. They do not do this for the sake of the gospel; but there are sufficient clues planted in the narratives that lead the reader to conclude that— through dramatic irony—the Romans end up being the channel through which God accomplishes his purposes. Thus, the Lord Christ is portrayed as exercising his authority even over the greatest contemporary power. This portrait is not at all dissimilar from those of potentates such as Cyrus and Nebuchadnezzar in the OT. It may be that Luke is showing his historiographic Jewish roots in this engagement with Rome.[2]

Third, I question whether we can, strictly speaking, call the speech in Acts 26 "Paul's self-defense," if by that we mean the apostle's argument for his own innocence vis-à-vis the Romans. The term employed by Luke to refer to the location of the hearing is *akroatērion*. This is a term which, on the majority of occasions, excludes a forensic sense and is thus to be envisioned more as an audience hall than a courtroom in its function.[3] Further, since Paul had already made use of *provocatio* in ch. 25, this could not have been a trial: the final verdict was to be made by the emperor himself, to whom Paul had astutely appealed. Barrett is thus probably correct when he states: "[The audience hall] is by no means necessarily a law court, and the use of the word suggests, or at least is consistent with, an informal hearing; this indeed it must have been. Once the appeal to the Emperor's court had been made and allowed no lower court had any right to try Paul."[4] This observation leads to my final critique.

Is it possible that, at the level of the historical event, Paul's speech before Agrippa was more of a direct attempt at *evangelism* than we often allow? I think Prof. Tiede has a similar view of this speech and its contemporary significance since he emphasizes toward the end of his paper our call to "make disciples of all nations" and to be "witnesses to the ends of the earth." Thus, this is not so much a critique as an attempt to refine his point. I give two reasons why I believe this speech should be viewed as an example of evangelism. First, as I stated above, after Paul had made use of *provocatio*, he could no longer have been tried by the authorities of the provinces. His final fate was to be decided by the emperor himself. This was his privilege as a Roman citizen. If that is the case, we should not approach this speech as forensic, attempting to show Paul's political innocence. Incidentally, it sheds light on the use of the term *apologia* (vv. 1, 2). The word appears to be shading into a reference to evangelism.

A second reason for viewing this speech as evangelistic rather than forensic is Paul's direct challenge to Agrippa towards the end:

> "King Agrippa, do you believe the prophets? I know that you believe." Agrippa said to Paul, "Are you so quickly persuading me to become a Christian?" Paul replied, "Whether quickly or not, I pray to God that not only you but also all who are listening to me today might become such as I am—except for these chains!" (Acts 26:27–29)

These are not the words of a man who is pleading his innocence before a Roman tribunal; they are the words of a preacher of the gospel! Consequently, to the extent that this text can be employed to map our contemporary engagement with culture, a more offensive stance is envisioned. That is, in engaging the contemporary political powers, Christians are to view their calling as a missionary one. If we take this text seriously, it means that our engagement is done, not only with our deeds, but also with a loving yet bold call to repentance. In this sense our stance may indeed become offensive in both senses of the word.

In my interaction with Prof. Tiede's paper, I have focused mainly on Rome as the culture being engaged in Acts 26. Let me conclude by dealing with the other culture that he proposes, namely the Jewish one. In this respect I find his comments puzzling. He makes the following statement: "The Pharisaic scriptural argument of Paul's speech is primarily an appeal to his fellow Jews, especially to those already belonging to the Way." This is questionable if he is referring to the ostensible historical audience recorded in Acts 26: it appears that there were no Jews in that audience. However, if he is referring to the real readers of Luke–Acts, then I think he has a point. As other congregations of early Christianity, I envision the church or churches which were the recipients of Luke–Acts as being made up of Jews (the majority) and gentiles—these latter being both former proselytes and God-fearers. What I find interesting in Paul's attempt to persuade his hearers of the messiahship of Jesus is his emphasis on the Jewish roots of the Jesus movement. It is because of Paul's hope "in what God has promised our fathers" that he stood before Festus and Agrippa. The coming of Jesus is the hope which the twelve tribes long to see fulfilled. He does not preach anything that goes beyond "the prophets and Moses." I think these statements are meant to go beyond the ostensible audience in Caesarea. They were meant to bolster the faith of the followers of Jesus who by now were scrimmaging with the synagogue. By showing that the OT promises applied to them because of Jesus, Luke wants to leave no doubt that they are the continuation of the people of God. Appealing to the Hebrew Scriptures to strengthen our identity, therefore, is nothing to be ashamed about but something to celebrate. In this I think Prof. Tiede and I heartily agree.

ENDNOTES

1. See Loveday Alexander, *The Preface to Luke's Gospel: Literary Convention and Social Context in Luke 1.1–4 and Acts 1.1* (Cambridge: Cambridge University Press, 1993); Lars Rydbeck, *Fachprosa, vermeintliche Volkssprache und neues Testament* (Uppsala, 1967).

2. I have dealt with this in more detail in *The Speeches of Outsiders in Acts: Poetics, Theology, and Historiography* (SNTSMS; Cambridge: Cambridge University Press, forthcoming).

3. See Plutarch, *Mor.* 45; 522E; 937D; Epictetus, *Dis.* 3.23.8; Heliodorus, *Aeth.* 2.21.6.

4. C. K. Barrett, *A Critical and Exegetical Commentary on the Acts of the Apostles* (2 vols; Edinburgh: T. & T. Clark, 1994–1998), 2.1145–1146.

CHRIST, CULTURE, AND THE SERMON ON THE MOUNT COMMUNITY[1]

PAUL LOUIS METZGER

CHRIST'S CHURCH'S MULTI-FACETED RELATION TO CULTURE

The church is a cultural community. This paper envisions the church as Christ's eschatological kingdom community that is itself a culture and that engages other cultures from Christ's kingdom vantage point.[2]

There can be no monolithic view of the relation of Christ to culture, for there is no ideal culture. God's kingdom culture embodied in the church always takes particular form in concrete contexts. This essay on the intersection and concrete engagement of Christ's church as a culture (which itself varies in diverse locations and over time) with other cultures involves the claim that the church's relation to other cultures is to be multifaceted and dynamic, in no way static, always particular, never abstract, ever contemporary, never remote. A quote attributed to Martin Luther states it well: "If you preach the gospel in all its aspects with the exception of the issues that deal specifically with your time, you are not preaching the gospel at all."

In view of Luther's exhortation, we would do no better than to look to the Lord himself to see how to preach the gospel in a manner that deals specifically with our own time. For his story includes our own. We will approach the subject through analysis of Christian Scripture, giving focused attention to the Sermon on the Mount. Our Lord's own approach to engaging human culture was multifaceted. In the Sermon on the Mount and its surrounding context we find indications of the Lord Jesus radically embracing and confronting the culture of his day. As the God-Man, Jesus is of his time and for his time while transcending and transforming it. The church as Christ's kingdom community envisioned in the Sermon on the Mount takes its cue from its Lord; just as Jesus' engagement of culture is multifaceted, so, too, must ours be.

Within this framework we will draw attention to the church's own history. Along the way we will take a special look at one of our Lord's finest followers,

Dietrich Bonhoeffer (1906–1945), who sought to live out the Sermon on the Mount in his community at Finkenwalde and in prison, and whose witness to Jesus even now assists us in the challenges we face. The church's relationship to culture has been understood in dramatically different ways throughout its history with models spanning a continuum from separation to transformation. We find various models exemplified in Bonhoeffer and the Christian community he envisioned. In the past and the present the church is a cultural community that is shaped by the surrounding culture and prophetically confronts that culture for the latter's own ultimate transformation. Outside culture there is no church, and outside the church of the triune God's eschatological kingdom there is no ultimate redemption of culture.

CHRIST AND CULTURE
THE BEATITUDES, BONHOEFFER, AND BEYOND

In what follows, we will take a look at various models, taking our cue from H. Richard Niebuhr's fivefold typology in *Christ and Culture*[3]: "Christ of Culture," "Christ against Culture," "Christ and Culture in Paradox," "Christ above Culture," and "Christ transforming Culture." The reason for using Niebuhr's types is their widespread currency.[4] We will not follow Niebuhr's order, depiction, valuation, and illustration of these types in a slavish manner; each type serves a useful purpose and has a role to play as part of the church's overarching framework for engaging other cultures.

Positively framed, Jesus exemplifies each of the five types: Jesus is *of* culture as its *protagonist*, *against* culture as its *antagonist*, God's "yes" and "no" to culture as the divine and human *dualist*, above culture as the great *synthesist*, and the one who ultimately transforms culture as the ultimate *transformationalist*. Given such exemplification, the church's aim in engaging culture is a simple one: to be about Christ-centered cultural encounters. However, what is signified by this aim defies simplistic forms of engagement. Bonhoeffer and his writing exemplify the multifaceted orientation required of every theologian and every Christian community in interfacing with the cultural situation. On the one hand, Bonhoeffer writes, "The *present* is not where the present age announces its claims before Christ, but where the present age stands before the claims of Christ;"[5] on the other hand, he claims, "The word of the church to the world must . . . encounter the world in all its present reality from the deepest knowledge of the world, if it is to be authoritative."[6] While there is much more to be said, these questions suggest that we have our work cut out for us, to say the least. What better place to turn first for assistance for tackling this mountain of a task than to the Bible and to what the Lord himself said in his longest and most famous sermon, the Sermon on the Mount.

Christ of Culture—Christ as Protagonist. The Sermon on the Mount, Jesus' state of the union address, follows on the heels of Matthew's discussion of Jesus' baptism with the Spirit descending as a dove from the Father (Matt 3:13–17), the Spirit leading Jesus into the wilderness to be tempted by the Devil (Matt 4:1), and Jesus beginning his public ministry in the power of the Spirit (Matt 4:17). Luke 4 tells us that the same Jesus of whom Matthew writes proclaims powerfully in word and deed the coming kingdom in the midst of the people through the Spirit's anointing (Luke 4:18–19). For his own part Matthew provides a summary statement of the Lord's radical intervention on behalf of the people:

> Jesus went throughout Galilee, teaching in their synagogues, proclaiming the good news of the kingdom, and healing every disease and sickness among the people. News about him spread all over Syria, and people brought to him all who were ill with various diseases, those suffering severe pain, the demon-possessed, those having seizures, and the paralyzed; and he healed them. Large crowds from Galilee, the Decapolis, Jerusalem, Judea and the region across the Jordan followed him. (Matt 4:23–25)

The people are drawn to Jesus and encircle him and his band of disciples (Matt 5:1–2) because he speaks profoundly and acts redemptively in addressing their concrete situation. They flock to him and are in awe of him, for he speaks with authority (Matt 7:28–29) and acts authoritatively as well (see Matt 8–9), unlike their religious leaders (Matt 7:29). In other words, Jesus is "relevant." We will return to this word later to clarify its meaning. For the time being, however, it is sufficient to note that Jesus is one who is a man of his times; he is from the people and of the people. Jesus understood the times and knew exactly what to do. To employ Niebuhr's categories, one might say that here the Lord exemplifies the "Christ of culture" model of cultural engagement.

Often, this phrase is taken negatively, as if to say that the person or group in question has compromised biblical convictions for cultural relevance. We will return briefly to discuss this phenomenon historically. Before doing so, however, it is important to stress that if one is *not* of culture one is *also* compromising biblical faith. For the eternal Word left heaven's security to accommodate himself to our creaturely and worldly limitations in dependence on the written Word and Spirit in order to redeem the creation from its fall to decay and destruction. Jesus could only transform humanity by becoming one with us in our concrete cultural setting. For as Gregory of Nazianzus said, "The unassumed is the unhealed."[7]

Bonhoeffer's life bears witness to the Lord's incarnational orientation. He was truly a man of his time, whose allegiance to Germany was so all-encompassing that he was willing to endure great sacrifice. During Hitler's reign Bonhoeffer could have stayed in America to avoid the mounting pressures on the church and its leaders, but instead he determined to come back to Germany to identify with the people, saying that he could not serve in the rebuilding efforts after the war if he did not endure the tragedies that had befallen the people. This is what it means to be "of the culture" in a positive sense.

The "German Christians," as they were called, typify the negative sense of what it means to be "of culture." They were church leaders who proclaimed an Aryan gospel apart from and besides the gospel of Jesus in service to the Führer—Lord Hitler—and to his Third (millennial) Reich (kingdom). The Barmen Declaration alludes to this Aryan gospel in the following denunciation:

> We reject the false doctrine, as though the church could and would have to acknowledge as a source of its proclamation, apart from and besides this one Word of God, still other events and powers, figures and truths, as God's revelation. . . . We reject the false doctrine, as though there were areas of our life in which we would not belong to Jesus Christ, but to other lords—areas in which we would not need justification and sanctification through him.[8]

These German Christians provide us with a negative example of the "Christ of culture" model. Following the spirit of the age they compromised their witness to the gospel of Jesus of Nazareth for power in the public square. The result was that they failed to proclaim the gospel in the power of the Spirit.

Similarly, the fundamentalist-evangelical church in North America (of which I am part), like its liberal antagonist, is in danger of exchanging the gospel of Christ's kingdom for the gospel of American power. United Methodist William Willimon argues regarding Jerry Falwell, Pat Robertson, the Religious Right, and the Religious Left:

> Pat Robertson has become Jesse Jackson. Randall Terry of the Nineties is Bill Coffin of the Sixties. And the average American knows no answer to human longing or moral deviation other than legislation. Again, I ought to know. We played this game before any Religious Right types were invited to the White House. Some time ago I told Jerry Falwell to his face that I had nothing against him except that he talked like a Methodist. A Methodist circa 1960. Jerry was not amused.[9]

Many conservatives and liberals have missed out on identifying the church's witness in terms of the power of the cross. All too often we place our confidence in legislating this or that morality as if it will save us here and now, not Christ's justification of sinners through his cross and resurrection and his promised return.

Being "relevant" does not necessarily suggest that we let culture shape the gospel to make it appealing. The gospel creates its own relevance. Followers of Jesus are not salespeople who sell a product but witnesses who are promoting a kingdom and who are participating in the life of the king as his people who give and receive from his abundance. The real question is not, "Is God relevant to culture?" but rather, "Are the church and surrounding cultures relevant to the triune God, who indwells, interrupts, and invites the society at large to participate in the church as the eschatological kingdom culture here and now?" The church is called to be a cultural community shaped profoundly by the eschatological kingdom of the triune God that Jesus proclaimed and embodied in the power of the Spirit. This Trinitarian and eschatological shaping will undoubtedly make the church relevant to God and will also undoubtedly lead the church into conflict with the world at large. In fact, going against the surrounding society in a redemptive manner in view of God will make the church as a distinctive culture most relevant to the world round about it, for the church will be challenging the surrounding cultures in view of what they most need to hear.

Christ against Culture—Christ as Antagonist. While Jesus identified with the surrounding culture(s) in which he lived, he also confronted it head-on in view of God's kingdom reality. Jesus challenged the dominant religious structures of his day, where legalists paraded righteousness but did not practice it, externalized spirituality, and ostracized those who did not live up to their self-imposed standards. In Matt 6:1–8 Jesus confronts such hypocrisy. Although religious, these spiritual guides are human-centered, seeking after human glory, not God's; they seek to be honored and seen by their peers (Matt 6:2, 5). As John makes clear in his own Gospel, unlike the religious rulers, Jesus does not seek after human glory, but God's (John 2:24–25; 5:41–44). Those who are concerned for human glory are one with the false prophets, who are inwardly "ferocious wolves," though they parade around in sheep's clothing (Matt 7:15).

It is interesting to note that the Lord prefaces his remarks on these hypocrites with an exhortation to enter through the narrow gate, for "small is the gate and narrow the road that leads to life, and only a few find it" (Matt 7:14). No doubt, Jesus' disciples were overwhelmed by the fact that the Lord told them: ". . . I tell you that unless your righteousness surpasses that of the Pharisees and the teachers of the law, you will certainly not enter the kingdom of heaven" (Matt 5:20). Those who think that external religion is actually more demanding than the spirituality Jesus embodies and espouses should think again.

Those who aspire to a righteousness that exceeds that of the Pharisees will sense their brokenness or bankruptcy before God.[10] Jesus demands that we die to our attempts at justifying ourselves so that we might truly live. As the beatitude makes clear, "Blessed are the poor in spirit, for theirs is the kingdom of heaven" (Matt 5:3). Such poverty in spirit is the result of the Spirit's movement in our lives. The Spirit brings us to the end of ourselves and forward as participants in God's kingdom, just as the Spirit descended upon, indwelt, and drove Christ forward on the heels of his self-denying and divine-dependent temptation to proclaim publicly in word and deed this same kingdom, which he inaugurated in his person. When the kingdom of God dawns and dwells in us, we perform righteous deeds; however, the flipside is not true, for a bad tree does not bear good fruit (Matt 7:16–20).

Human power fails us when it comes to the transformation of the human heart. Only God can perform this work, and it is very costly. It cost the triune God his Son, and it costs us our lives as well, taking us to the end of ourselves. We must die to ourselves and depend wholly on Christ for our life and righteousness, as Bonhoeffer himself reasons in his depiction of Luther. According to Bonhoeffer, Luther had gone to the monastery void of everything but his piety, but piety does not justify. God had to strip him even of his devotion.[11] Grace takes us to the end of ourselves, as well as to the end of obedience to Christ, no matter where it will lead us.

Bonhoeffer's Luther championed grace, not as cheap, but as costly.[12] Grace costs us our lives whereas salvation by works leaves us intact. The latter does not cost us nearly enough. Works salvation is very other-worldly and worldly at the same time. It separates "saints" from simple Christians and "the humble work of discipleship" and turns "the self-renunciation of discipleship into the flagrant spiritual self-assertion of the 'religious.'"[13] "The monk's attempt to flee from the world turned out to be a subtle form of love for the world."[14] Not only is pious self-assertion worldly, but also the search for obtaining grace at the cheapest price is also worldly. God's grace will cost us our day by day existence as well as our lives.[15]

In commenting on Matt 5:3 (the poor in spirit), Bonhoeffer writes:

> They are the "poor" *tout court* (Luke 6.20). They have no security, no possessions to call their own, not even a foot of earth to call their home, no earthly society to claim their absolute allegiance. Nay more, they have no spiritual power, experience or knowledge to afford them consolation or security. For his sake they have lost all. In following him they lost even their own selves, and everything that could make them rich. Now they are poor—so inexperienced, so stupid, that they have no other hope but him who called them.[16]

For Bonhoeffer poverty or affluence is not in and of itself the goal. Rather, "everything depends on faith alone . . . it is possible to have wealth and the possession of this world's goods and to believe in Christ—so that a man may have these goods as one who has them not."[17] For Bonhoeffer, such self-abandoned faith has an eschatological component: ". . . this is an ultimate possibility of the Christian life, only within our capacity in so far as we await with earnest expectation the immediate return of Christ."[18]

Bonhoeffer speaks to the difference between Jesus' disciples (old and new) and the system of affluence and influence: "Jesus knows all about the representatives and preachers of national religion, who enjoy greatness and renown, whose feet are firmly planted on the earth, who are deeply rooted in the culture and piety of the people and moulded by the spirit of the age."[19] A church that is "moulded by the spirit of the age" can never be led by the Spirit of freedom—the Spirit of the Messianic age, nor can it offer hope of liberation to those so molded. Karl Barth wrote that if the church is to remain free it must never demand rights and recognition from the state: "Whenever the Church has entered the political arena to fight for its claim to be given public recognition, it has always been a Church which has failed to understand the special purpose of the State, an impenitent, spiritually unfree Church."[20] It must concern itself with Christ's all-encompassing demand upon its own life. Only then can it offer hope to this decaying and darkening world. The church's hope is not in this world as such, but in the inbreaking of the triune God's eschatological kingdom in our midst. As an authentic witness to the triune God's eschatological kingdom, it offers hope to the world.

The church serves society at large as a redemptive counterculture. As a counterculture the church serves the world as a preserving and penetrating influence of salt and light respectively. If the church were to lose its saltiness, it would be thrown out and trampled underfoot. Thus, it must retain its distinctive saltiness and continue serving as a light to the world through its good works (Matt 5:13–16).

Bonhoeffer speaks of the church as a mediatory people called out from the world, yet for the world, by the reigning and returning Christ:

> Amid poverty and suffering, hunger and thirst, they are meek, merciful, and peacemakers, persecuted and scorned by the world, although it is for their sake alone that the world is allowed to continue, and it is they who protect the world from the wrath and judgement of God. They are strangers and sojourners on earth (Heb. 11.13; 13.14; I Pet. 2.11). They seek those things that are above, not the things that are on the earth (Col. 3.2). For their true life is not yet made manifest, but hidden with Christ in God. Here they see no more than the reflection of what they shall be. Here all that is visible is their dying, their secret daily death unto the old man, and their manifest death before the world. They are still hidden from themselves, and their left hand knows not what their right hand does. Although they are a visible society, they are always unknown even to themselves, looking only to their Lord. He is in heaven, their life is with him, and for him they wait. But when Christ, who is their life, shall be manifested, then they too shall be manifested with him in glory (Col. 3.4).[21]

The church is a kind of first fruits which offers hope to the world of deliverance from God's judgment and wrath.

The preceding discussion demonstrates that Jesus and his disciple Bonhoeffer, as well as those Christian communities who have followed their lead in the past, cannot be identified simply with either pole—"Christ of culture" or "Christ against culture." Their means of engagement is just too complex; in light of their example the contemporary church, no matter its location, should also engage the society at large in a multifaceted manner. Unfortunately, my own cultural heritage, the fighting fundamentalistic-evangelical movement, often fails to recognize the need for complexity. Its adversarial orientation fails to reflect Jesus' and Bonhoeffer's redemptive countercultural engagement of the society at large on behalf of that society's own redemption through the mediatory witness of the church. The same could be said of the Religious Left. By the sound of the culture-war rhetoric, one might be led to believe that Jesus came to save us from liberals or conservatives, dependent of course on our political party vantage point!

Each of Niebuhr's models possesses some merit, for they are all reflected in some measure in the Gospels. The two noted at length so far—Christ as protagonist of culture and Christ as antagonist of culture—when not balanced with the others, become extreme. Jesus' and Bonhoeffer's lives illustrate the truth that we flesh out various models of cultural engagement at various times and places, sometimes at the same place and time. This being said, there are three more models to consider: Christ as dualist, Christ as synthesist, and Christ as transformationalist, each of which may be found in Christ and Bonhoeffer.

The dualist, synthesist, and transformationalist positions stand somewhere on the spectrum between the protagonist and antagonist perspectives, and somewhere between the eschatological extremes of the "now" and "not yet" standing in opposition to one another. Geoffrey Wainwright argues that with the antagonist position, one finds an eschatology of the "not yet," perhaps even of the "never";[22] with the protagonist position, the "now" overwhelms the "not yet."[23] According to Wainwright, both forms of spirituality are "cripplingly deficient from the eschatological point of view. Either the Kingdom of God can never be achieved or its achievement was never necessary in the first place."[24] Both poles—"now" and "not yet"—are required if we are to account for the biblical story.

This "now" and "not yet" pattern is found at the outset of the Sermon on the Mount. A present tense description or prescription is followed by a promise of future realization and reward. Note how each beatitude in Matt 5:3–10 begins: "Blessed are the poor in spirit," ". . . those who mourn," ". . . the meek," ". . . those who hunger and thirst for righteousness," ". . . the merciful," ". . . the pure in heart," ". . . the peacemakers," ". . . those who are persecuted because of righteousness." Each beatitude gives rise to promises of certain future blessings: ". . . theirs is the kingdom of heaven," ". . . they will be comforted," ". . . they will inherit the earth," ". . . they will be filled," ". . . they will be shown mercy," ". . . they will see God," ". . . they will be called sons of God," ". . . theirs is the kingdom of heaven." This kind of people—namely Christ's poor in spirit and persecuted community—*are* blessed, *for* they *will be* blessed. They follow in the footsteps of Jesus and the prophets and participate in the kingdom that is to come (Matt 5:11–12).

Jesus speaks to his community of followers in the Sermon on the Mount (Matt 5:1–2), describing to them what the eschatological community of the triune God looks like, what it values, and how it lives out Jesus' mandate and mission. The church today is called to live out the Sermon on the Mount as Jesus' community in the present. The message we seek to proclaim in heart, word, and deed is a message of judgment and hope. It is a message for and against culture, accounting for the cross and resurrection. The Christ of culture orientation, on its own, does not account for the judgment of the cross. The Christ against culture orientation, on its own, does not account for the transformative work of the resurrection. The following three models offer mediating possibilities.

Christ and Culture in Paradoxical Relation—Christ as Dualist. The dualist position is the most difficult one to understand because it is so paradoxical. Niebuhr describes the dualist position in the following terms:

> . . . the dualist joins the radical Christian in pronouncing the whole world of human culture to be godless and sick unto death. But there is this difference between them: the dualist knows that he belongs to that culture and cannot get out of it, that God indeed sustains him in it and by it; for if God in His grace did not sustain the world in its sin it would not exist for a moment.[25]

Luther spoke of the Christian life in paradoxical terms. Believers are wholly righteous and wholly sinful simultaneously and throughout their lives.[26] One also finds a paradox in Luther's view of the church's relation to the state:

> There are two kingdoms, one the kingdom of God, the other the kingdom of the world. . . . God's kingdom is a kingdom of grace and mercy, not of wrath and punishment. In it there is only forgiveness, consideration for one another, love, service, the doing of good, peace, joy, etc. But the kingdom of the world is a kingdom of wrath and severity. In it there is only punishment, repression, judgment, and condemnation to restrain the wicked and protect the good. . . . Now he who would confuse these two kingdoms—as our false fanatics do— would put wrath into God's kingdom and mercy into the world's kingdom; and that is the same as putting the devil in heaven and God in hell.[27]

Niebuhr argues that such a distinction is not a division. The kingdoms of God and the world are "closely related. The Christian must affirm both in a single act of obedience to the one God of mercy and wrath, not as a divided soul with a double allegiance and duty."[28]

Regardless of how one reads Luther, many Lutherans at the time of Hitler maintained that the two kingdoms thesis meant for them that they submit to Hitler in the sphere of the state and to Christ in the sphere of the church. Barth's objection to Luther's translation of Rom 13 is relevant. Barth argues that, "Luther's translation speaks of 'being *subject*' . . . , which is something dangerously different from what is meant here. The last thing this instruction implies is that the Christian community and the Christian should offer the blindest possible obedience to the civil community and its officials."[29] Barth maintains that the church is to subject itself to Christ in the sphere of the state, for Christ's kingdom includes both the church and the secular domain. Neither the church nor the state then is an end in itself. Thus, the church must not subject itself to the state in blind obedience.[30] Both church and state are instruments of the kingdom, and they only submit to one another in their respective service to that one kingdom.

Dualists today among fundamentalist-evangelicals—and liberals for that matter—often fail to recognize the church and state as mutually subject to Christ. Earlier we stated that many conservatives and liberals have missed out on identifying the church's witness in terms of the power of the cross. Such moves on the part of fundamentalist-evangelicals and liberals are bound up with inadequate attention to ecclesiology and eschatology. On the one hand, both movements often tend to individualize the faith rather than conceive the faith in social or ecclesial terms. For all the talk against privatization of faith by fundamentalist-evangelicals today in their criticism of those who seek to relativize faith, the individualization of faith by the Religious Right—not to mention the Religious Left—does not fare much better.

Cynthia Moe-Lobeda's critique of H. Richard Niebuhr's brother, Reinhold Niebuhr, could be made against fundamentalist-evangelicalism as well. Moe-Lobeda states that liberalism and Reinhold Niebuhr embraced two conflicting claims: (a) "Personal relationship with God" is "the centerpiece of faith" and (b) "Personal relationship with God" is "*not* a centerpiece" of the Christian's political and public life. These two conflicting claims

> reflect the theological anthropology of liberalism's legacy. . . . That anthropology is viewed clearly in the work of Reinhold Niebuhr who held that the individual is the primary human unit in relationship with God; the self—although a social being—stands before God as an individual. The result is a public-private dichotomy in which the moral knowledge and norms that faith offers are understood and enacted by individuals, rather than by social groups.[31]

Both the Religious Right and Religious Left often make the individual the primary human unit for the Christian's political and public life, not the church. Many today view the church as a voluntary association of religious individuals, whose true allegiance lies elsewhere (the explicit or implicit endorsement of political candidates/parties from pulpits and opening of doors to them to share their wares come election time impact negatively the church's understanding of itself as a distinctive polis with its own political practices, such as Baptism and the Lord's Supper). Such emphasis on the private and/or individual has negative consequences. As Moe-Lobeda argues, "The social construction of human-divine intimacy as private has served the interests of established power structures, for singularly private relationship with God cannot issue in public challenge."[32]

The privatization-individualization-subjectivization of the faith in Bonhoeffer's day created a vacuum for a monster such as Hitler to arise[33] and serves as a serious warning to us in the States today. Bonhoeffer's close friend and colleague, Eberhard Bethge, found nothing benign about Rev. Falwell's church with its emphasis on "American Christianity." While having a great admiration and affection for the United States, he was deeply troubled when he entered the church:

> As we entered the foyer, an usher stepped forward and gave me two badges to fasten to my lapel: the one on the left said, Jesus First and on the right, one with an American flag. . . . I could not help but think myself in Germany in 1933. . . . Of course, Christ, but a German Christ; of course, "Jesus First," but an American Jesus! And so to the long history of faith and its executors another chapter is being added of a mixed image of Christ, of another syncretism on the American model, undisturbed by any knowledge of that centuries-long and sad history.[34]

If only the badge opposite Jesus had been the church! While nationalistic monsters today may appear more benign, there is nothing benign about public-private dualities and dichotomies regardless of their form. Such dichotomies weaken and threaten the church's pure witness as a public—Christ's kingdom community.

While there is a distinction between church and state, there is no public-private dichotomy for Christian existence. The church is called to engage the state as a public facing another public, not as a subsidiary of the state. The failure of the church to see itself as a distinct public engaging other publics such as the state is likely "one reason it is susceptible to becoming the bearer of national and other identities and projects, securing for itself thus as a national or civil religion a measure of public relevance within the framework of the public arena of society at large," as Reinhard Hütter argues.[35] This failure of self-understanding and subservience to the state also signifies that the church loses its prophetic voice to speak out in society at large.[36]

Biblically speaking, the church—not the individual or state for that matter—is the primary human unit in effecting God's kingdom purposes, for the church is the embodiment of Christ's kingdom mission, not the isolated individual Christian, and certainly not the state. The privatization of faith to the realm of the individual is non-Trinitarian, for the triune God is by nature social and communal. Such privatization is also due to an imbalanced eschatology of the kingdom.

Emphasis on the individual (not the social and ecclesial—except when the ecclesial is viewed as the collection of individuals where the parts are greater than the whole) and preoccupation with the distant future (without seeing that the church is the now of the not yet kingdom) leads to the improper politicization of the faith whereby the church becomes subservient to the state. Where there is inattention to this communal and contemporaneous Trinitarian eschatological kingdom reality, those least suspected of politicizing the faith—dispensationalists—are sometimes most guilty of it. Given such inattention, supposed rapture-and-retreat fundamentalists—following the lead of the late Jerry Falwell, Tim LaHaye of *Left Behind Series* fame, and Pat Robertson—have aligned themselves with the Republican Party to take back centers of power for God and country. Their strange mixture of pretribulation theology and postmillennial practice fails to account for the fact that Christ's kingdom community must radically confront the world's kingdoms and parties. The confrontation takes place in proclamation and participation in Christ's story of cross and resurrection in the present and in view of the day when Christ's kingdom will reign on this earth in all its fullness.[37]

The historical move by many dispensationalists to limit the Sermon on the Mount's import to Israel and keep it off limits for application to the church's engagement inadvertently keeps the church off limits from the public sphere as Christ's kingdom community, a city on a hill. Capitol Hill ends up replacing it! The Sermon on the Mount makes clear that the Lord of the church publicly engages and confronts the fallen powers. Our Lord does not privatize the faith. He and his kingdom were viewed as a threat to the Romans. We find this in the Sermon on the Mount when he tells his community of disciples to turn the other cheek and carry the load a second mile, and at his trial when he tells Pilate that his kingdom is not from this world. His kingdom is a kingdom of grace, mercy, and love, as Luther maintains (see above), not that of retribution; and so, his kingdom threatens the very foundations on which "the Romans" have built theirs—then and now.

Jürgen Moltmann argues that while Pilate was mistaken in taking Jesus to be a "Zealot rebel" he clearly perceived Jesus with his divine "law of grace" to be an affront to "the *Pax Romana* and its gods and laws" of oppression and retribution.[38] Jesus was not a political revolutionary in the manner of the Zealots; in fact, for all his affinities to them, he stood in diametrical opposition to their vision and aims at key points. Thus, while both Jesus and the Zealots condemned the mistreatment of the poor, Jesus, contrary to the Zealots, "did not call upon the poor to revenge themselves upon their exploiters nor the oppressed to oppress their oppressors."[39]

Jesus' kingdom of grace and mercy is not one of passivity though. Walter Wink says of turning the other cheek and walking the second mile that Jesus is instructing his followers: "Do not continue to acquiesce in your oppression by the Powers; but do not react violently to it either. Rather, find a third way, a way that is neither submission nor assault, flight nor fight, a way that can secure your human dignity and begin to change the power equation. . . ." Jesus' teachings are meant to "recover for the poor a modicum of initiative that can force the oppressor to see them in a new light. . . . The logic of Jesus' examples in Matthew 5:39b–41 [turning the other cheek] goes beyond both inaction and overreaction to a new response, fired in the crucible of love, that promises to liberate the oppressed from evil even as it frees the oppressor from sin."[40] This approach makes it possible for the oppressed to oppose the enemy while holding out the possibility for the enemy to become just. Jesus avoids the extremes of acquiescence and violent reaction by creating the church as an alternative politics—the theo-political communal presence of the not yet eschatological kingdom that submits all judgment to God and loves the enemy, thereby destabilizing the kingdoms of this world.[41]

The preceding discussion reflects a certain dialectical two kingdom approach. The church does not take up arms, but it does fight. The problem with many two kingdom positions surfaces when people do indeed acquiesce, saying that Jesus' politics of living in authentic community where we turn the other cheek and go the extra mile has no bearing on the Christian life and his or her calling. It is a text reserved simply for improving our state of mind and life of the soul. This is a common occurrence in the evangelical church and reflects a spiritual and hermeneutical abnormality. As one of my friends once said, he knew that something was wrong with evangelicalism when so much of his Gospels class in his Christian college consisted of being taught what Jesus didn't *really* mean by what he said.[42]

For Bonhoeffer, Jesus really *did* mean what he said. That is why he found it so hard to join in the assassination plot against Hitler. Bonhoeffer never sought to justify his actions, but neither could he ever justify the separation of powers where the Christian submits his soul to God and his body to the state.[43] While Bonhoeffer struggled with the Lutheran two kingdom view as well as with Jesus' words about turning the other cheek, he believed he must join the resistance movement in its assassination plot, regardless of the consequences. All this goes to show that Bonhoeffer was no pure dualist. It also shows him to be a representative figure for all of us in dealing with the host of complexities surrounding cultural engagement and the different approaches so many of us embody in our day to day lives, including the synthesist orientation.

Christ above Culture: Christ as Synthesist. With the synthesist model the foundation stones for the gospel are laid in culture. While culture needs "to be purified and lifted," there are positive dimensions to it.[44] There is an end to which culture strives through supernatural enablement. On this model grace does not destroy but perfects nature (*gratia non tollit sed perficit naturam*), as many Roman Catholics and defenders of natural theology maintain.

Hints of the synthesist orientation may be found in several places in the Gospels. The synthesist model is incarnational and organic.[45] God's kingdom sprouts and grows in the world like a mustard seed and spreads like leaven through dough (Matt 13:31–33). Jesus often appealed to people's secular or earthy sensitivities in his images and parables of the life of the kingdom, making use of birds and lilies (Matt 6:25–34) and shrewd managers (Luke 16:8–9) and affirming the faith and contriteness of pagan tax collectors while rebuking the religiosity and pride of the Pharisees (Luke 18:9–14). Jesus says in the Sermon on the Mount that "evil" parents know how to give good gifts to their children, going further to say that God gives even better gifts, and more abundantly (Matt 7:9–11).

This discussion on how the secular and pagan can have sacred ends calls to mind a story that John Doberstein recounts from Bonhoeffer's student days. While participating in one of Barth's seminars in Bonn, Bonhoeffer quoted the earthy saint Luther approvingly: "The curse of a godless man can sound more pleasant in God's ears than the Hallelujah of the pious."[46] This secular sentiment also surfaces in Bonhoeffer's *Letters and Papers from Prison* written near the end of his life. Bonhoeffer speaks there of man come of age. Humanity no longer needs the hypothesis "God" to function in life. Faced with this state of affairs as well as with the emptiness and absence of the all-powerful God who rescues us from *gaps* (*deus ex machina*) but who had not liberated Germany and the church from the Hitler menace, Bonhoeffer finds God's presence and fullness in the weakness and poverty and sorrow of the God-forsaken God on the cross. As Bonhoeffer writes,

> God would have us know that we must live as men who manage our lives without him. The God who is with us is the God who forsakes us (Mark 15.34). The God who lets us live in the world without the working hypothesis of God is the God before whom we stand continually. Before God and with God we live without God. God lets himself be pushed out of the world on to the cross. He is weak and powerless in the world, and that is precisely the way, the only way, in which he is with us and helps us. Matt. 8.17 makes it quite clear that Christ helps us, not by virtue of his omnipotence, but by virtue of his weakness and suffering.[47]

Bonhoeffer is not calling for a Christless and churchless spirituality but for a "religionless Christianity" where Jesus is viewed as "the man for others" and the church as his body that "exists for others." Bonhoeffer says, "The Church is the

Church only when it exists for others."[48] We must stop looking to God to intervene in our struggles and remove us from crises, but instead face those crises with the awareness that God suffers our affliction with us and calls us to identify with others in their suffering.

While I do not deny that there are times in the church's history where God has intervened with his righteous right arm to redeem the church from oppression and suffering, I also realize that the church has often failed to see that God so profoundly and pervasively demonstrates his omnipotence through the weakness of the cross—in Christ and in his church. While it is not always the case that the blood of the martyrs is the seed of the church, much of the time it is. The church is growing most rapidly today in places where it is poor and oppressed, whereas in America most growth is through transfer of membership and attendance. When the church realizes that Jesus' identity is in and with and for others in the midst of affliction, and that it too is to exist for others in this way, it will gain ultimate affluence and influence with God.

We as the church have much to learn from secular humanity's coming of age, for it teaches us that we too as God's church need to come of age. This worldly age served as a stepping stone, if not a foundation stone, for Bonhoeffer, who recognized more and more clearly that

> . . . it is only by living completely in this world that one learns to have faith. One must completely abandon any attempt to make something of oneself, whether it be a saint, or a converted sinner, or a churchman (a so-called priestly type!), a righteous man or an unrighteous one, a sick man or a healthy one. By this-worldliness I mean living unreservedly in life's duties, problems, successes and failures, experiences and perplexities. In so doing we throw ourselves completely into the arms of God, taking seriously, not our own sufferings, but those of God in the world—watching with Christ in Gethsemane. That I think is faith, that is *metanoia*; and that is how one becomes a man and a Christian (cf. Jer. 45!). How can success make us arrogant, or failure lead us astray, when we share in God's sufferings through a life of this kind?[49]

Worldly affluence and political influence—success by our standards—are often counterproductive by God's standards. Bonhoeffer's own abiding influence is in many respects the result of his having died to affluence and influence, giving up everything to gain Christ. Bonhoeffer understood well that it is the poor in spirit, the meek, those who mourn and who are persecuted because of their union with Christ, who are truly affluent and influential.

Bonhoeffer's form of discipleship and "religionless Christianity" did not take him out of the world but further into it. While persecuted, he gave himself all the more fully to bringing about a more just society. In fact, he suffered at the hands of those who claimed to speak for the Christian God—Hitler and the

German Christians—even while suffering for Jewish people who did not share his Christian beliefs. He gave sacrificially of himself to take back Germany from the nationalistic Christians for the "unbelieving" people of God, seeking to build on new and better German foundations. As a result of reading Bonhoeffer's *Letters and Papers from Prison*, one such unbelieving Jewish person told Eberhard Bethge, the volume's editor, that he was now "beginning to see for the first time why Jesus could be regarded as divine."[50]

We American evangelicals have gained a lot of influence in centers of American power in recent years but have lost America's heart in the process. The appearance of taking back America for our own kind of people and Jesus for ourselves needs to be replaced by the reality of giving up our lives for America, just as Jesus, "the man for others," gave of himself unreservedly for the people of his day—irrespective of their relation to him. The "God of the gaps" and "Take Back America" way of thinking needs to give way to God in the gallows. This will involve getting our hands dirty and moving increasingly toward downward mobility and heterogeneity in our church life and outreach. Instead of going back to the religion of our founding constitutional fathers, who did not truly see all humans as created equal (Jefferson for one owned slaves), we will seek to go back to the religion founded by Jesus, which has hardly taken root in our nation and religion, becoming slaves for Christ so that everyone else might become truly free in body and spirit through him, especially the poor and other "least of these" groups. We do this so that we ourselves might become truly free in the process.

Our American nationalistic religion perceives Jesus, not as a man for others, but as a God for ourselves who exacts revenge on our enemies. Like Bonhoeffer who was concerned for building a more spiritual church and more civil state, we must seek to build the church and the nation on better foundations, foundations that hearken back to our religion's founder. Our Lord sought to do away with Pharisaical religiosity in favor of a worldly spirituality in his Sermon on the Mount (Matt 6:1–18), and instead of exacting revenge on his enemies, he gave up his life at the hands of the religious so that the world might live (Matt 27:41–44).

The church can only serve as a preservative and penetrating light in society by joyfully facing persecution for its union with Jesus (Matt 5:11–16) and by not seeking to preserve itself like the religious leaders of Jesus' day did by sacrificing Jesus to preserve the people, the temple, and their own position (Matt 27:18 and John 11:45–53). A transformation of the American church's spirituality is in order. Before it can take the sawdust out of the nation's eye, it must take the plank out of its own (Matt 7:3). Only then can it serve as a reforming and transforming force in the culture at large.

Christ Transforming Culture: Christ as Transformationalist. Now we come to the last of the five categories—Christ as the transformer of culture. This view of Christ's engagement of culture requires culture's radical purification, but not its replacement. Here the positive reality of the creation and incarnation balance consideration of the negativity of the fall.[51] On this model, according to Wainwright,[52] there appears to be no division of history into two autonomous spheres—sacred and profane. The church is to be an "adumbration," "perhaps even an anticipation of the final Kingdom of God."[53]

The Sermon on the Mount certainly portrays Christ's community as an anticipation of the final kingdom of God and Christ himself as the one who inaugurates and eventually consummates that kingdom. In fact, we would go so far as to say that the Sermon on the Mount and its surrounding narrative signify that Jesus recapitulates or transforms Israel's history. After Jesus submitted himself to John's baptism—a baptism of repentance—to identify with his people (Matt 3:13–17), the Spirit drove Jesus into the wilderness to undergo temptation by the devil for forty days and forty nights, mirroring Israel's forty years of temptations and trials (Matt 4:1–11). Upon his return Jesus began his public ministry, proclaiming in word and deed that the eschatological kingdom is at hand in his person (Matt 4:12–25). Then, whereas Moses went up the mountain to receive the Law, Jesus went up the mountain to give the Law of the kingdom (Matt 5:1–2). His disciples become the new teachers of the Law, standing in the line of the OT prophets and replacing Jesus' opponents among the scribes and Pharisees (Matt 13:10–23) who had hardened themselves toward the Spirit's work of inspiring and empowering Jesus in word and deed (Matt 12:24–32; 13:10–23).

Jesus is the ultimate prophet, priest, and king—summing up, perfecting, and transforming the whole of the OT story so that it becomes part of his own. This calls to mind the opening lines of Heb (1:1–3):

> In the past God spoke to our forefathers through the prophets at many times and in various ways, but in these last days he has spoken to us by his Son, whom he appointed heir of all things, and through whom he made the universe. The Son is the radiance of God's glory and the exact representation of his being, sustaining all things by his powerful word. After he had provided purification for sins, he sat down at the right hand of the Majesty in heaven.

God speaks conclusively through his Son, the prophet Jesus, who is also the great high priest, who has provided purification for humankind's sin once and for all, and who now sits enthroned as God's ascended and reigning Messiah.

No wonder the writer of Hebrews can say that whereas Moses was faithful in all God's house, Jesus, God's Son, is faithful over all God's house. Christ's church is that house—holding firmly to the hope which is ours in Christ (Heb 3:1–6). No wonder too that Jesus said that he came to fulfill or perfect the Law and the Prophets in his person (Matt 5:17–20). Jesus countered the traditions that distorted the Law and deepened the Law's significance, especially as it bore witness to him (Matt 5:17–6:8; 7:12, 24–29; see also Luke 24:25–27). John's Gospel reveals that Jesus cast his shadow over the Law and Prophets as he served as antitype for its various images. He is the ultimate bread of heaven (John 6:30–35; cf. Exod 16:1–22), the true light of the world (John 8:12; cf. 7:1–10 and Lev 23:33–44),[54] the Good Shepherd (John 10:1–18; cf. Ezek 34:1–10), the resurrection and life (John 11), and the good and true vine (John 15:1–8; cf. Isa 5:1–7).

The Law of Moses and the traditions of men certainly shaped the culture in which Jesus was embodied, which Jesus had come to confront, redeem, perfect, and transform. Yet, Jesus did not consummate the kingdom in his first coming. This point is often lost on the church. The founding fathers of Calvin's Geneva and the proponents of Manifest Destiny in the States failed to recognize the line of demarcation between the "now" and "not yet" of Christ's kingdom. The church is God's eschatological *polis*—the city set on a hill, not the state; while the gospel is the politics of Christ's kingdom and intersects and impacts this world's *polis* and politics, the church must never be confused with the latter.

Whereas classic forms of dispensationalism have tended to subsume the "now" of the kingdom under the "not yet," theonomist versions of covenant theology have tended to subsume the "not yet" under the "now."[55] These moves parallel their respective approaches to Israel's relation to the church. Dispensationalism has often tended to divide Israel and the church,[56] whereas covenantal theology has often tended to displace Israel in favor of the church.[57] In contrast to both perspectives there is a distinct though inseparable relation between Israel and the church according to which Christ is Lord over Israel and the church and where the church is the fulfillment (not replacement) of Israel.

Calvinists such as John Winthrop and many other early colonists journeyed to America to create a Christian society.[58] They looked at the church as the New Israel and America as a new Promised Land, which they were destined by God to inhabit and rule. When advocates of Manifest Destiny took up the call, it proved disastrous for the native peoples of the land. Such proponents of Manifest Destiny treated the indigenous peoples like the Canaanites in Joshua's day.

Bonhoeffer gave much thought to what Germany would look like in the event of Hitler being overthrown. However, Bonhoeffer entertained no hope of a nation where the church becomes the state. He was too Lutheran for that.[59] But, he did hope and plan for a better future for Germany and for the church. In *Letters and Papers from Prison*, he speaks against a "silly, cowardly kind of optimism," on the one hand, and those pessimists who "think that the meaning of present events is chaos, disorder, and catastrophe; and in resignation or pious escapism . . . surrender all responsibility for reconstruction and for future generations." Bonhoeffer would only stop hoping and planning for a better earthly future once the day of judgment dawns: "It may be that the day of judgment will dawn tomorrow; and in that case, though not before, we shall gladly stop working for a better future."[60]

The church in America today should work for a better future for the church and for America. The church first and foremost is always to bear witness to the politics and economics of the coming kingdom in light of which it engages the society at large. It does this through its own practices such as baptism, the Lord's Supper, and redistribution of resources on behalf of the poor. At the outset of this chapter we indicated that the church is a cultural community that is shaped by the surrounding culture and that prophetically confronts that culture for the latter's own ultimate transformation. Outside culture there is no church, but outside the church of the triune God's eschatological kingdom, there is no ultimate redemption of culture. The church is joined to Jesus as his body and bride. Thus, it is called to embody his kingdom values and proclaim them in word and deed to the surrounding world. The church is to be the now of the not yet kingdom. It is to be a kind of first fruits and foretaste (not rotten fruit and a bitter aftertaste) of the kingdom in the here and now (James 1:18). It is to be salt and light, a city set on a hill whose light all can see, and whose good works serve to enlighten all (Matt 5:13–16).

A CITY ON A HILL

In 1630 John Winthrop preached a sermon titled "A Model of Christian Charity" in which he warned the Puritan colonists of New England that the world would be watching them as they would "a city upon a hill." Drawing from the imagery of salt and light in the Sermon on the Mount, Winthrop wrote:

> For we must consider that we shall be as a city upon a hill. The eyes of all people are upon us. So that if we shall deal falsely with our God in this work we have undertaken, and so cause Him to withdraw His present help from us, we shall be made a story and a by-word through the world. We shall open the mouths of enemies to speak evil of the ways of God, and all professors for God's sake. We shall shame the faces of many of God's worthy servants, and cause their prayers to be turned into curses upon us till we be consumed out of the good land whither we are going.[61]

The church as a public, as a distinct culture engaging other particular publics and cultures, must seek to be that city on the hill that sheds its light in such a manner that those who see it would be led to glorify God rather than curse us. The church can only be this shining light as it demonstrates charity toward its members and toward the world at large.

The Puritan community did not always practice the love toward one another that Winthrop's sermon on charity commended. Nor are the Puritans usually remembered for exercising charity and tolerance toward those who believed differently than they did. As a result, they opened the mouths of the American church's enemies to speak evil of the ways of God. We no longer live under Christendom or in a utopian Christian society, though many Christians still long for it and lobby on Capitol Hill to take it back. While the church will always have its fair share of enemies, the church must ever live to bless those communities with whom it coexists rather than seek to take back America from its enemies or wall itself off from them as a separatist society. As Christ's eschatological kingdom community the church should not aspire to be taken out of this world. Rather, it is to exist as salt and light among this world's kingdoms and their communities as first fruits and as a witness to that kingdom that will be consummated when Christ returns.

It is not the church's role to judge the world but to serve it. It is not the American church's place to take back America or its cities like Portland, Oregon, where I minister, but to "love on Portland," as Pastor Rick McKinley of Imago Dei Community often says. In place of a theology of disengagement with a God of the gaps who will come to rescue us from this evil world, we need a theology of engagement with a God on the gallows, a theology framed by the same Jesus who did not come to take back Jerusalem from his enemies but to give up his life for his enemies on Golgotha outside the city's gates so as to win them over to God.

Whereas Christ the transformer of culture has often presupposed Christendom and a church-state's use of force to impose its rule, the church in America today can only go forth as Christ's alternative kingdom culture in pursuit of transformation of the surrounding cultures in our pluralistic society by bearing its cross. But, bearing the cross alone is not sufficient to calm fears. The cross has often been used to promote Manifest Destiny's ambitions. As Native American Vine Deloria Jr. has said, "Where the cross goes, there is never life more abundantly—only death, destruction, and ultimately betrayal."[62] The American church today must not simply bear the cross, but be willing to be hung upon it on behalf of the surrounding world—and in the gallows, too, like Bonhoeffer before us. The transformationalist kingdom model espoused here is Christ-centered, cruciform, and ecclesially framed.[63] Otherwise, we may transform Christ and his cross—distorting them—to serve as illustrations of the hardships we will face before we climb the mountain and set up our standard on the Hill in the City of the New Jerusalem through which the Potomac River runs.

In "Armaments and Eschatology," John Howard Yoder wrote, "People who bear crosses are working with the grain of the universe,"[64] even while working against the grain and against the stream in a society dominated by the culture wars. Bonhoeffer served as such a witness to this universal pattern as he hung on the gallows on behalf of the endangered Jewish people and in view of his hope for a transformed Germany. Unless a kernel of wheat falls to the ground and dies, it can bear no fruit (John 12:24). Only as Christ's followers bear their persecution joyfully rather than bitterly, as Bonhoeffer did before them, can they serve as Bonhoeffer did as salt and light and as a brilliant city set upon a hill that leads others to glorify our Father in heaven (Matt 5:11–16; cf. Heb 11–13).

ENDNOTES

1. An expanded version of this essay will appear as chapter seven in my forthcoming book with Brad Harper titled *The Bride: An Ecumenical and Evangelical Ecclesiology* (Brazos).

2. "Culture" may be defined as the totality of human activity in all spheres, both work and leisure, and includes language and social norms—whether spoken or unspoken—that shape people's lives and worldviews and guarantee rites of passage in society. Culture is also taken to refer to the heights of human achievement in the realms of the sciences, the arts, ethics, or sports. Lastly, culture may be seen to refer to the whole of a particular society or civilization, which may either be viewed as inclusive of the church or as distinct from its religious or spiritual counterpart. In this essay, we are thinking specifically of culture as a community with a given language and social norms, which shape that community's values, actions, and practices.

3. H. Richard Niebuhr, *Christ and Culture* (New York: Harper & Brothers, 1951).

4. For other helpful treatments of Christ's relation to culture through the centuries, see the following works: Robert Webber, *The Secular Saint: A Case for Evangelical Social Responsibility* (Eugene, Or.: Wipf & Stock, 2004); Jaroslav Pelikan, *Jesus Through the Centuries: His Place in the History of Culture*, with a new preface by the author (New Haven: Yale University Press, 1999). This last book shows Christ's impact on culture through the various epochs; each age's predominant image of Christ presented here provides a lens for viewing that particular era. Two important critiques of Niebuhr's paradigm are John Howard Yoder, "How H. Richard Niebuhr Reasoned: A Critique of Christ and Culture," in *Authentic Transformation: A New Vision of Christ and Culture* (ed. Glen Stassen and D. M. Yeager; Nashville: Abingdon, 1996), 31-89; and Craig A. Carter, *Rethinking Christ and Culture: A Post-Christendom Perspective* (Grand Rapids: Brazos, 2007).

5. Dietrich Bonhoeffer, *No Rusty Swords* (ed. Edwin H. Robertson, et al.; London: Collins, 1970), 306.

6. Quoted in Larry Rasmussen, *Dietrich Bonhoeffer: Reality and Resistance* (Nashville: Abingdon, 1972), 25.

7. Gregory of Nazianzus, "Epistle 101: To Cledonios," in *Patrologia Græca,* Vol. XXXVII, col. 181C.

8. Karl Barth, "The Barmen Declaration," quoted in *The Church's Confession Under Hitler* by Arthur C. Cochrane (Philadelphia: Westminster, 1962), 239–240.

9. William H. Willimon, "Been There, Preached That: Today's Conservatives Sound Like Yesterday's Liberals," *Leadership: A Practical Journal for Church Leaders* 16.4 (Fall 1995): 76.

10. John R. W. Stott speaks of poverty in spirit as "spiritual bankruptcy" in *The Message of the Sermon on the Mount, Matthew 5–7: Christian Counter-Culture* (The Bible Speaks Today; Downers Grove: InterVarsity, 1978), 39.

11. Dietrich Bonhoeffer, *The Cost of Discipleship* (2d ed.; New York: Macmillan, 1959), 50–51.

12. Ibid., 50–53.

13. Ibid., 50–51.
14. Ibid., 51.
15. Ibid., 52–53.
16. Ibid., 120.
17. Ibid., 90–91.
18. Ibid., 91.
19. Ibid., 120.
20. Karl Barth, "The Christian Community and the Civil Community," in *Against the Stream: Shorter Post-War Writings, 1946–1952* (ed. R. G. Smith; trans. E.M. Delecour and S. Godman; London: SCM, 1954), 31.
21. Bonhoeffer, *The Cost of Discipleship*, 303–304.
22. Geoffrey Wainwright, "Types of Spirituality," in *The Study of Spirituality* (ed. Cheslyn Jones, Geoffrey Wainwright and Edward Yarnold; New York: Oxford University Press, 1986), 595.
23. Ibid., 596.
24. Ibid., 597–598.
25. Niebuhr, *Christ and Culture*, 156.
26. Luther wrote, ". . . a Christian man is righteous and a sinner at the same time, holy and profane, an enemy of God and a child of God. None of the sophists will admit this paradox, because they do not understand the true meaning of justification." Martin Luther, *Luther's Works*, vol. 26, *Lectures on Galatians*, 1535, chapters 1–4 (ed. Jaroslav Pelikan; Saint Louis: Concordia, 1963), 232–233.
27. Martin Luther, "An Open Letter on the Harsh Book Against the Peasants," in *Luther's Works*, vol. 46, *The Christian in Society* (ed. Robert C. Schultz; Philadelphia: Fortress, 1967), 69–70. See also Bonhoeffer's dialectical depiction of the relation of Christ, church, and state in *Christ the Center* (trans. Edwin H. Robertson; San Francisco: Harper SanFrancisco, 1978), 63–64.
28. Niebuhr, *Christ and Culture*, 172.
29. Karl Barth, "The Christian Community and the Civil Community," 24.
30. Ibid., 29.
31. Cynthia D. Moe-Lobeda, *Healing a Broken World: Globalization and God* (Minneapolis: Fortress, 2002), 106.
32. Ibid., 106.
33. See also Alan J. Torrance's discussion of the situation at the time of Hitler in his introduction to Eberhard Jüngel's *Christ, Justice and Peace: Toward a Theology of the State in Dialogue with the Barmen Declaration* (trans. D. Bruce Hamill and Alan J. Torrance; Edinburgh: T. & T. Clark, 1992). Torrance speaks of how nationalism's rise in Germany led to the subjectivizing of spirituality and the relativizing of the "imperatives of the Gospel" (p. xi). Also see Paul Louis Metzger, *The Word of Christ and the World of Culture: Sacred and Secular through the Theology of Karl Barth* (Grand Rapids: Eerdmans, 2003), 165–166.
34. Bethge's remarks are found in John W. de Gruchy, *Daring, Trusting Spirit: Bonhoeffer's Friend Eberhard Bethge* (Minneapolis: Fortress, 2005), 200–201.
35. Reinhard Hütter, *Suffering Divine Things: Theology as Church Practice* (Grand Rapids: Eerdmans, 1999), 11.
36. See Kristen Deede Johnson, "'Public' Re-Imagined: A Reconsideration of Church, State, and Civil Society," in *A World for All? Global Civil Society in Political Theory and Trinitarian Theology* (ed. William F. Storrar, Peter J. Casarella, and Paul Louis Metzger; forthcoming from Eerdmans), 14–15.

37. Falwell was a very complex figure. As an antagonistic fundamentalist distancing himself from secular America, he promoted the Christ against culture model. As a reconstructionist trying to take back America, he promoted the Christ as the transformer of culture model. However, Falwell also inadvertently promoted Christ and culture in paradox, given his subjugation of the church to the state in promoting culture's transformation. Falwell functioned as a kind of dualist in that he did not see the church as the primary agent for bringing about society's transformation; for this he turned to the state. The church was awarded a subservient role to the state in bringing about society's transformation.

38. Jürgen Moltmann, *The Crucified God: The Cross of Christ as the Foundation and Criticism of Christian Theology* (Minneapolis: Fortress, 1993), 143–144.

39. Ibid., 141.

40. Walter Wink, *The Powers That Be: Theology for a New Millennium* (New York: Doubleday, 1998), 110–111.

41. Suffice it to say that Jesus' claim that he is king, and that his kingdom is here though not yet fully realized but will be realized at his second coming, has always made the Caesars apprehensive. Barth was ousted from Germany in the early 1930s for claiming in the Barmen Declaration that there is no other Führer than Jesus Christ. Japanese pastors during World War II were imprisoned for preaching the return of Christ. The problem for Führers and Tojos, Caesars and Caiaphases alike, is that the resurrected and reigning Jesus serves as a check on their ambitions and spoils their garden parties.

42. See Bonhoeffer's discussion of interpretive sophistry when dealing with Christ's claims in *The Cost of Discipleship*, 87–91.

43. Regardless of how Luther intended them, his remarks that while the body is under Caesar's authority the soul is under God's alone certainly opens the door for Christians to offer blind and reckless submission to the state. See Martin Luther, "Temporal Authority: To What Extent It Should Be Obeyed," in *Luther's Works*, vol. 45, *The Christian in Society* (ed. Walther I. Brandt; Philadelphia: Fortress, 1962), 111. Ultimate authority over our souls and bodies belongs to the one who alone can throw both soul and body in hell (Matt 10:28). See William T. Cavanaugh's discussion of the problem of separating authority over the body/temporal and the soul/spiritual in Roman Catholic circles in "The Minimum of Body," in *Torture and Eucharist: Theology, Politics, and the Body of Christ* (Oxford: Blackwell, 1998), 157–165.

44. Wainwright, "Types of Spirituality," 598.

45. Wainwright claims that the incarnation and resurrection receive particular attention in the synthesist model; this orientation bears the marks of the biological and the infused, which impact the entire race of humanity. Wainwright, "Types of Spirituality," 598. Wainwright sets forth 2 Tim 1:10 (the infusion of divine life into the whole race through Christ) as representative of this form of spirituality (pp. 598–599).

46. Dietrich Bonhoeffer; quoted by John W. Doberstein in his introduction to Dietrich Bonhoeffer's *Life Together* (New York: Harper & Row, 1954), 9.

47. Dietrich Bonhoeffer, *Letters and Papers from Prison* (ed. Eberhard Bethge; rev. ed.; New York: Macmillan, 1967), 188.

48. Ibid., 203.

49. Ibid., 193–194.

50. Eberhard Bethge, "Foreword," in Dietrich Bonhoeffer, *Letters and Papers from Prison*, xv.

51. See Wainwright, "Types of Spirituality," 603.

52. Ibid., 604.

53. Ibid., 605.

54. It is quite possible that Jesus proclaimed "I am the light of the world" against the backdrop of the lights from the booths scattered on the hills surrounding Jerusalem during the Feast of Tabernacles.

55. Theonomists maintain that the church is to strive to make America a Christian nation where God's OT Law is enforced. For a representative work see Gary North and Gary DeMar, *Christian Reconstruction: What It Is, What It Isn't* (Tyler, Tex.: Institute for Christian Economics, 1991).

56. See the critique of classic forms of dispensationalism as it concerns separation of Israel and the church in Craig A. Blaising and Darrell L. Bock, *Progressive Dispensationalism* (Wheaton: BridgePoint, 1993), 50–51.

57. See the discussion of supersessionism (the church displacing Israel) in Scott Bader-Saye's *Church and Israel After Christendom: The Politics of Election* (Radical Traditions; Boulder: Westview, 1999), 67, 74, and 76.

58. See Perry Miller's discussion of Winthrop in *Errand into the Wilderness* (Cambridge: The Belknap Press of Harvard University Press, 1956), 4–6.

59. Thus, he was no theonomist, but he was no Anabaptist either. Unlike Anabaptists Bonhoeffer was not reticent to get involved in confronting and/or promoting governmental or social structures as a Christian. Usually, when Anabaptists get involved socially, they speak as a community. It would be out of character for them to seek public office. While Bonhoeffer does not see the church as a voluntary association of religious individuals whose ultimate public allegiance is to the State, he did see that he as an individual Christian had a public role beyond participation in Christ's *polis*, the church. Thus, he involved himself in various efforts nationally and internationally in the fight against the Hitler menace.

60. Bonhoeffer, *Letters and Papers from Prison*, 16.

61. The quotation is taken from John Winthrop, "A Model of Christian Charity," http://religiousfreedom.lib.virginia.edu/sacred/charity.html, (August 6, 2007).

62. Vine Deloria, Jr., *God Is Red* (Golden: Fulcrum, 1994), 261.

63. Niebuhr's model(s) is neither Christ-centered, cruciform, nor ecclesially framed. Concerning Jesus, he wrote: "[Christ] is not a center from which radiate[s] the love of God and of men, obedience to God and Caesar, trust in God and nature, hope in divine and human action. He exists rather as the focusing point in the continuous alternation of movements from God to man and from man to God. . ." See Niebuhr, *Christ and Culture*, 29. When Christ in his particularity as the crucified and risen Messiah is not taken seriously in our reflections on the church's engagement of culture, the danger exists that the church will take matters into its own hands when facing the world's opposition rather than entrust judgment to God. Christ's cross instructs us to undergo judgment and persecution, and Christ's resurrection encourages us to hope in God to deliver and redeem us in his time and in his way. As stated above, the problem with Niebuhr's model is not limited to Christ's particularity. Christ's particular embodiment in the church does not figure significantly in Niebuhr's reflections on Christ's relation to culture. Without seeing the church as key to the matrix, Christ is abstracted from his concrete embodiment in culture. When Christ is abstracted from the church, there is nothing to safeguard the Christian individual from being conformed to the patterns of the fallen powers, including the state or market. Christ and his kingdom are crucial to the church as its transcendent ground, providing firm hope. The church is also of critical importance in that the church is the concrete manifestation of Christ's kingdom, providing the context for the demonstration of this hope as contemporary witness. As Stanley Hauerwas and Mark Sherwindt write, "Without the Kingdom-ideal, the church loses her identity-forming hope; without the church, the kingdom loses its concrete character." Stanley Hauerwas and Mark Sherwindt, "The Kingdom of God: An Ecclesial Space for Peace," *Word & World*, 2.2 (1982): 131.

64. John Howard Yoder, "Armaments and Eschatology," quoted by Stanley Hauerwas, *With the Grain of the Universe: The Church's Witness and Natural Theology* (Grand Rapids: Brazos, 2001), 6.

RESPONSE TO METZGER

G. SUJIN PAK

I want to express my deep appreciation to Prof. Paul Metzger for his very engaging essay that lays out some key interstices between the Sermon on the Mount, H. Richard Niebuhr's typology of Christ and culture, and the life and ministry of Dietrich Bonhoeffer. Using Niebuhr's fivefold typology, Prof. Metzger argues that in the Sermon on the Mount Jesus Christ exemplifies all five types: Jesus is the protagonist, the antagonist, the dualist, the great synthesist, and the ultimate transformationalist of culture. In sum, then, Jesus models for the church the way the church's relationship with culture should be "multifaceted and dynamic," rather than adhering to just one mode of Niebuhr's typology. Likewise, Prof. Metzger uses Dietrich Bonhoeffer's response to his own times concerning rising German nationalism, the Hitler regime, and the proper role of the German churches in order to demonstrate how the church is to be "a cultural community that is shaped by its surrounding culture and prophetically confronts that culture for the latter's own ultimate transformation."

In the course of accomplishing these stated objectives, Prof. Metzger also offers salient warnings about the pitfalls threatening the faithful embodiment and practices of the church within each of Niebuhr's five types. Namely, the temptations within the protagonist of culture is to exchange the gospel of Jesus Christ for a national agenda or to conform the church's "relevance" to the surrounding culture rather than asking if either of these are "relevant" to God and God's purposes. The temptation of the antagonist of culture is to forget that the overriding objective is the transformation of culture, not its elimination, nor a complete separation from it. The possible pitfall of the dualist is the creation of separate public and private sectors, in which faith is privatized and the primary player for the Christian's political and public life becomes the individual rather than the church. The temptation of the synthesist of culture is to act for the benefit and advantage of its own self rather than to act faithfully for others, which will mean the readiness to suffer persecution and to give up life for others (i.e., the way of the cross). Finally, the transformationalist of culture needs to remember that there is always a "not yet" aspect of the church's work in the world, a "not yet" that can only be fully completed by the ushering in of the final kingdom of God by Jesus Christ himself. These are all cautions that the church today would be very wise to heed.

Indeed, I believe Prof. Metzger is exactly right to argue that the church's relationship with culture does not—and should not—adhere to any one type of Niebuhr's model but must be multifaceted. I also applaud the wise warnings about the various temptations contained within the practices of each of Niebuhr's types. I might, however, question whether we want even to use Niebuhr's typologies at all.[1] Should we fit Scripture to Niebuhr's five-fold typology, or can we find in the Sermon on the Mount a *scriptural* paradigm with which to understand and view culture?

I profoundly affirm Prof. Metzger's consistent and clear use of Scripture to make his arguments. This is not something to be taken for granted in our times, as too often theological arguments are made and buttressed apart from clear references and grounding in Scripture. Overall, though, I would have liked to see the Sermon on the Mount used more as the guiding model for the essay. What might this look like? The Beatitudes speak of a community defined by the virtues of humility, compassion, meekness, righteousness, mercy, purity, peace, and martyrdom (Matt 5:1–12). It is also a community identified by its practices of being salt and light in the world (Matt 5:13–16) and observing and teaching the law (Matt 5:17–20). The Sermon on the Mount calls forth a community grounded in the practices of reconciliation, which includes guarding against anger and actively seeking forgiveness for wrongs done (Matt 5:21–26). It is a community summoned to righteous valuation and protection of its women, for it is called to act righteously and justly in areas where women can be most vulnerable (Matt 5:27–32). Furthermore, it is a community called to truthfulness and the keeping of one's word (Matt 5:33–37) and one called to peacefulness and love of enemies (Matt 5:38–48). Jesus summons the Sermon on the Mount community to right practices of worship over and against self-aggrandizement (Matt 6:1–16). Moreover, it is a community beckoned to serve one Master and abhor all the various forms of idolatry (Matt 6:19–34). Finally, Jesus summons the Sermon on the Mount community to practices of discernment and wisdom, particularly proper self-discernment and defense against self-deception (Matt 7:1–23). What would a culture look like with these characteristics? My hope is that we can say that the faithful church looks like this and that such a "culture" would encompass but also surpass the world's delineation of "culture" in predominantly racial, ethnic, and national terms.[2]

In sum, my point is that I would love to see more common in the practice of theologians the return to Scripture to provide the defining paradigms to be used—that *Scripture* forms and informs the models we employ—rather than conforming Scripture to a schema outside of itself.³ In other words, it seems to me that the Sermon on the Mount sets forth a calling of who the church should be in the world in such a way that it reveals that the *primary* aim of the church is not as the protagonist, antagonist, dualist, synthesist, or even transformationalist of the culture(s) of the world but, rather, to be faithful—to inhabit its true, faithful embodiment—to be *the church*. It is only when the church fulfills this calling that it can then be the salt and light in the world; only then can the church faithfully effect God's transformative purposes.

Given that my own field of expertise is the history of the Protestant Reformation and, particularly, the lives and theologies of Martin Luther and John Calvin, I am especially pleased to see Prof. Metzger's generally positive references to Martin Luther on this topic, albeit mostly through the lenses of Karl Barth and Dietrich Bonhoeffer. Nonetheless, more often than not, the references to Luther on the topics of church and state and his doctrine of the two kingdoms are overwhelmingly negative. For example, Luther's response to the German Peasants' Revolt is often cited as a case in point of the dangers of his two-kingdoms theology. Though I, too, have definite issues with the way Luther handled this situation, his response *could* be read in certain aspects as much in keeping with several of the arguments made in the current essay under consideration. Namely, Luther does not tell the peasants that they have no good reason for their rebellion; he affirms that they are unjustly oppressed.⁴ His chastisement concerns their taking up of arms for their own cause and doing so in the name of Christ.⁵ Instead, Luther admonishes the peasants by telling them that there is no place for Christians to take up arms *for their own cause* and that the faithful response is to *take on suffering for others*.⁶ At least in these ways, Luther is trying to bring the peasants, who call themselves Christians, back to the right practices of the kingdom of God as shown through the teachings of Christ in the Sermon on the Mount.⁷

A final question also points to a great strength of this essay. My question is this: In talking about the prophetic voice of the church in the world, particularly in the typologies of Christ against culture and Christ as transformationalist, is there not also an important place to talk about a prophetic voice *to the church* herself, to which I believe the Sermon on the Mount clearly directs us? Prof. Metzger names the church as a cultural community, but throughout the essay it appears that the primary "culture" with which Christ and the church interact is the world. Yet, clearly in the Sermon on the Mount, Jesus is also addressing the "church" of his day, particularly in the sixth chapter of Matthew where he condemns false, self-promoting worship practices. I would have liked to see the author more clearly take up not only the call for the church to participate faithfully in Christ's transformation of the world but also daily to undergo that transformation herself—that, indeed, the transformation of the world cannot occur without the continual transformation of the church to become more Christ-like. Yet, Prof. Metzger himself embodies this very call for transformation in the church when he admonishes his own particular faith community, the "fundamentalist-evangelicals," concerning their temptations toward an adversarial orientation, the privatization of faith, inadequate attention to ecclesiology, alignment of nation with faith, and the attitude of "taking back" rather than "giving up our lives for others." Is this not what the Sermon on the Mount teaches—that in order to be salt and light in the world, the church herself must daily be transformed and conformed to the righteous virtues and practices of the kingdom of God?

ENDNOTES

1. One of the problems with using Niebuhr's five-fold typology is that its use of culture has the strong tendency to view culture monolithically. Whose culture, which culture, are we talking about?

2. By this I do not mean the erasure of racial, ethnic, or even national cultures; rather, the embodiment of the virtues and practices taught in the Sermon on the Mount may very well have different nuances within Asian Christianity or African Christianity or Latino/Latina Christianity, but its character, grammar, and ethics have a shared core.

3. Indeed, I would liken this to the differentiation Bonhoeffer makes between reading the Bible for himself and reading Scripture over against himself, as articulated by Stephen Fowl and L. Gregory Jones in the chapter "Living and Dying in the Word: Dietrich Bonhoeffer as Performer of Scripture" in *Reading in Communion: Scripture and Ethics in Christian Life* (Grand Rapids: Eerdmans, 1991), 140. Scripture is to set forth the paradigm, to question our lives, rather than making Scripture relevant to an external agenda (ibid., 145). Similarly, Geffrey B. Kelly and F. Burton Nelson trace Bonhoeffer's transformation from a biblical interpreter taught to conform to the principles of biblical interpretation common in his day (i.e., historical criticism) to one who operated with openness to the movement of the Spirit and conformity to God's guidance given in Scripture. See "Dietrich Bonhoeffer's Theological Interpretation of Scripture for the Church," *Ex Auditu* 17 (2006): 1–4. I would argue that Martin Luther, along with Bonhoeffer, is another excellent example of what it looks like to be a theological interpreter of Scripture in response to the cultures of his day.

This criticism, of course, betrays my own particular biases. I am a historian, particularly a scholar of the history of biblical interpretation and of the Protestant Reformation, which had as one of its primary aims the return to the centrality of the Word of God. Thus, I am a keen proponent of those who aim to bridge the gap between biblical studies and theology that abounds in American theological academies today. As Stephen Fowl points out, Thomas Aquinas would not understand the separation of the tasks of the biblical scholar and the theologian (*Engaging Scripture: A Model for Theological Interpretation* [Oxford: Blackwell, 1998], 16). The same could be said of Martin Luther and John Calvin.

4. See Luther's *Admonition to Peace: A Reply to the Twelve Articles of the Peasants in Swabia* in *Luther's Works* (*LW*), Volume 46, pages 19–23. Luther writes to the princes and lords, "We have no one on earth to thank for this disastrous rebellion, except you princes and lords . . . as temporal rulers you do nothing but cheat and rob the people so that you may lead a life of luxury and extravagance . . . since you are the cause of this wrath of God, it will undoubtedly come upon you, unless you mend your ways in time. . . . It is not the peasants, dear lords, who are resisting you; it is God himself, to visit your raging upon you" (*LW* 46:19–20). And further on Luther writes, "The peasants have just published twelve articles, some of which are so fair and

just as to take away your reputation in the eyes of God and the world and fulfill what the Psalm [107:40] says about God pouring contempt upon princes" (*LW* 46:22).

5. Luther's first charge against the peasants is that they have taken up this revolt in the name of Christ, identifying themselves as a "Christian association." He warns them that this is akin to breaking the second commandment of taking the Lord's name in vain (*LW* 46:24). Secondly, Luther asserts that they are going diametrically against the teachings of Scripture by taking up the sword in the name of Christ (*LW* 46:24–25).

6. Indeed, here Luther appeals to the Sermon on the Mount to make his point: "For if you claim that you are Christians and like to be called Christians and want to be known as Christians, then you must also allow your law to be held up before you rightly. Listen, then, dear Christians, to your Christian law! Your Supreme Lord Christ, whose name you bear, says in Matthew 6 [actually 5:39–41], 'Do not resist one who is evil. If anyone wants to take your coat, let him have your cloak too. If anyone strikes you on one cheek, offer him the other too.' Do you hear this, O Christian association? How does your program stand in the light of this law? You do not want to endure evil or suffering, but rather want to be free and to experience only goodness and justice. . . . Suffering, suffering! Cross, cross! This and nothing else is the Christian law!" (*LW* 46: 28, 29). And even more clearly, later on Luther adds, "Christians do not fight for themselves with sword and musket, but with the cross and with suffering, just as Christ, our leader, does not bear the sword, but hangs on the cross" (*LW* 46:32).

7. Indeed, Luther appeals to the Sermon on the Mount throughout his rebuke of the peasants. See *LW* 46:26, 28, 29, 33, 34. However, especially one aspect of Luther's rebuke of the German peasants is deeply troubling: his appeal to natural law in such a way that he renders the authority given to every secular ruler an authority given by God, and thus, there is no proper place to question this authority or overturn it without also questioning and "treading underfoot" the authority of God and putting oneself above God. See *LW* 46:25–26.

DISCERNING THE SPIRIT IN CULTURE: OBSERVATIONS ARISING FROM REFLECTIONS ON GENERAL REVELATION

ROBERT K. JOHNSTON

Christian theologians have too often looked at general revelation as a "cup half-empty," even while their own experience of God's Spirit, like that of others in the culture around them, has been of a "cup half-full." The difference has proven more than semantic. It has described the "spectacles" we have worn as we have engaged both biblical text and cultural context. It has defined either a posture of suspicion or one of appreciation through which we have filtered the witnesses of others (and ourselves) to the Spirit's illumining presence in our lives. Is C. S. Lewis's experience of "Joy's" "bright shadow" or John Updike's experience of "supernatural mail: decisive but illegible" of any account? How seriously are we to take experience as a theological source? What difference might it make to reread the biblical text with the experience of these artists, as well as our own, in mind? Could our own spirituality be deepened and our witness enhanced through recognizing the testimony of the Spirit in and through creation, conscience, and creativity?

In her novel *All New People* Anne Lamott has Nanny Goodman, her quasi-autobiographical young heroine, say about her parents, "Now my father didn't believe in God, but he believed in the existence of the sacred, of the holy; it was pretty hard not to believe in anything in the face of Bach, or our mountain. . . . My mother believed that God lit the stars and spoke directly through family and friends, musicians and writers, madmen and children, and nature—and not, as she had been raised to believe, through a booming voice from the heavens."[1] One of the characters in Ingmar Bergman's film *Fanny and Alexander* speaks more succinctly of the arts providing "supernatural shudders."[2] Writing in a similar vein, John Updike has one of his characters, David Kern, speak of an experience he had as "supernatural mail on foreign soil." His transcendent experience took place as he helped a dying cat that had been hit by a car while on his way home from the hospital where his wife was giving birth to their daughter. The juxtaposition of death and life came together for him as a moment in time, yet out of time. David concludes, "The incident had the signature, decisive but illegible."[3]

Such witnesses to God's presence in life are common throughout the arts, but they are not limited to imaginary worlds. In fact, similar reflections are the testimony of many, perhaps most, people. David Hay and Kate Hunt reported for example that in 2000 in a national sample in England, while less than ten percent of those polled went to church, seventy-six percent reported having a spiritual experience of some kind.[4] Hay observed that their findings were consistent with the evidence from comparative religion, where there are few, if any, limitations on where or when such "moment(s) of religious awareness can take place": "There are records of such moments during childbirth, at the point of death, during sexual intercourse, at a meal, during fasting, in a cathedral, on a rubbish dump, on a mountain top, in a slum, in association with a particular plant, stone, fish, mammal, bird and so on *ad infinitum*. . . . (T)hough it is worth repeating that there seems to be no way of 'switching them on.'"[5]

For Paul Tillich such an experience came while in Berlin on furlough from his duty as an army chaplain during World War I. Gazing at Botticelli's *Madonna and Child with Singing Angel* while visiting a museum, he had what he later described as a "breakthrough." This early experience was for him "revelatory ecstasy."[6] For C. S. Lewis these experiences sporadically occurred throughout his youth—as he played with a toy garden his brother made for him in the lid of a biscuit tin, as he listened to his mother read to him Beatrix Potter's *Squirrel Nutkin*, as he smelled a currant bush, as he later listened to Wagner, read Norse mythology, studied Euripides' *Hippolytus*, and encountered George MacDonald's *Phantases*. These experiences provided him the title for his autobiography *Surprised by Joy*. He reflected, "It was as though the voice which had called me from the world's end were now speaking at my side. It was with me in the room, or in my body, or behind me. If it had eluded me by its distance, it now eluded me by its proximity—something too near to see, too plain to be understood, on this side of knowledge."[7] Or to give still a third example, Albert Einstein went to a concert early in the career of the violinist Yehudi Menuhin. After the concert Einstein said to the musician, "Thank you, Mr. Menuhin; you have again proved to me that there is a God in heaven."[8] In narrating the story Richard Viladesau concludes, "Aesthetic experience seems to play a major role—at least for some people—in the exercise of the practical judgment for belief in God—perhaps a great deal more than the traditional 'proofs' of God's existence set forth in apologetic theology."[9] Confirming such a judgment, George Barna in a poll taken in 2000 found that twenty percent of Americans turned to "media, arts and culture" as their primary means of spiritual experience and expression.[10]

In my teaching in theology and the arts it is a common experience for me to hear students relate stories of their own transcendent experiences that they have had while reading a book or viewing a movie: *March of the Penguins, Magnolia, The Year of Living Dangerously, Field of Dreams, The Last Temptation of Christ*—the list of movies referenced by them includes secular and religious themes, documentaries and feature films, movies that are "G" rated and "R" rated, gritty and romantic.[11] Others speak of such revelatory moments as occurring at the birth of their child as with David Kern, or when on a mountain top, or when listening to music, or when joining others in a march for justice. One cannot predict or produce these revelatory moments, but they are nonetheless the experience of many. The experiences do not come from the arts alone, nor are they only a response to encountering nature or participating in the furtherance of goodness. They come randomly, but persistently, from human creativity, creation, and conscience. *What are we to make theologically of these repeated descriptions of experiences that are understood as "revelatory"?*

GENERAL REVELATION: A LARGELY NEGLECTED TOPIC

Revelation, said Karl Barth, "is what human beings cannot tell themselves."[12] It is, in Tim Gorringe's words, "the bridge between heaven and earth, human experience and the transcendent."[13] Yet we have largely ignored that bridge when it has occurred outside the Christian community and without direct reference to Jesus Christ. Perhaps this is because we are unsure how to sort out human projections from such revelation—"the making-known of what we truly *cannot* tell ourselves in and through the events we experience and in our language," to again quote Gorringe.[14] It appears to many, particularly in the evangelical wing of the church, that to paraphrase Barth, those testifying of transcendent experiences are simply speaking of God by shouting "man/woman." But though some of us are quick to posit such judgments, we also live uneasily with our own sporadic experiences of the "More," with those moments that seem to put all other moments into perspective, with those liminal occurrences that cross the threshold beyond human projection. As C. S. Lewis came to realize, the joy he experienced through art and nature was not of his making, but was his response to a joy which he encountered from beyond. But how can we be sure? And, is the joy resident in creation, or does it infuse nature/conscience/creativity from beyond? Again, the question intrudes: *How are we to understand theologically such "sacred" encounters?*

There have been in the last fifty years relatively few monographs written on "general revelation," the term given to that communion with the divine that takes place outside the church and its Scriptures and without direct reference to Jesus Christ. There have been even fewer of late. Perhaps here is the reason for the present disconnect between the burgeoning literature on spirituality in our broader, postsecular culture and the specifically Christian literature on spirituality and church life that has simultaneously arisen, texts either turned inwardly to a focus upon building up the body of Christ through worship and contemplation or outwardly in service, whether to humanity or the environment. Among the few theological studies on general revelation, one thinks of Avery Dulles's *Revelation Theology* (1969), Bruce Demarest's *General Revelation* (1982), H. Richard Niebuhr's *The Meaning of Revelation* (1941), Jürgen Moltmann's *The Spirit of Life: A Universal Affirmation* (1992), H. D. McDonald's *Theories of Revelation: An Historical Study, 1700–1960* (1979), T. J. Gorringe's *Discerning Spirit: A Theology of Revelation* (1990), and C. G. Berkouwer's *General Revelation* (1955), though the purview of several of these studies is broader than general revelation per se. More typically, there have been historically grounded studies on "common grace," or "prevenient grace," or "natural revelation," or "natural theology," related subjects to be sure, but also distinct. *Why this dearth of reflection on God's revelatory presence in the world, in the arts, and in the experience of non-Christians, particularly when the topic is increasingly a central concern for postmoderns?*

Surely part of the answer as to why Protestants, in particular, have undervalued the topic has to do with Scripture itself, which centers on God's mighty acts in history culminating in the birth, life, death, and resurrection of Jesus Christ, that is, with saving grace. Special revelation's focus on salvation has tended to define the conversation, delimiting its boundaries. But we must also ask if all of Scripture has truly been listened to. That is, have we come to the Bible in its entirety asking the right questions, wearing the right "spectacles"?[15] Or have we allowed past priorities and past questions to color present interpretation unduly, so that portions of Scripture are overlooked or wrongly interpreted? What of the Bible's creation-centered texts, for example? Why has this portion of God's Word been largely ignored in discussions of revelation? Or conversely, why is it that the biblical discussion of general revelation has usually been focused on an interpretation of Rom 1 and 2, John 1, and perhaps Acts 17? What of the recorded experiences in Scripture of men and women who were outside the covenant community and yet experienced God's revelation? Melchizedek? Abimelech? King Neco? King Lemuel? Why are their stories largely ignored in discussion of general revelation, giving priority by default to the overarching, second order reflections of NT writers seeking to spell out the way of salvation? Theology's bias towards the redemptive over the creational and towards the propositional over the narrative is perhaps one explanation for the relative paucity of theological thinking on general revelation. First order, primary experience has been ignored, and thus, biblical source material limited. As a result, general revelation is more typically judged to be a side issue, a necessary inference from other theological loci, but little more.

Equally important with regard to the marginalization of most theological reflection on general revelation has been the theological judgment that sin has so clouded and warped human receptivity to divine revelation that general revelation, even though present, is of little if any value other than to confirm our sin and our "hardness of heart." Here in a nutshell is the theological interpretation many give to Rom 1 and 2, and John 1. While general revelation is acknowledged, the effects of sin are thought by some to be so devastating as to preclude any positive contribution from God's continuing presence among us through conscience, creation, and human creativity. Avery Dulles labels this typically "Reformed" approach to general revelation "Revelation as Doctrine," associating it with the biblically centered, more propositional theology of conservative evangelicals like B. B. Warfield, Carl Henry, and J. I. Packer.[16]

Perhaps most representative here is G. C. Berkouwer in his monograph on *General Revelation* for his *Studies in Dogmatics*.[17] Although Berkouwer takes pains to distance himself from those like Barth who would equate the exclusivity of salvation in Jesus Christ with the exclusivity of revelation in Jesus Christ, in practice this important distinction seems to matter little. In particular, although Berkouwer recognizes that there is a "natural" knowledge of God and his will that is outside of the revelation of Jesus Christ, he allows general revelation to be overwhelmed by human depravity. Though revelation is present to us, we simply remain ignorant of it as human beings. When Scripture seems to suggest otherwise, Berkouwer "finds" other explanations of what the text must mean.

For example, Berkouwer believes that the nature psalms do not really suggest that a knowledge of God is possible for all in and through creation, though this is what they might seem to be saying. Rather, such knowledge is dependent on redemption categories. Those psalms which glory in creation (e.g., Pss, 8, 19, 29, 65, 104, 147) are actually rooted in "faith knowledge," arising out of the community of Israel as a response to the saving acts of God. Creation alone is insufficient to mediate God's presence to us regardless of what these psalms seem to say. Berkouwer writes, "The Creator of heaven and earth is adored even as the Redeemer of Israel is praised: for Israel the two are identical. Hence it is impossible to appeal to the 'nature psalms' on behalf of a natural theology."[18]

At one level, Berkouwer is no doubt correct. The psalms are Israel's hymnbook, her response to the saving acts of YHWH. But can creation theology be so easily conflated with redemption theology and then dismissed? Surely the wisdom literature of the OT would resist such leveling. Berkouwer is again correct to resist "natural theology," if it means something apart from the continuing illumination and activity of God through his Spirit. But, things are somewhat more complex than Berkouwer suggests. For if "natural theology" is more to be equated with "natural revelation," with God speaking in and through his creation, then the nature psalms do give voice to a general revelation through nature.

Similarly, Berkouwer discusses Elijah's confrontation with the prophets of Baal on Mt. Carmel, concluding that "Elijah shows, on the basis of the irrefutable facts of God's deeds, that there is no *revelation* in the Baal worship."[19] No power, yes, but does Elijah's confrontation with the priests of Baal irrefutably show that God cannot be seen in creation, even as he shines in all that is fair? Idolatry has wrongly been generalized outward to include all experiences with nature. Or again, Berkouwer's sense of human depravity is so far-reaching that when he comments on Paul speaking in Rom 1:25 about the Gentiles "knowing" God, he must reinterpret Paul, saying that Paul was simply using "hyperbole." That is, because of our sin, real knowledge of God is not possible. Paul could not mean what he seems to have said. Although for Berkouwer "knowledge and revelation are *not* identical,"[20] the fact of human blindness cancels out any value or possibility that general revelation might have. Thus, though Berkouwer tries to distinguish between "salvation as being only in Christ" and "revelation being also outside of Christ," in the end this is a formal distinction without substance, having no experiential consequence except to condemn humankind given the hardness of human hearts. There is no possibility for Tillich's "revelatory ecstasy" or David Kern's "supernatural mail" or Yehudi Menuhin's violin.

Reacting, in part, to the German misuse of general revelation to baptize Hitler's ascent to power, Berkouwer concludes that, though revelation has priority over knowledge, because of sin general revelation is sufficient only to reveal to humankind our guilt. Berkouwer writes, "Contact with God in the community of life is broken and man [sic], though continuing to take his place in created reality, accordingly no longer understands its purpose, the language or song of creation. God's greatness and glory are no longer observed by a lost humanity."[21] But, is this true? *What are we to make of the repeated testimony to God's greatness and glory that those outside the church give to God, based in their experiences of creation, conscience, and human creativity?* How are we to understand the repeated witness of humankind to revelatory experiences of a *mysterium* that is simultaneously *tremendum* and *fascinans*.[22] If truth is one, should not our understanding of God through our experience of him and the narratives of others in our wider culture match Scripture's and tradition's understanding of how God has in fact revealed himself? We are thrown back upon the question of theological hermeneutics. Who qualifies as God's messenger (Hermes)? How do we hear God's revelation to us? That culture/experience is theology's context and application is today little debated; but can culture/experience also be more than this, a means as well of hearing God's story?

THE QUESTION OF THEOLOGICAL HERMENEUTICS

Jürgen Moltmann tells the story of Galileo, who wanted to show his opponents Jupiter's satellites, but they refused even to look through the telescope. They believed, as Bertolt Brecht puts into their mouths in his *Life of Galileo,* "that no truth can be found in nature—only in the comparison of texts." Rather, argues Moltmann,

> There are no words of God without human experiences of God's Spirit. So the words of proclamation spoken by the Bible and the church must also be related to the experiences of people today, so that they are not—as Karl Rahner said—merely "hearers of the Word," but become spokesmen of the Word, too. But this is only possible if Word and Spirit are seen as existing in a *mutual relationship,* not as a one-way street.[23]

Barth says it more simply when he speaks of the theologian having a Bible in one hand and the newspaper in the other. That is, the theologian's task is a dialogical one. My colleague Bill Dyrness understands theological method in similar terms, believing the theologian must bring together in reflective obedience the telling of our stories and the hearing of God's stories.[24] One can add components to this basic schematic, but theology's two-way dialogical task remains. The hearing of God's story is heard not only through Scripture but through the church past and present. Our stories also reflect both our own experiences (sometimes of God) and those of the wider culture (including those of the Transcendent). My own understanding is that the theologian has five resources at his or her disposal through the work of the Spirit. All are interactive, even while the Bible's ultimate theological authority for faith and practice is recognized. Hearing God's story has three components—one's particular worshipping community, the whole of the Christian tradition, and Scripture—while telling our stories includes both experience and culture. In my book on theology and film, *Reel Spirituality,* I expressed it as follows: "We read the authoritative biblical text from out of a worshipping community, in light of centuries of Christian thought and practice, as people embedded in a particular culture, who have a unique set of experiences. Here is the theological process."[25]

Rather than an hermeneutic of suspicion, or even of caution, with regard to human experience and culture, I would understand the revelatory experiences of Lewis and Tillich, David Kern and Nanny Goodman's mother, as inviting dialogue with, and even appropriation by, theologians interested in understanding general revelation. Scripture and the dogma of the church cannot be ignored, but neither can the witness of our culture and our own personal experiences. A robust two-way conversation is called for. Not only can Scripture provide an interpretive grid for our experiences (Calvin uses the metaphor of "spectacles" for this), but experiences from out of our individual and collective lives can also become the "spectacles" through which we reread the Scriptures, looking for insight from God's Word that might provide further interpretation and illumination to such experiences, and vice versa.

The experiences of those individuals with whom I began the paper, and scores like them, are not simply subjectivity in disguise, though that remains at times a possibility. It is not creation or human creativity apart from God's continuing presence that is revelatory. Berkouwer provides the helpful example of astrology to illustrate the truth that revelation is not to be thought of as being resident in creation or creature independent of God's illumining Spirit. The Romantics often made the mistake of confusing the artist with the divine muse, as if we could conjure up revelation by an act of the imagination. Rather, it is through creation, conscience, and human creativity that we can observe how God acts and hear him speak. Each retains the possibility of actually being an encounter with God's Spirit. There is, in Jürgen Moltmann's words, an "immanent transcendence," paradoxical but not dialectic, unifying rather than competing.[26] Here is the subject matter of general revelation, and it is to be seen as complementary to special revelation.

The nonoppositional nature of general and special revelation is perhaps best seen in Ps 19. Here the psalmist relates, "The heavens are telling the glory of God. . . . There is no speech, nor are there words . . . yet their voice goes out through all the earth" (Ps 19:1, 4). It is the experience of ʾĔlōhîm within nature that elicits the songwriter's praise. Creation's "wordless speech" finds its analogy, perhaps, in C. S. Lewis's description of Joy's experience as a "bright shadow," something on this side of knowledge, too close to be seen or heard. Such is the "immanent transcendence" of the Creator God. The encounter of this psalmist is not with YHWH, Israel's covenanting God; it is with ʾĔlōhîm, the generic name for the God of the universe.

The psalmist follows his praise of God's glory in creation with parallel praise for God's revelation through his word, the Law. The songwriter experiences YHWH's commandments as vivifying, making wise, causing rejoicing and enlightenment, as being true, righteous, and enduring, as preeminently desirable, and like fine gold or honey. Here the focus is on God who has revealed his name, YHWH, to his people and covenanted with them, providing them further revelation as to how to live. Creation and the Law, ʾĔlōhîm and YHWH, general revelation and special revelation—the paradox is united, but never confused, in the experience of the songwriter. God is to be praised, both as creator and as redeemer.

ALLOWING FOR AN EXPERIENTIAL FOCUS

It is worth noting that it is experience that allows the psalmist in Ps 19 to unite that which otherwise might remain distinct, whether in creation or redemption, whether in general or in special revelation. It is this same experiential focus which offers the best potential for a more robust biblical theology of general revelation today, one that would no longer reduce general revelation to little more that the "footprint" of God's past activity or subsume general revelation under special revelation, creation theology under salvation theology, the work of the Spirit in Creation under the Spirit of Christ. Given the witness of those within and without the church as to the present presence of God's Spirit in their lives, given, that is, the witness of many to revelatory experiences through creation, conscience, and human creativity, we need to read the Scriptures again as to what they might be saying to us in this regard. In particular, how might we reread the Scriptures so as to fall prey neither to a natural theology that reduces general revelation to traces of God's past activity nor to a redemptive triumphalism that reduces general revelation merely to the grounds by which humankind is declared guilty by God and in need of his saving grace?

Proverbs. As I have begun to reread the Bible with my experience of general revelation as my "spectacles," new texts have come to life. A beginning point has been the wisdom literature of the OT. Here the focus is reflection on the goodness of created life, not the narration of the story of salvation history, though later Jewish writers would conflate creational and redemptive themes (see Sirach, Wisdom of Solomon, and the epilogue of Ecclesiastes). Job, Proverbs, Ecclesiastes, Song of Songs, and selected Psalms focus on the "kerygma of life," to borrow the felicitous phrase of Roland Murphy. These books, as Walther Zimmerli reminded modern scholarship forty years ago, think resolutely within the framework of creation theology. Mention of God's saving acts in the Exodus event is largely lacking. So too is appeal to the Law. Instead the power and authority of these texts is rooted in the experience of life itself. Shockingly to some, these texts have as one of their sources the wisdom—do I risk saying "spiritual insight"?—of those outside of the covenant community of faith.

Proverbs, for example, is a collection of collections of proverbs. Its theological introduction (1:1–9:18) is followed by "the proverbs of Solomon" (10:1–22:16), "the words of the wise" (22:17–24:22), "also sayings of the wise" (24:23–34), "other proverbs of Solomon that the officials of king Hezekiah of Judah copied" (25:1–29:27), "the words of Agur son of Jakeh" (30:1–33), "the words of King Lemuel . . . that his mother taught him" (31:1–9), and a final description of a capable wife (31:10–31). That many of the proverbs are attributed to Solomon comes as no surprise. After all, Scripture records that "God gave Solomon very great wisdom, discernment, and breadth of understanding as vast as the sand on the seashore, so that Solomon's wisdom surpassed the wisdom of all the people of the east, and all the wisdom of Egypt" (1 Kgs 4:29–30). What is surprising is the stated source of some of the other proverbs. Agur, son of Jakeh, is not an Israelite name, and there is no indication that the source of his wisdom is to be interpreted as coming from within the covenant community of Israel. Rather, Israel seems to have recognized in the international wisdom of its neighbors God's revelatory truth and thus included Agur's proverbs as part of their inspired Scriptures. Here, general revelation and special revelation unite concretely. In a similar way King Lemuel's words, based on his mother's teaching, seem also to have an international source. For the list of Israel's kings makes no mention of a "Lemuel." Yet, the wisdom his mother taught him was thought by Israel to be God's revelation to them.

It is not just these two collections of proverbs by "outsiders" that have become part of the Book of Proverbs' sacred canon. Most scholars are in agreement that the compiler of Proverbs also made use of a collection of proverbs based in the thirty sayings of the Egyptian *Instruction of Amenemope* (22:17–24:22). The sayings have been freely adapted and the opening proverbs in the section contain more allusions to this Egyptian work than those closer to the end. The writer of this collection of proverbs does not hide his non-Israelite source. Near to the beginning of his admonitions, he writes:

> Have I not written for you thirty sayings
> of admonition and knowledge,
> to show you what is right and true,
> so that you may give a true answer to those who sent you? (Prov 22:20–21)

Translators struggled for centuries with the seeming non sequitor in these verses. Why in the midst of "the words of the wise" (22:17) would the writer mention "thirty sayings," since it is by no means clear to any reader of Proverbs where these "thirty" sayings are. Failing to find a meaningful referent, translators tried amending the word "thirty" to "triplely," and then interpreting the resultant adverb allegorically as meaning "excellently" or "fully." Unfortunately for this view, the text has no hint of corruption, so the alternate reading has lacked any textual basis.

The riddle was not solved until the twentieth century when an Anglican librarian in the British Library was reading *Amenemope* and noted what he thought were familiar sounding proverbs. He turned to the OT where he discovered repeated similarities with Prov 22:17–24:22. Also, *Amenemope* had thirty sayings! Here again, it is God's general revelation from outside of Israel as discovered in the human observations (through "conscience" and "creativity") of Egyptian culture that has been brought into Israel's life and even made a part of its special revelation, the Scripture that Jesus himself used. The final redactors recognized in these sayings an immanent transcendence. God had revealed the sacred shape of created life to those neither part of the covenant community nor believers in YHWH. This revelation as received was not seen by Israel as oppositional to the Law. In fact, those late in Israel's history would understand the Law and such wisdom as having the same source—the Most High who was both "the Creator of all things" and the giver of "the law that Moses commanded us" (Sir 24). In Proverbs these two sources of revelation are kept distinct. Creation is not yet folded into redemption.

Chronicles. A more careful reading of the biblical text through the "spectacles" of general revelation also brings to light new perspectives on Chronicles. It could be that both Proverbs in its final form and Chronicles reflect a similar *Sitz im Leben*, the postcaptivity period when questions about Israelite faith and life included not only the need to explore the shape of a renewed worship life, but also the role of Israel's God given the presence of other cultures that did not worship YHWH. These OT writers/editors had a similar question in mind: In what sense was YHWH to be understood as God of the whole world, as well as the covenanting God of his people?

One means by which the Chronicler addressed this more international concern was by reshaping the stories of how Israel's kings interacted with other royalty in the Ancient Near East. Two accounts in particular stand out upon closer reading, for they have been altered from their original source material in 1 Kings and reshaped theologically. The first is the account of Josiah and King Neco in 2 Chron 35:20–27. Here the Chronicler adds an additional incident to the account of Josiah which had been recorded in Kings. After narrating the "faithful deeds" of this great king, deeds "in accordance with what is written in the law of the Lord," the writer relates the account of King Neco, who, while on his way to fight in Carchemish on the Euphrates [modern day Iraq], sent envoys to Josiah saying that he was not coming to fight Judah, but rather the "house with which I am at war," and "God [*Ĕlōhîm*] has commanded me to hurry." The envoy spoke for Neco, the Egyptian pharaoh, saying, "Cease opposing God [*Ĕlōhîm*], who is with me, so that he will not destroy you." That is, let me pass through your territory unopposed for this is God's will. But Josiah, who had always done "what is right in the sight of the Lord [YHWH]" (34:2), who had "repair[ed] the house of the Lord his God" (34:8) and had "found the book of the law of the Lord given through Moses" (34:14), who was penitent and had "made all who were in Israel worship the Lord their God" (34:33), and keep "a Passover to the Lord in Jerusalem" for the first time since the days of Samuel (35:1), did not believe Neco. After all, it was Josiah who knew YHWH by name, not Neco; it was Josiah who had rediscovered Israel's Scriptures, the Lord's special revelation to his people, and had them read, not Neco; and it was Josiah who worshipped the Lord in Jerusalem, not Neco. By

Discerning the Spirit in Culture

what possible logic could he conclude that Neco was speaking accurately about God's desire for Josiah? Surely his words were based in deceit or projection.

So King Josiah rejected Neco's words as being from God and instead disguised himself to fight. Then the text reflects: "He [Josiah] did not listen to the words of Neco from the mouth of God [*ʾĔlōhîm*], but joined battle in the plain of Megiddo" (35:22), and Josiah was killed. The Chronicler relates that all Jerusalem mourned the passing of Josiah, even Jeremiah who uttered a lament. What is telling in this recounting of Josiah's actions is the theological failure of Josiah to recognize that YHWH might also be revealing himself to an Egyptian pharaoh. His "generic" spirituality—his reference to *ʾĔlōhîm*—seemed paltry and mistaken, given Josiah's lifetime of covenantal faithfulness. Surely it was the people of God who should be telling this pharaoh what it was that the Lord YHWH desired. After all, they read his Law. After all, it was they who worshipped him aright in Jerusalem. Would many in the church today think any differently? But, the Chronicler is at pains to remind his readers that the Lord is God of the whole world, even Egypt, and he reveals himself to others, not just the covenant community.

That the Chronicler was interested for theological reasons in noting God's involvement with those outside of his chosen people is arguably reinforced by his narration of a second encounter between one of Israel's kings and a neighboring one. The Chronicler records in 2 Chron 2:7 how King Huram of Tyre was asked by Solomon to send "an artisan skilled [the word is *ḥākām*, 'to be wise at'] to work in gold, silver, bronze, and iron, and in purple, crimson, and blue fabrics, trained also in engraving, to join the skilled workers who are with me in Judah and Jerusalem, whom my father David provided" (2 Chron 2:7). So King Huram sent Solomon Huram-abi, a skilled artisan. He is said to be "the son of one of the Danite women, his father a Tyrian" (2 Chron 2:13–14). What is telling in this recounting is that the Chronicler has altered the description of Huram-abi's mother from being "a widow of the tribe of Naphtali" (1 Kgs 7:14) to being "one of the Danite women."

Why would the tribal background be changed by the Chronicler? Why would it matter? It seems probable that here was a way for the Chronicler to connect Huram-abi with another "wise" artisan (one skilled in his craft, *ḥokmāh*), Oholiab, who worked not on the temple but on an earlier house of God, the tabernacle. For Oholiab is described in Exodus as being of the tribe of Dan and he, with Bezalel, was said to have an ability (literally, *ḥokmāh*), a divine gifting, that came from God (Exod 31:3, 6). The Chronicler's readers were to believe similarly that Huram-abi's skill/wisdom as an artisan (*ʾîš ḥākām*) was like Oholiab's, a wise gifting that found its parallel in the *ḥokmāh* given Solomon himself. Thus, an artisan from outside of the people of God, but gifted with a divine skill (*ḥokmāh*), would join Solomon who was himself also gifted (*ḥokmāh*) by God in jointly constructing the temple. That such is the probable meaning of the text is reinforced by the words of King Huram, who in dispatching Huram-abi to Solomon, writes: "Blessed be the Lord God of Israel who made heaven and earth, who has given King David a wise son (*bēn ḥākām*), endowed with discretion and understanding, who will build a temple for the Lord, and a royal palace for himself" (2 Chron 2:12). Huram recognizes Israel's God as the creator of heaven and earth. It is that God who has gifted Solomon with the wisdom/skill to rule and Huram-abi with the skill/wisdom to create. God is God over all the world, bestowing similar gifts on Israelites and non-Israelites alike.

Acts 17. This text provides us a third window into a theology of general revelation, one of the few biblical narratives that have often been referenced in traditional discussions about the topic. The text recounts Paul's dialogue with citizens of Athens. Not all interpreters have found Paul's theology to be helpful or adequate. Some commentators are uneasy with Paul's seemingly "soft" approach to idolatry as he begins his reflection recognizing (complimenting?) the Athenians for being "extremely religious," given their worship of an "unknown god" (v. 23). These commentators criticize Paul for not being more prophetic, more condemnatory of idolatry, and more forthright about God's judgment of their sin. No wonder, the critique goes, that Paul was not more successful in his preaching that day—only a few responded. Contrast Paul's indirect apologetic with Peter's more theologically rooted sermon where he preached that his listeners had crucified and killed Jesus, with the result that three thousand converts responded (Acts 2:41). One cannot afford to be soft on sin, so the judgment goes.

Apart from the fact that there is no textual evidence to support such an interpretation that somehow Paul's preaching in Athens is an example of "ineffectual" preaching, this interpretation also fails to recognize in the text itself the extent to which Paul affirmed the validity of a general revelation residing outside of the church, even among pagans. He is not simply being manipulative by seeming to compliment his audience by saying something he does not really believe. In v. 28 Paul quotes with approval the poets Epimenides ("in him we live and move and have our being") and Aratus ("For we too are his offspring") in order to support his argument that the Athenians should want to know more about this unknown God who wants them to find him. Shockingly for many contemporary Christians, these classic poets that Paul affirms are not writing about a generic sense of spiritual well-being arising out of their humanity, or even about a general notion of God arising out of Jewish belief. No, these poets are referencing Zeus! The Cretan poet Epimenides (c. 600 B.C.) puts on the lips of Minos, Zeus's son, these words:

> They fashioned a tomb for thee, O holy and high one—
> The Cretans, always liars, evil beasts, idle bellies!
> But thou art not dead; thou livest and abidest for ever,

> For in thee we live and move and have our being. (*Horae Semiticae X*)

Similarly, Paul quotes from the Cilician poet Aratus (c. 315–240 B.C.). The longer text reads: "It is with Zeus that every one of us in every way has to do, for we are also his offspring" (*Phaenomena* 5).

Rather than simply criticize the Athenians for their idolatry, an idolatry that Luke has already mentioned as being deeply distressing to Paul (v. 16), Paul chose instead to recognize that in their groping after God (v. 27) the Athenians have evidenced a genuine sensitivity to God "who made the world and everything in it, he . . . is Lord of heaven and earth" (v. 24). Paul moved back and forth between affirmation and correction as he addressed the Athenians. He wanted them to know that this God does not live in their shrines, nor does he need anything. Instead it is God himself who "gives to all mortals life and breath and all things" (v. 25), as even their poets have recognized. That is, though their understanding of revelation is partial and confused, their poets have also sensed something profoundly right. Our lives are dependent on God who has made us and who continues to uphold us. Paul was not manipulating his hearers but seeking to build on perceived common ground based in the revelation of God the Creator.

Such creational insight rooted in general revelation is not for Paul sufficient for salvation, and given their evidenced ignorance and idolatry, Paul believed that the Athenians need to repent and believe in him who was raised from the dead (v. 30–31). Paul recognized as well that there was also something correct in what the Athenians sensed. The Creator has upheld them until now and invites them to know him further. In his preaching to a Gentile audience with no context or background through which to interpret or understand the gospel message, Paul turned neither to Scripture nor to Christianity's Jewish background but to general revelation, to those intimations of spirituality experienced within the wider culture, that while partially confused, also reflect revelational sensitivity that Christians can build upon. The account concludes by confirming that indeed the bridge from general revelation to special revelation can be effectively traversed, that the two can be united, for "some of them (the Athenians) joined him and became believers, including Dionysius the Areopagite and a woman named Damaris, and others with him" (v. 34).

RECOGNIZING THE SPIRIT'S ROLE: A TURN TO THE PNEUMATOLOGICAL

There are of course multiple reasons for the scant attention that has been given theologically to God's revelation of himself outside of the church and without direct reference to Christ, but central has been a narrowing of our understanding of the Spirit's role. The Spirit is involved (1) not only in God's incarnation in Jesus Christ, continuing today to make him known, and (2) not only in God's life-giving and sanctifying work in and through the church, but the Spirit is also, to quote the Nicene Creed, (3) "the Lord and giver of life."

John Calvin, commenting on Gen 1:2, asserts:

> ... the beauty of the universe (which we now perceive) owes its strength and preservation to the power of the Spirit. . . . For it is the Spirit, who, everywhere diffused, sustains all things, causes them to grow, and quickens them in heaven and in earth. . . . in transfusing into all things his energy, and breathing into them essence, life, and movement, he is indeed plainly divine.[28]

It was the Spirit of God who moved over the face of the waters in Gen 1:2. It is the Spirit (*rûaḥ* in Hebrew and *pneuma* in Greek) who gives "breath" (life) to the body (Gen 6:17), who makes humans understand (Job 32:8; Gen 41:38) and imagine (Exod 31:3–4, where artistic excellence is the Spirit's work). It is the Spirit who reveals what is good, causing us to desire it (Ps 51:10–11). The Spirit provides the power to live (Eccl 12:7; Ps 33:7; 104:29); his influence is expansive (Ps 31:8).

Yet, the Spirit's ongoing revelatory role in and through creation has tended to be ignored. The Spirit's creational role has been largely reduced to his providential care. When general revelation has become the biblical focus, there has typically been a narrowing to those texts whose intention is more clearly soteriological, e.g., Rom 1 and 2, John 1, and depending upon the interpreter, Acts 17. This is somewhat understandable, however regrettable, given theology's traditional concentration on the first two articles of the creeds. The Spirit becomes by default simply the expression of "the Father and the Son," largely lacking his ("its") own personal center (cf. the sixth century addition to the Nicene Creed of the phrase "*Filioque*": "who proceedeth from the Father *and the Son*"). This is also to be explained by the Reformers' more primary theological intention to counter those theological aberrations which would suggest that one could obtain salvation by some works of one's own. Their focus was not on God's gifting and revealing outside the church and without direct reference to Jesus Christ. The Spirit's work was thus truncated, being reduced to his role in redemption and sanctification. In the process the Spirit's work in creation and his concomitant revelation in and through creation, conscience, and creativity was downplayed or ignored.[29]

Even more recently in the history of theology, as the third article of the creeds has again become a more regular topic, the focus has still been on the work of the Spirit in redemption and the church, not in creation. This is what has captured the church's theological attention. The rise of the pentecostal and charismatic movements that have swept through the church worldwide has only reinforced this tendency to neglect the role of the Spirit in creation in favor of the Spirit in redemption.

However, the Spirit must also be identified with the divine presence in life. As Epimenides wrote, "In him we live and move and have our being" (Acts 17:28). In the words of John Taylor, the Spirit is the "Go-between God," revealing God to us.[30] Luther can say:

> Spirit is everything that is worked in us through the Spirit . . . loving the wife, procreating children, governing the family, honoring the parents, being obedient to the magistrate, etc., which in themselves are secular and of the flesh, are fruits of the Spirit. Blind people do not distinguish the things that are of the good creatures of God from vices.[31]

But though blind people do not see, the testimony of many others is that they can and do, however partially. They are like Nanny Goldman's mother who recognized, "God lit the stars and spoke directly through family and friends, musicians and writers, madmen and children, and nature—and not, as she had been raised to believe, through a booming voice from the heavens."

CONCLUSION

A doctrine of general revelation is clearly open to theological abuse, from baptizing culture in the name of revelation to confusing creation with Creator. We are not free from the danger of unbelief. But, a truncated doctrine of God's wider revelation also carries with it its own dangers: an ineffective witness to those lacking a functioning Jewish/Christian background, but having authentic spiritual experiences; a stunting of one's own spiritual growth by closing off the presence of the Spirit of God in the wider arena of life; and a silencing of those outside the church, a failure to hear God's witness/prophetic critique through them in order that the church might be renewed by the witness of the Spirit in her midst.

Surely our knowledge of God through his Spirit remains partial, whether creationally (Eccl 3:1–11), existentially (Rom 11:33–36), or relationally (1 Cor 13:12). But having said this, Protestants have too often let caution and defensiveness, given the Fall, dominate their understanding of God's revelatory presence. Fearing what Berkouwer labeled "the suction power of natural theology,"[32] they have emptied God from the world, closing him up in the church. They have let salvation history categories drain creation theology of any vitality and meaning. The sacramentality of life has been denied.

We need to hear again the words of Elizabeth Barrett Browning in her poem "Aurora Leigh":

Natural things
And Spiritual, —who separates those two
In art, in morals, or the social drift,
Tears up the bond of nature and brings death,
Paints futile pictures, writes unreal verse,
Leads vulgar days, deals ignorantly with men,
Is wrong, in short at all points. . . .
Earth's crammed with heaven,
And every common bush afire with God;
But only he who sees, takes off his shoes—
The rest sit round it and pluck blackberries. . . .[33]

ENDNOTES

1. Anne Lamott, *All New People* (Washington, D. C.: Counterpoint, 1989), 29, 37.

2. *Fanny and Alexander* (directed, Ingmar Bergman, 1982).

3. John Updike, "Packed Dirt, Churchgoing, A Dying Cat, A Traded Car," in *Pigeon Feathers and Other Stories* (Greenwich, Conn.: Fawcett Crest, 1962), 172.

4. David Hay and Kate Hunt, *Understanding the Spirituality of People Who Don't Go to Church: A Report on the Findings of the Adults' Project at the University of Nottingham,* http://www.etbi.org.uk/downloads/com/documents/0008%20David%20Hay%20Final%20Report.doc, August 2000.

5. Ibid.

6. Paul Tillich, *On the Boundary: An Autobiographical Sketch* (New York: Scribner's Sons, 1966), 27–28; Paul Tillich, *On Art and Architecture* (ed. John Dillenberger and Jane Dillenberger; New York: Crossroad, 1987), 12; cf. Paul Tillich, *My Search for Absolutes* (San Francisco: Harper & Row, 1967), 28, 129–130.

7. C. S. Lewis, *Surprised By Joy* (New York: Harcourt, Brace & World, Harvest Books, 1955), 180–181.

8. Albert Einstein, quoted in Richard Viladesau, *Theological Aesthetics* (New York: Oxford University Press, 1999), 104.

9. Viladesau, *Theological Aesthetics*, 107.

10. George Barna, *Revolution!* (Wheaton, Ill.: Tyndale, 2005), 48–49.

11. For my student David Johnson, his encounter with God came while watching the movie *Grand Canyon* (directed, Kasdan, 1991); for another student, Chris Min, it was *Magnolia* (directed, Anderson, 1999). For me it was the movie *Becket* (directed, Glenville, 1964).

12. Karl Barth, quoted in T. J. Gorringe, *Discerning Spirit: A Theology of Revelation* (Philadelphia: Trinity Press International, 1990), 6.

13. Gorringe, *Discerning Spirit*, 6.

14. Ibid.

15. In using the metaphor of "spectacles" I am of course playing with an image from John Calvin but reversing its meaning. It is not Scripture that provides us "spectacles" by which to look at culture but culture which can provide us a new set of questions and experiences (i.e., new "spectacles") by which to look at Scripture.

16. Cf. Avery Dulles, *Models of Revelation* (Maryknoll, N.Y.: Orbis Books, 1994).

17. G. C. Berkouwer, *General Revelation* (Studies in Dogmatics Series; Grand Rapids: Eerdmans, 1955).

18. Ibid., 137.

19. Ibid., 124–125.

20. Ibid, 314.

21. Ibid, 312; cf. 305–314.

22. Cf. Rudolph Otto, *The Idea of the Holy* (New York: Oxford University Press, 1923).

23. Jürgen Moltmann, *The Spirit of Life: A Universal Affirmation* (Philadelphia: Fortress, 1992), 3, 28.

24. William Dyrness, "How does the Bible Function in the Christian's Life?" in *The Use of the Bible in Theology: Evangelical Options* (ed. Robert K. Johnston; Atlanta: John Knox, 1985), 159–174.

25. Robert K. Johnston, *Reel Spirituality: Theology and Film in Dialogue* (2d ed.; Grand Rapids: Baker Academic, 2006), 114.

26. Moltmann, *The Spirit of Life*, 7, 17.

27. According to F. F. Bruce, "This quatrain is quoted in a Syriac version by the ninth-century commentator Isho'dad (cf. M. D. Gibson, *Horae Semiticae* X [Cambridge, 1913], p. 40." See F. F. Bruce, *The Book of Acts* (Grand Rapids: Eerdmans, 1954), 359.

28. John Calvin, *Institutes of the Christian Religion* (ed. J. T. McNeill; Philadelphia: Westminster, 1960), 1.138 (1, 13:14).

29. Cf. the Westminster Confession: "Although the light of nature and the works of creation and providence do so far manifest the goodness, wisdom and power of God, as to leave men inexcusable; yet are they not sufficient to give that knowledge of God, and of his will, which is necessary unto salvation."

30. John V. Taylor, *The Go-Between God: The Holy Spirit and the Christian Mission* (London: SCM, 1972).

31. Martin Luther, *WA* 40 I, 348, 15–20, in *Epistolam S. Pauli ad Galatas Commentarius 1531*, in his comments on Gal 3:3, quoted in Hans Schwartz, "Reflection on the Work of the Spirit outside the Church," *Neue Zeitschrift für Systematische Theologie und Religionsphilosophie* 23 (1981): 207.

32. Berkouwer, *General Revelation*, 56.

33. Elizabeth Barrett Browning, "Aurora Leigh," book 7, in Elizabeth Barrett Browning, *Aurora Leigh, and Other Poems* (New York: James Miller, 1866), 263, 265, 266.

RESPONSE TO JOHNSTON

JIM DEKKER

How are we to understand the human experience of "revelatory ecstasy" or "supernatural shudders"? In our evangelical circles we are generally "a people of the word"—the written text. I am personally fond of that text and willing to tie myself to it. However, a word on the page hardly captures the phenomena we experience in the movement of the Spirit. Needless to say, wind becomes word, becomes text, and particularly the biblical text. Doing theology in the movement of the Spirit is turning breath into text, or art, or maybe even science, but when the movement of the Spirit is seen only as text, we may be limiting ourselves and the Spirit's voice. Maybe Lamott, Updike, Tillich, and Lewis are all unsatisfied with their textual account of their liminal experience, but then we have Beethoven and Michelangelo who have created more than a thousand words in one picture or a movement. But why stop there? Why not consider Broadway and Hollywood producers, maybe even Hip Hop artists with their supernatural shudders too. Key to all of this is the term "discernment."

As a church we often deal strictly with the text of Scripture. We deploy the very particular discipline of hermeneutics to a very real text on a page. In some ways this has created a particular culture of conversations around the text, a culture that has its own walls and stained glass lenses. If we are to propose that general revelation, including human art in broader culture, carries a form of divine revelation/experience, what might the hermeneutics of that revelation be? To quote Johnston, "How are we to understand theologically such 'sacred encounters'?"

The question of definition. Johnston makes the case for appreciating revelatory value in various non-Christian experiences and activities. He identifies the created order, human creative expression, and the liminal experience as revealing something of God. In speaking so broadly about revelation one might get lost in how to appreciate each category or all of them in general. Do we understand all to be functioning within the one category "general revelation"? Do we speak differently of subjective liminal experience? Is human creativity different from God's creativity, and does the difference speak to how we understand any particular person's creative expression? These notions may hold their own set of theological concerns, and it may be less helpful simply to combine or speak of the supernatural shudders generally.

Theological perspective. Johnston proposes two possible reasons for the unfortunate marginalizing of general revelation. First: "Theology's bias toward redemptive over creational, propositional over narrative . . ." and, second: the notion that "sin has so clouded and warped our receptivity to divine revelation that general revelation . . . is of little if any value other than to confirm our sin. . ." Johnston finds these notions in Berkouwer's work and offers a welcome challenge for those following them. Though the assessment of Berkouwer makes sense, his forefathers at the Free University of Amsterdam, Abraham Kuyper and to a greater extent Herman Bavinck, offer more helpful theological reflections than a noncomplementary view of redemption and creation, propositional and narrative, or even the sin and common grace theology.

Bavinck over Berkouwer. Herman Bavinck speaks very directly to "the importance of creation and human culture as good gifts of God." He says "revelation existed even prior to the fall. Creation itself is the first, rich revelation of God, the foundation and beginning of every subsequent revelation." After quoting much of the same Scriptures listed by Johnston, Bavinck states, "There is thus a rich revelation of God even among the heathen—not only in nature but also in their heart and conscience, in their life and history, among their statesmen and artists, their philosophers and reformers. There exists no reason at all to denigrate or diminish this divine revelation."[1]

Bavinck goes on to make the case that Israel's religion is built on two pillars, the God of Creation and the God of the Covenant—*Ĕlōhîm* and YHWH. From this we understand that God is a redeeming God and reveals himself as such in both general and special revelations, in both creation and the covenant, before the text and in the text. It makes sense then when Bavinck moves on to talk of Christ as both co-creator and covenant fulfiller, the union of both general and special revelation. In Christ, therefore, we have the communion of creation or common grace and covenanting grace (text) extended to humanity. Like Johnston, Bavinck laments the unfortunate separation of these two in the churches of his day.

Finally, Bavinck, like Johnston, closes the article with the notion that doing theology is itself born out of grace found in the community—a common grace that though sanctified by faith remains part of the created consciousness of humanity. "Consequently, theology accords to the other sciences their full due. Theology's honor is not that she sits enthroned above them as the queen of the sciences and waves her scepter over them but that she is permitted to serve them all with her gifts."[2] In many ways Bavinck's reformed theology values a complementary approach to general and special revelation.

Although for some a theology of redemption moves them away from a theology of creation, it need not. Nor does a theology of sin necessitate a narrow appreciation of creation, limiting it to mere conviction for sin. We cannot dismiss the impact of sin in the conversation of common grace expressed by "the heathen." Nor can we suspend the voice of redemption when enjoying the warmth of common grace. When discussing general revelation as Johnston has, we still need to address the theologies of sin and redemption, but they need not be destructive of the good seen in common grace.

Scripture. In Job we see a man in his culture wrestling with theological questions. He is confronted with the common theology of his day (possibly pre-Abrahamic covenant) and with creation. In the face of creation revelation he recognizes his sin and repents, and then we see grace abounding all the more as he receives flocks, and family, and restored relationships. The story seems to pivot on the two sequences of encounters with creation: one set that tears him down and the other set that brings him to his knees in repentance and restoration. The intermediate wrestle is with the nature of sin, justification, righteousness, and the theology of his day. Here we have a picture of someone confronted with common grace, theology of sin, and redemption all working together.

Johnston identifies several cases in Scripture where God's voice is heard beyond the community of God's people. The Acts 17 sermon to the Athenians is a strong case for the appreciation of culturally rooted ideas formed among those outside of Israel but nonetheless revelatory to some extent. Such examples call us to listen for God's revelation beyond ourselves and to those we are not accustomed to hearing. Johnston's case calls us to look beyond our stained glass to hear the voice of the Spirit in the world, but this is intimidating since we may struggle to find common language with those in the theater or Hollywood or Hip Hoppers.

The World. Listening for the Spirit in the culture may appear to be messier than listening for the Spirit in the church. The language and rhythms and pictures are different, but nonetheless they tell us something. The rapper KRS One speaks of Hip Hop as a language that continues to evolve so as to capture the intensely creative mind within Hip Hop culture. According to him rap is the attempt to formulate a language that gathers people within a culture by which they understand themselves and maybe even God.[3] Evanescence's song "Bring me to Life" is a profound song with pounding rhythms calling out for redemption: "Wake me up inside, wake me up inside, call my name and save me from my dark . . . save me from the nothing I've become."[4] Lead singer, Amy Lee, and all those relating to these lyrics call out for a conversation regarding the meaning of life and redemption. The same can be said of 2Pac's "Thugz Mansion" where he speaks of an eschatology from the urban culture[5] or DMX's "Prayer," a spoken word piece where he articulates a moving prayer of suffering.[6]

Finally, Zach Helm and Lindsay Doran wrote and produced the movie "Stranger than Fiction," where we hear the author/narrator Karen Eiffel describing her main character in her book as she writes: "This is a story of a man . . . Harold Crick . . ." The movie follows Harold throughout his 'life' as Karen narrates it until Harold begins to discover his existence is rooted in the mind of an author. Harold attempts to resolve his inner conflict between self-awareness and the idea that his author is determining his steps. Eventually, Harold meets Karen face to face, the creator with the created, and discovers that the story of Harold's life will end soon in a profound death, a death he learns to accept.[7] Are Helm and Doran telling us something of their theological understanding of free will and God's sovereignty or the nature of God's participation within the narration of history? Is KRS One giving us a language lesson in street theology? Is DMX becoming vulnerable by inviting us into his prayer and suffering? Is Amy Lee calling for a theology of redemption?

Johnston's concern for a more thorough pneumatology needs to be underscored, especially in the face of culture's theological concerns. Common grace exists and theology is being done beyond the stained glass windows of the church. However, in stepping out of the church to do theology in culture, we still need a hermeneutic, but not necessarily the same hermeneutic we use with Scripture. We need a discernment that comes from understanding what these forms of general revelation are and a discernment that holds theologies of sin and redemption in complementary ways with common grace.

ENDNOTES

1. Herman Bavinck, "*Common Grace*," trans. Ray VanLeeuwen, *Calvin Theological Journal* 24 (1989): 39, 41.

2. Ibid., 65.

3. KRS One, "Spirituality" on the compilation "Ruminations" (July 25, 2003; Welcome Rain; Har/Com Edition).

4. Evanescence, "Bring me to Life" on the album "Fallen" (March 4, 2003; Wind-Up Records).

5. 2Pac, "Thugz Mansion" on the album "Better Dayz" (November 26, 2002; Interscope Records).

6. DMX, "Prayer" on the album: "It's Dark and Hell is Hot" (May 19, 1998; Def Jam Records).

7. *Stranger than Fiction*, directed Marc Forster, 2006.

PROPRIETY AND TRESPASS: THE DRAMA OF EATING[1]

ELLEN F. DAVIS

". . . I eat
my history day by day."[2]

CULTURE AND AGRICULTURE

In this essay I am addressing the symposium topic of "Christianity's engagement with culture" in the most literal sense. The Latin word *cultura* refers to the act of cultivating or demonstrating care in a variety of senses, the most basic of them being the care of fields—agriculture. For some fifteen years now I have been teaching a seminar on what the Hebrew Scriptures have to say about land care; to my (initial) surprise, they are pervasively interested in the subject. On reflection, this agrarian interest of the biblical writers seems less surprising, since throughout the Iron Age and into the Persian Period at least, the vast majority of Israelites—eighty-five percent or more[3]—were farmers. So, even if many or most of the biblical writers and editors were urbanites holding "desk jobs," they had grown up and still lived in close quarters with agriculturalists. Also, most urban residents in ancient Israel engaged in tilling the fields within walking distance of the city. By background, as well as by propinquity and osmosis, they knew something most of us have forgotten, namely that agriculture is a theologically significant enterprise. If the notion of agriculture's theological significance seems odd to most of us, then that in itself testifies to the dangerous peculiarity of our modern industrialized culture, and specifically to its irreverence about eating. For thousands of years agriculture has been the most widespread form of cultural activity. It is our most basic artifact, and agriculture has always (until recently) been imbued with religious significance. To this day it remains far and away our largest industry, the heaviest consumer of water and energy (the latter, primarily in the form of petroleum products). According to the 2005 United Nations sponsored Millennium Ecosystem Assessment, agriculture as currently practiced may also constitute the "largest threat to biodiversity and ecosystem function of any single human activity."[4] In sum, as evolutionary biologist and Kansas farmer Wes Jackson observes, "It is in agriculture . . . that human culture and the creation totally interpenetrate."[5]

To the biblical writers that statement might have seemed only too obvious. They took it as a matter of course that human work approaches God's work most regularly through agriculture. Therefore, throughout the Hebrew Scriptures the condition of the land serves as the best index of the health, or conversely the ill health, of the relationship between God and humanity, and God and Israel in particular. Good farming was an aspect of Israel's religious obligation and witness. That is hard for us to comprehend, and so in order to understand what the Bible may have to say to us in this matter, it is necessary to consider how we raise and process food in industrial societies, in a system so different from traditional farming practice that it is more accurately labeled "agribusiness."

One of the most pronounced features of a fully industrialized culture is its willingness (indeed, its need) to leave its members in nearly total ignorance about the sources of their food and the other essential stuff of life. We are ignorant because we are not involved: less than one percent of the U. S. population is engaged in fulltime farming; prisoners outnumber farmers in our society. On a global scale crucial decisions about how we eat are overwhelmingly made by a few multinational conglomerates that control a system increasingly characterized by horizontal consolidation and vertical integration, from seed to supermarket.

This system of food production is not only the largest but also the most consequential industry the world has ever known. Sixty years of petro-chemical "inputs" have increased food production to an unprecedented degree, enabling the world population to grow by four and one-half billion. At the same time industrial practices have caused damage on an unprecedented scale: erosion, drastic reduction of the seed base, draining of rivers and aquifers, chemical poisoning of soil and water supply, and release of deadly floods of effluents and greenhouse gases. Returns on chemical farming are now decreasing; it is evident that we have purchased short-term abundance at the cost of the health of the whole "land community"—to evoke Aldo Leopold's important concept, which implies that land is not so much an "it" as a "we." The land community is soil and water and air, combined with the plants and motile creatures, human and nonhuman, that depend upon those living elements for their own life.[6] Our community is sick, and the symptoms of our disease are everywhere visible: the widespread impoverishment of rural towns and regions; high rates of rural violence and farmer suicides worldwide; the trauma injuries and abbreviated lives of people working in both field and factory;[7] drastic reduction of genetic variety within all major food crops; the short, sick lives of industrially confined animals and the collapse of some populations, wild or semi-domesticated. With respect to this last, the worst news may be the latest: in Europe and the U. S. widespread "Colony Collapse Disorder" among commercial honeybees, pollinators for many of our crops.[8]

"Catastrophic agriculture,"[9] as we now practice it, will end in the foreseeable future. (That is the good news, sort of.) The oil that makes it possible for us to eat this way now will give out. Yet, already half the topsoil in Iowa is gone; about forty percent of the arable soils worldwide are significantly degraded.[10] So the question is: What will be left for the coming generations to work with—to eat from—when the dominance of industrial agriculture ends? The urgency of that question has generated a quite large (and rapidly growing) body of contemporary agrarian literature. For the first time in history the philosophy of agrarianism has been fully articulated, with a body of *belles lettres* to back it up. Some of that literature, especially the essays, fiction, and poetry of Wendell Berry, is among the best work of North American writers. The modern agrarians are diverse in interests and backgrounds; they include farmers and city dwellers, biologists, economists, professors of philosophy, literature, ecology, and even a few theologians. What they all share is a worldview that holds together the health of "land" (in the broad sense) and culture. They are concerned about the integrity of biotic communities, their food and energy flows, and equally the integrity of human communities, their economic, political, and spiritual wellbeing. My own research is now focused on bringing the insights of "secular" agrarian writers to bear on biblical texts. I believe that the practice of "reading the Bible through agrarian eyes" leads to better exegesis, through the recovery of a way of thinking that was native to many or most writers of the Hebrew Scriptures.

The rest of this essay models such an agrarian reading of the first three chapters of Genesis. The biblical writers, I shall argue, demonstrate both recognition of the phenomenon of biological integrity within creation and also concern about its threatened loss. They do so specifically in the attention they give to food and its immediate source, the fertile soil. "Land," "soil," "food," "eat"— all these are very common terms in the primeval history (Gen 1–11) and especially in these first chapters, which, seen from one perspective, constitute a drama about the moral dimensions of eating.

GENESIS ONE: PROPRIETY

For ecologically concerned contemporary readers the first chapter of Genesis is generally viewed as something to get past—at least, a few verses of it are, when humans are created in God's image and charged to "subdue the earth" (vv. 26–28). Norman Habel suggests that what may once have been an "Earth-centered" account of creation has been editorially "interrupted" by a radically anthropocentric story that reduces Earth "to a force or thing that must be subjugated."[11] However, rather than positing an interruption in a passage (Gen

1:1–2:4a) that virtually all other scholars acknowledge to be a tightly unified composition, it is preferable to ask how that charge to the human may be integral to the larger earth-sensitive story in which it appears.

One hundred years ago, the great German biblical scholar Hermann Gunkel taught us that identifying the literary genre of a piece is a crucial first step to its interpretation. It is widely acknowledged that Gen 1 comes from the so-called Priestly tradition. Therefore, I suggest, it is best viewed as a piece of liturgical poetry,[12] a genre designation that implies at least three things.

First, the text seeks to open up a deepened perception of God's presence in and to the world, a perception that translates fairly directly into human experience and behavior. This poem is giving us a God's-eye view of creation, with particular attention to how humans fit in that design. We are the only creatures with the capacity to think about our proper place, the only ones who can recognize when we fall short of it. So this is a poem that instructs us in *propriety*, in conforming our behavior to the limits of the world as God has made it and in realizing hopeful possibilities for the world.

Second, because a liturgical poem is carefully structured and designed primarily for the ear, literary devices such as rhythm, repetition, and verbal framing are important. When an established rhythm is broken, that is noteworthy.

Third, each word of a good poem is carefully chosen. This being the first chapter of the Bible, it is safest to assume careful composition. If a word seems awkward or ill chosen, it is probably important.

I focus on just two aspects of the poem, two places where it seems to be trying to arrest attention—in the first instance by an awkward break in rhythm, and in the second, by an offensive word choice. Notably, in each case that part of the poem has something to do with eating.

The break in rhythm is evident because of the regular beat established on the first two days of creation. The events of those days are recounted in the elegantly terse diction of divine summons and execution: "Let there be light. . . . And there was light." There are no descriptive details at all, until the middle of the third day, when "the dry land" appears. At that point, however, the poet suddenly becomes verbose:

> And God said: "Let the earth sprout-out sprouts (*tadšeʾ hāʾāreṣ dešeʾ*), plants seeding seed (*mazrîaʿ zeraʿ*) fruit trees making fruit, each of its own kind—with their seed in them—on the earth," and it was so. And the earth brought forth sprouts, plants seeding seed each of its own kind, and trees making fruit with its seed in it, each of its own kind. . . .
> (vv. 11–12)

Too many seeds, it would seem. Yet, it is worth considering that an able poet sacrifices good style only in order to make a point. If this poem is about propriety, then its seemingly excessive emphasis on seed must have something to do with the place that humans occupy in the created order, as an Israelite might have understood it. In fact, any Israelite had good reason to be interested in seed, because the most important botanical fact about the land Israel occupied is its remarkable abundance of plant diversity. In terms of genetic heritage this is one of the nutritional centers of the whole earth, both for human beings and for animals. Its liminal location—contiguous, or nearly so, with three continents—gives that small corridor of land a natural gene flow with few parallels worldwide. Botanical fact led to cultural development; ten or twelve thousand years ago the first permanent human settlements appeared in the uplands and foothills bordering the Fertile Crescent, where hunter-gatherers built stone houses and storage facilities for wild grains: emmer wheat, einkorn wheat, and barley, as well as leguminous grains such as lentils, peas, chickpeas, and vetch. Eventually wild harvests were succeeded by domesticated ones, the first farmed crops.[13] Notable in this context is the fact that the rare enabling condition for the emergence of agriculture in the Fertile Crescent was not rich soil; it was readily harvestable seed. What is most unusual about the native plant distribution is the presence of cereals and legumes, high-protein grains, with nonshattering seed heads—a minor genotype that the early farmers selected and gradually made prevalent.[14] Seed-retaining, life-sustaining grains—this is the phenomenon the poet captures with that apparently pleonastic phrase, "plants seeding seed . . . with their seed in them." Genesis 1 celebrates the familiar yet inexhaustible mystery of fruitfulness as the Israelites experienced it.

This understanding of the first awkwardness in this chapter may help us deal constructively with the second, namely the assertion of human "dominion" (as it is commonly construed) in v. 28:

> And God blessed them and God said to them: "Be fruitful and multiply and fill the earth and conquer it (*wĕkibšūhâ*), and exercise mastery among (*ûrĕdû b-*) the fish of the sea and among the birds of the sky and among all living things creeping on the earth."

Four aspects of this verse are important for our understanding of the human place in creation. First, an observation about what is missing: we are never told that the divine command is fulfilled. Normally, there is some indication that God's intention in making the creatures has been fulfilled: e.g., "…and there *was* light" (1:3); "Let there be a firmament. . . . And it was so" (1:6, 7). In this case, however, fulfillment of the divine command remains in the future, out ahead of where the creation story ends.[15] So, as readers we are in a position to render some critical judgment on ourselves with respect to our progress in fulfilling the charge we were given "in the beginning."

Second, concerning the command "*pĕrû ûrĕbû*, "Be fruitful and multiply," the most important thing is that God has uttered it before. On the fifth day of creation, one day before the humans come on stage, God blessed all the "animate creatures" (*nepeš ḥayyâ*, Gen 1:20, cf. 21) of sky and sea and charged them, "Be fruitful and multiply and fill the waters of the seas, and let the birds multiply on earth" (Gen 1:22). Juxtaposition and echo are literary devices whereby the biblical writers customarily signal meaningful connection, so when on the following day the land creatures are formed and the human is likewise blessed and charged to multiply, we must assume that the second iteration of the commandment is conditioned by the first. Legitimate human fruitfulness cannot be secured to the detriment of life forms that are equally blessed by God. Judged by that standard, the twenty-first century evidence would seem to tell against us, living as we do in our planet's sixth age of massive species extinction, with humans now functioning as "a geophysical force."[16] Humans have driven to extinction as much as a quarter of the earth's bird species, and thirty percent of fish species are currently under threat.[17] The blessing of the creatures of the fifth day of creation has been turned to a curse.

A third point to note is that the Hebrew phrase *rĕdû b-* (Gen 1:28) is rendered here, not as conventionally "exercise dominion *over*," but as "exercise mastery *among*." While the verb may denote harsh rule (Lev 25:43, 46; 26:17; Neh 9:28), its primary connotation seems to be firmness rather than harshness (see Ps 72:8). Koehler and Baumgartner observe that "the basic meaning of the verb is not 'to rule'; the word actually denotes the traveling around of the shepherd with his flock."[18] The crucial point for interpretation of the phrase in this context is that humans are blessed and charged to exercise mastery with respect to the very same creatures of sea and sky who have just received their own blessing and charge to multiply. Therefore, the human vocation can only be fulfilled if we take our place *among* the nonhuman species. Although Gen 1 and the divine speeches in Job are generally considered to be polar opposites in terms of their view of the human place in the cosmos, this reading reveals some affinity between them.

A fourth point concerns the one word in the poem that seems designed not just to prompt reflection but to stop us dead in our tracks: ". . . fill the earth *wĕkibšūhâ*, 'and *conquer* it'" (Gen 1:28). The implied object is *ʾereṣ*, "earth" or "land." "Conquer the land"—elsewhere in the Priestly tradition the notion of "conquered land" (Num 32:22, 29; Josh 18:1) refers to the promised land of Canaan. Since the verb *kabaš* ("conquer") is altogether infrequent in the Bible, this echoing of the conquest tradition must be regarded as deliberately egregious. The two divine commands are parallel: to the humans, "Conquer the *ʾereṣ*/earth"; to the Israelites, "Conquer the *ʾereṣ*/land." The intention in each case is that humans should be present in the land as representatives of God's benevolent sovereignty over it.

Yet, more can be said about that word choice, in light of what a poet working in the Priestly tradition would likely have understood about the conquest of Canaan. Two points about the Priestly account of the conquest are relevant to its foreshadowing in the first chapter of the Bible. First, that account celebrates the God-given fruitfulness of the land; memorably, it tells of grape clusters so large that two men were required to carry even one of them (Num 13:23). Just as Israel's faithfulness is meant to perpetuate the fruitfulness of Canaan, so the human exercise of mastery among the creatures is associated with God's provision of food for all. That association is implied by another instance of juxtaposition and echo. Immediately following the charge to the human is a second notice about seeds and the self-perpetuating fruitfulness of the earth:

> And God said: "Look, I give to you every plant seeding seed that is on the face of all the earth, and every tree that has on it tree-fruit seeding seed; for you it shall be, for eating. And to every living thing of the earth . . . every kind of green herbage for eating. (Gen 1:29–30b)

In modern scientific language, then, it would seem that the proper exercise of human mastery among the creatures has centrally to do with maintaining the integrity of the food chains on which all creatures depend—or even enhancing their long-term productivity, as indigenous farmers may once have done in the Middle East and on the North American continent and elsewhere.[19] As we have seen, that kind of mastery is very far from our present exercise of domination over the planet.

The disparity between the effects of human behavior, on the one hand, and the divine intention as set forth by this poet, on the other, points to a second aspect of the Priestly understanding of Israel's entry into Canaan: the "conquest" ultimately ended in failure and exile. This is a fact that would have been known to those who composed and heard Gen 1, which almost certainly reached its present form during the period of the Babylonian Exile. In that historical context the reminder of the conquest of Canaan recalled Israel's recent failure in the land even while it also encouraged exiles to believe that God still intended for them a future in the land and more broadly on the earth—both connotations of 'ereṣ—now that Israel was dispersed among the nations. In our own generation we might hear in this verse a warning that the human project on earth could fail altogether, for we are the first to face the real historical possibility that, if we do not exercise our "mastery" with propriety, the fruitfulness of the whole planet may be lost. As we shall see, the second chapter of Genesis accords with this reading and gives a more detailed understanding of the difficulties and the promise that such an exercise of mastery entails.

GENESIS TWO AND THREE: VOCATION AND TRESPASS

In the following chapter the Yahwistic writer famously recounts: "YHWH God formed *hāʾādām* ("the human being") from *hāʾădāmâ* ("the fertile soil"), "human from humus," and with the inspiration of divine breath, the human became "an animate being," *nepeš ḥayyâ* (Gen 2:7)—the same term that occurs three times in Gen 1 to designate the *nonhuman* creatures of sea and land (1:20, 21, 30). Thus the compound creation account, from both the Priestly and Yahwistic writers, points to the biological integration of all life. The essential relatedness of all living things is underscored when the Yahwist recounts further that "God caused to grow from *hāʾădāmâ* every desirable tree" (2:9) and formed from the same substance every other "animate being" on earth and in the sky (2:19). The complex relationship between *ʾādām* and *ʾădāmâ* is both "genealogical" and vocational: "And YHWH God took the human being and set him in the garden of Eden to . . ." (Gen 2:15)—to do what? *Lěʿobědāh ûlěšoměrāh*, the Hebrew says; a standard rendering is "to till it and tend [or 'keep'] it" (NJPS, NRSV). That is to some degree misleading, for neither Hebrew verb is primarily an agricultural term, and each has an ambiguity that is lost in translation. *ʿĀbad* means "work," in the broad sense of the English word. Occasionally it refers to working a substance, specifically soil (e.g., Gen 2:5; 3:23; 4:2), yet in the overwhelming majority of its uses the verb means to work *for* someone, to serve a master. So the phrase *lěʿobědāh* invites a question: who is in charge here? *ʾĀdām*, who comes from *ʾădāmâ*, also works *ʾădāmâ*. We exercise some degree of control over the soil, and at the same time we are controlled by it, limited to what it is able or willing to give (Gen 3:18). The farmer Cain is condemned for his violence through the soil's bloody "mouth" (Gen 4:10–12); as a result it withholds from him its strength. Thus, the whole question of who has priority—*ʾādām* or *ʾădāmâ*—is called radically into question.

The second verb, *šāmar*, is at least as ambiguous as the first, because it has a broader semantic range. A basic meaning is to "watch over, protect," as in Cain's question: "Am I my brother's *šōmēr*?" (Gen 4:9). Frequently it may be rendered "observe," with a variety of nuances: to acquire wisdom by observation of the workings of the world (Ps 107:43; Isa 42:20), to observe behavior with the goal of imitating it (Ps 37:37), to observe guidelines, specifically divine commandments or the dictates of justice (Hos 12:7; Isa 56:1), even to observe certain natural rhythms (Jer 8:7). Humans are thus charged to work the soil and watch it, to serve it, observe it, and preserve it. In short, they are charged to learn from it and respect the limits it sets, to "consult the genius of the place in all." This phrase, from Alexander Pope's verse epistle on gardening written to Lord Burlington, serves as a motto for farmer and evolutionary biologist Wes Jackson in his work at the Land Institute in Salina, Kansas.

The Natural Systems Agriculture being developed at the Land Institute seems to me a direct application of that charge, for it proceeds from three questions: "What is (or was) here?" "What will nature require of us (or permit us to do) here?" "What will nature help us to do here?"[20] These questions acknowledge that the first step to working the land responsibly is observing it: "What [is] here?" Further, they bespeak a concern for propriety: working respectfully *with* nature, what must or might we do here? The recurrent word "here" is crucial; each place has its own answers to yield.[21] Further, these questions point to the complex truth underlying the ambiguous verbs of Genesis. Because there is power on both sides of the relationship between ʾādām and ʾădāmâ, and potential for lasting benefit or harm, then it must be a relationship of mutual service. When we humans neglect our first vocation, the bond with the soil is not broken or even attenuated, even if we are oblivious of it. Rather, it becomes twisted, and the relationship becomes one of mutual suffering and death.

Against this background it can hardly be a coincidence that the first trespass of the limits of the created order is an eating violation. At the moment when the woman makes her fateful decision the narrator slows down and (uncharacteristically for biblical storytelling) moves inside her head, so we see with her and know precisely how she reasons: "And the woman saw that the tree was good for eating and that it was appealing to the eyes, and the tree was desirable for 'enlightenment,' and she took some of its fruit, and she ate" (3:6). The woman "saw that the tree was good"—the near echo of God's seeing all that was good in the first days of the world underscores the fact that her perception of the desirable leads her away from God's intention for creation; God made every tree *except* this one "good for eating" (2:9). Only in the woman's mind does mere consumption yield enlightenment; in fact, the only thing the humans learn from their experience is that they are naked. Based on what we have found in Gen 2, it seems likely that God meant the humans to gain insight into the workings of the world gradually—literally, "by steps"—through walks with God "in the breezy time of day" (Gen 3:8) and through patient "observation," in all its senses, in the garden (2:15). Instead, "she took some of its fruit, and she ate." She took without thought of tending, and further, without gratitude or memory. This is the first time a creature appears as the subject of the verb *lāqaḥ*, "take";[22] she took, forgetful or ignorant of the simple agrarian understanding that there is "nothing taken that was not first a gift."[23]

In this trespass immediate desire is the standard for action vis-à-vis God and the other creatures. Environmental philosopher J. Baird Callicott proposes that here "knowledge of good and evil" denotes the power "to *determine* what is right and what is wrong *in relation to self*."[24] Once the humans have "consumed" that knowledge, then they regard themselves as "an axiological point of reference . . . an intrinsically valuable hub to which other creatures and the creation as a whole may be referred for appraisal"[25]—and, I would add, for appropriation. It is not hard to see why the humans' adoption of that new standard would create a rupture in their relationship with God, who shortly afterward poses to the man this incredulous question: "From the tree that I commanded you not to eat from it . . . you ate??!" (3:11). The question shows that God does not distinguish between woman and man in terms of culpability—although through the centuries "theological" interpreters have often ascribed chief responsibility to Eve. If it is significant that the *woman* first takes and eats and then gives the food to the man, then the logic of the narrative is probably grounded in social practice: food preparation in the ancient world was primarily the responsibility of women.

The rupture in the created order affects more than the humans' relationship with God. It is fair enough that they should have to leave Eden, but from now on the soil suffers a curse for their sake (3:17). In order to see the propriety of that curse, one has to adopt an agrarian perspective and standard for human behavior. Some years ago I studied this passage with a group of young farmers and plant biologists at Wes Jackson's Land Institute. I told them that my theology students (at that time, in urban New Haven, Connecticut) found the curse on the soil troublesome and arbitrary: this must be a classic instance of the grumpy God of the Old Testament. When I asked the Land Institute interns for their view, they answered without a second's hesitation: "When humans are out of touch with God, the soil is the first to suffer." Note, these people were not theologians, nor in most cases were they conventionally religious. Yet they easily intuited and, further, accepted the biblical view that there is an unbreakable three-way connection among people, God, and land, a connection so tight that when the first humans eat against the rules, disturbance in the divine-human relationship is evidenced in the landscape:

> Thorns and thistles it will sprout for you, and you shall eat the grass of
> the field. By the sweat of your face you shall eat bread, until you return
> to the soil, for from it you were taken. (3:18–19a)

Thorns and thistles are signs of eroded and desiccated soil. Thus the biblical poet is writing in a few lines a short but accurate history of land transformation and degradation in the uplands of the ancient Near East. First tree cover—Eden seems to be an arboreal garden[26]—was cleared for cultivation and grazing. Too often the bared sloping ground was further denuded by overgrazing and incautious cultivation; as a result, more marginal land had to be cleared and mined for its fertility.[27] Humans and land together "fell" into the world the Israelites knew.[28] Living in a fragile landscape that was already damaged in ancient times, the Israelite knew they could eat from the soil, generation to generation, only through unrelenting labor and good service to the soil—that is, by working to maintain the health of the land and even gradually to heal it of its wounds.

The first three chapters of Genesis demonstrate the biblical writers' understanding that the drama of human eating is fraught with tension, trouble, and potential tragedy. It is sobering to reread those chapters, mindful of the agricultural practices that currently dominate industrial systems of food production, many of them centered in North America and ramifying throughout the globe. Millions of North American Christians now passionately assert the "authority" of the biblical account of creation in the context of the debate about creationism vs. evolution. How much more hopeful would our situation be if those who seek moral guidance from the Bible were to heed the warning present in that account and begin to reexamine our careless, destructive, and potentially catastrophic eating practices? Such an outcome of our reading could open before us a future that God might yet judge to be "very good."

ENDNOTES

1. The research for this paper was sponsored in part by the Lilly Theological Research Grants Program.
2. Wendell Berry, "History," *Collected Poems* (San Francisco: North Point, 1985), 175.
3. Edward F. Campbell, "A Land Divided," in *The Oxford History of the Biblical World* (ed. Michael Coogan; Oxford/New York: Oxford University Press, 1998), 229.
4. Millennium Ecosystem Assessment, *Ecosystems and Human Well-Being*, vol. 1, *Current State and Trends* (Washington: Island, 2005), 777.
5. Wes Jackson, *Becoming Native to This Place* (Lexington: University Press of Kentucky, 1994), 22.
6. See Aldo Leopold's classic essay "The Land Ethic," in *A Sand County Almanac* (New York: Oxford University Press, 1966), 237–264.
7. The average life expectancy of Latino farmworkers in the U. S. is about one-third less than for the general population: 49 years, compared to 73 to 79. Gary Holthaus, *From the Farm to the Table: What All Americans Need to Know about Agriculture* (Lexington: University Press of Kentucky, 2006), 140.
8. While the cause of the die-offs is not determined at the time of writing, it appears to be an unidentified virus compounded by other factors such as drought, the resulting undernutrition, and the practices of industrialized beekeeping. See Andrew C. Revkin, "Virus Is Seen as Prime Suspect in Death of Honeybees," *New York Times* (September 7, 2007): A–16, and also the website http://www.eurekalert.org/bees.
9. On the concept of "catastrophic agriculture," see Richard Manning, *Against the Grain: How Agriculture Has Hijacked Civilization* (New York: North Point, 2004).
10. Wes Jackson of The Land Institute, Salina, Kansas, commonly cites the figure of thirty-eight percent for global land degradation. Similar figures are given by Jonathan A. Foley et al., "Global Consequences of Land Use," *Science* 309 (July 22, 2005): 570; see also L. R. Oldeman *et al.*, *World Map of the Status of Human-Induced Soil Degradation: An Explanatory Note* (2d ed.; Wageningen/Nairobi: International Soil Reference and Information Centre/United Nations Environment Programme, 1991), 28. According to James Gustave Speth (citing the U. N. Environment Programme's *Global Environment Outlook*), "about three-fourths of the world's drylands are degraded, and about a fourth of all land is degraded to a degree sufficient to reduce its productivity" (*Red Sky at Morning* [New Haven: Yale University Press, 2004], 31).

11. Norman Habel, "Geophany: The Earth Story in Genesis 1," *The Earth Story in Genesis* (ed. Norman Habel and Shirley Wurst; Sheffield/Cleveland: Sheffield Academic Press/The Pilgrim Press, 2000), 47.

12. For the sake of convenience I designate the Priestly poem of creation (Gen 1:1–2:4a) as "Gen 1." I follow Walter Brueggemann in classifying it as a liturgical poem (*Genesis* [Interpretation Series; Atlanta: John Knox, 1982], 30), although Brueggemann himself does not explore the implications of that genre designation.

13. Oded Borowski notes: "The domestication of cereals . . . took place sometime before 7000 B.C.E. in the Near East. . ." (*Agriculture in Iron Age Israel* [Winona Lake, Ind.: Eisenbrauns, 1987], 87).

14. See Daniel Hillel, *Out of the Earth: Civilization and the Life of the Soil* (New York: Free, 1991), 72–73.

15. The notice of fulfillment in Gen 1:30 refers to the divine provision of food for all creatures.

16. E. O. Wilson observes that "Homo sapiens has become a geophysical force, the first species in the history of the planet to attain that dubious distinction" (*The Future of Life* [New York: Alfred A. Knopf, 2002], 23). On species loss, see Richard E. Leakey, *The Sixth Extinction: Patterns of Life and the Future of Humankind* (New York: Doubleday, 1995).

17. In 1997 a team of terrestrial ecologists from Stanford University reported that extinction rates for plant and animal species are "now on the order of 100 to 1000 times those before humanity's dominance of Earth. . . . [A]s many as one-quarter of Earth's bird species have been driven to extinction by human activities over the past two millennia" (Peter Vitousek and Harold A. Mooney, "Human Domination of Earth's Ecosystems," *Science* 277 [July 25, 1997]: 498). See also James Gustave Speth, *Red Sky at Morning: America and the Crisis of the Global Environment* (New Haven/London: Yale University Press, 2004), 15, 34. An indicator of the recent decline of bird populations is a 1998 report to the British Government's Joint Nature Conservation Committee, which revealed that in twenty-five years habitat loss and agricultural biocides had drastically reduced the populations of several of the (formerly) most common birds: for example, tree sparrows by ninety-five percent; grey partridges by eighty-six percent; turtle doves by sixty-nine percent (Alistair McIntosh, *Soil and Soul* [London: Aurum, 2004], 38).

18. Ludwig Koehler and Walter Baumgartner, *The Hebrew and Aramaic Lexicon of the Old Testament* (Leiden: Brill, 2001), 2.1190.

19. J. Baird Callicott suggests that the abundance of plant and animal life found in the Americas by the first European invaders and settlers was not purely "natural" but instead reflects the land management practices of the native inhabitants. See "Genesis and John Muir," *Covenant for a New Creation* (ed. Carol S. Robb and Carl J. Casebolt; Maryknoll, Md.: Orbis, 1991), 133–134.

20. Both Wendell Berry and Wes Jackson take these questions as the starting point for their thinking. See Wes Jackson, *New Roots for Agriculture* (Lincoln, Neb.: University of Nebraska Press, 1985) and also Wendell Berry, "Wildness," in *Home Economics* (New York: North Point, 1987), 137–151.

21. On local adaptation as "the inescapable governing principle of agriculture" (in contrast to industrial agriculture's "governing principle of uniformity"), see the correspondence between Wendell Berry and Wes Jackson, "Letters from a Humble Radical," in Jason Peters, *Wendell Berry: Life and Work* (Lexington: University of Kentucky Press, 2007), 170.

22. Notably, the same three words or phrases—*rāʾāh*, "see"; *kî ṭōb*, "how good"; and *lāqaḥ*, "take"—occur together in another account of trespass within the primeval history, when "the divine sons *saw* the human daughters, *how good* they were, and *took* for themselves wives" (Gen 6:2).

23. Wendell Berry, "Sabbath 1998, VI," *Given* (Washington, D. C.: Shoemaker & Hoard, 2005), 61.

24. J. Baird Callicott, "Genesis and John Muir," 123.

25. Ibid., 123–124.

26. J. Baird Callicott speaks of Eden as "an agroforest permaculture" ("Genesis and John Muir," 118).

27. On the stages of land degradation in Israel and its environs, see Daniel Hillel, *The Natural History of the Bible* (New York: Columbia University Press, 2006), 22–23.

28. In response to my essay Prof. Frank Yamada has questioned the notion of a "Fall" and raised the question, "Wouldn't more knowledge help and not hurt when it comes to the use of environmental resources?" The biblical writers, however, do not treat knowledge as valuable in the abstract, nor do they assume that more is better. What is both valuable and rare is knowledge of the world conjoined with mindfulness of and obedience to God ("fear of YHWH"). That combination is what the sages of Proverbs call *ḥokmâ*, "wisdom" (Prov. 1:7, etc.).

NEW from Baker Academic

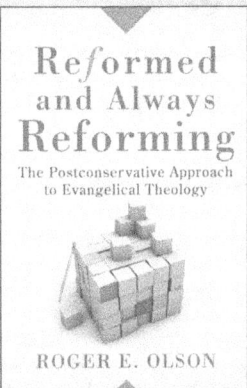

Reformed and Always Reforming
THE POSTCONSERVATIVE APPROACH TO EVANGELICAL THEOLOGY
Roger E. Olson
9780801031694
256 pp. • $19.99p

"Olson has become a major interpreter of American evangelical theology and an advocate of a postconservative approach. What we have lacked is a clear guide to this perspective within evangelicalism. In his new book, Olson sets forth a genuinely evangelical theology that rejects modernity and fundamentalism. His focus on a personal relationship with Christ over propositions and the need to continually revise theology in light of the Word of God are important corrections to conservative evangelical tendencies. Anyone interested in a truly gospel-oriented theology will benefit from engaging with his arguments."
—**Alan G. Padgett**, Luther Seminary

What Would Jesus Deconstruct?
THE GOOD NEWS OF POSTMODERNISM FOR THE CHURCH
John D. Caputo
9780801031366
160 pp. • $19.99p

"This is a marvelous little book. It enables readers to understand deconstruction as the hermeneutics of the kingdom of God and provides a glimpse of what this concept might look like in the hands of Jesus as applied to the church. This will be difficult therapy, and many of us will be inclined to resist. However, let us remember that while discipline is painful in the moment, it produces a harvest of peace and righteousness in the long run. May the church learn from the wisdom found in these pages."—**John R. Franke**, Biblical Seminary

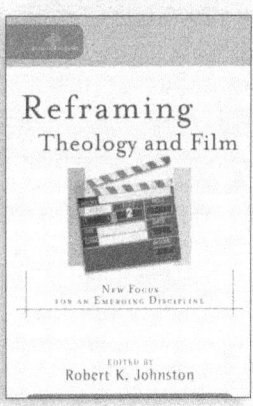

Reframing Theology and Film
NEW FOCUS FOR AN EMERGING DISCIPLINE
Robert K. Johnston, editor
9780801032400
336 pp. • $24.99p

"Here is a fine collection of essays full of rich detail, engaging insights, and provocative suggestions. The impressive cast of authors points beyond many of the usual frames of study, offering original perspectives and new approaches. Without exception, the chapters make a valuable contribution to ongoing dynamic conversations. This is a 'must-read' for anyone with an interest in film and theology."—**Jolyon Mitchell**, Edinburgh University

Resounding Truth
CHRISTIAN WISDOM IN THE WORLD OF MUSIC
Jeremy S. Begbie
9780801026959
416 pp. • $22.99p

"Jeremy Begbie's thinking emerges out of a fusion of the best musical thinking about theology and the best theological thinking about music. The resulting text is charged with energy and insight—and not just for musicians and theologians. This vital work is poised to energize and strengthen the entire Christian community for a way of life together that is marked by grace, truth, beauty, and genuine self-giving service."—**John D. Witvliet**, Calvin College and Calvin Theological Seminary

Baker Academic
Extending the Conversation

Available at your local bookstore, www.bakeracademic.com, or by calling 1-800-877-2665
Subscribe to Baker Academic's electronic newsletter (E-Notes) at www.bakeracademic.com

CASCADE Books
199 W. 8th Ave., Eugene, OR 97401 • www.wipfandstock.com

THEOLOGICAL INTERPRETATION *of* SCRIPTURE
Stephen E. Fowl

978-1-55635-241-6 / Available Winter 2008

Christians have been interpreting Scripture with an aim of deepening their life with God and each other from the very beginning of the church. Now, in the past twenty years or so, we have witnessed an explosion of scholarly writing devoted to the theological interpretation of Scripture. Stephen Fowl's companion explores some of the connections between this long running and essential Christian practice and this more recent body of scholarly literature. As one who has contributed to the contemporary conversation, Fowl is able to help readers navigate their way through the literature by introducing them to people, texts, and issues that have become important to discussion over the years.

READING BONHOEFFER
A Guide to His Spiritual Classics and Selected Writings on Peace

Geffrey B. Kelly

978-1-55635-236-2 / Available Spring 2008

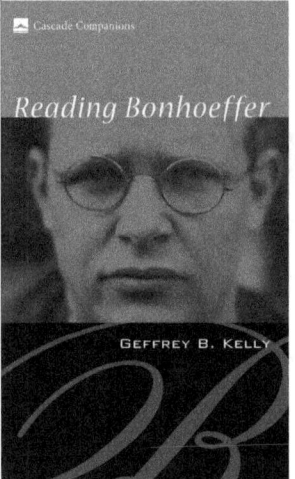

The German theologian Dorothee Soelle once wrote, "Dietrich Bonhoeffer is the one German theologian who will lead us into the third millennium." As we near the end of the first decade of the third millennium, Bonhoeffer continues to inspire new generations of those who recognize in him a spiritual guide for their actions on behalf of peace and social justice. Geffrey Kelly's *Reading Bonhoeffer* provides a critical analysis and reading guide to two of Bonhoeffer's spiritual classics—*Discipleship* and *Life Together*. In a final section, Kelly excerpts and analyzes three significant texts by Bonhoeffer on the need for world peace against the rising militarism and continued glorification of war in Germany and other European nations.

Forthcoming from Cascade Companions

CREATION AND EVOLUTION
by Tatha Wiley
ISBN: 978-1-55635-291-1
Summer 2008

iPOD, YOUTUBE, Wii PLAY
Theological Engagements with Entertainment
by D. Brent Laytham
ISBN: 978-1-55635-509-7
Fall 2008

CHRISTIANITY AND POLITICS IN AMERICA
by Chad C. Pecknold
ISBN: 978-1-55635-242-3
Winter 2008

available in bookstores | Tel.: (541) 344-1528
orders@wipfandstock.com | www.wipfandstock.com

RESPONSE TO DAVIS

FRANK M. YAMADA

I will begin my response with a confession of sorts and a self-designation. If someone would have asked me, "What do Wes Jackson and Hermann Gunkel share in common?" or "What are the interconnections between the Land Institute and *'āpār min-hā'ădāmâ*, 'the dust of the ground'?" or better yet, "What does Eden have to do with Kansas?" I would have shrugged my shoulders and given the overused response that most professors give in such situations—the pedagogical gem, "I don't know, let me get back to you on that one."

I have invested a lot of time and energy in these first three chapters of Genesis as a teacher, scholar, and theologian. They have inspired, troubled, and angered me, at times all in one sitting. I have also tried, although admittedly not as hard as I should, to live a life that is conscientious when it comes to the earth, the environment, and the creaturely world. However, I have not often thought of these commitments in relationship to each other, that is, to consider "the theological significance of agriculture" to use my colleague's words. If I were to find myself in Dr. Davis's paper, I would admittedly be one of those urban persons who stands in ignorance outside of the garden when it comes to food supply and consumption. I have Dr. Davis to thank for her insights that have sparked afresh in me another possible reading of Gen 1–3. I find her interpretation compelling and her ethical insights challenging. She has found yet another way to live into Fernando Segovia's imperative to make real the "flesh and blood" reader of the biblical text as she seeks to read the Edenic story through "agrarian eyes."[1]

Ordinarily, when people discuss and debate Gen 1–3 in the context of Christianity and culture, the topic revolves around the debate of evolution vs. creationism or intelligent design. Within these discussions the real theological issue under scrutiny is biblical authority, or to what extent the biblical witness is true and in what way (scientifically, historically, factually, etc.). I agree with Dr. Davis that her topic is much more interesting and morally compelling than the creation/evolution debate. I find myself drawn, however, to similar questions of scriptural authority. In what way does the biblical text speak truthfully about human experience, and, similarly, about which narrative or narratives are we talking?[2] My response and my questions to Dr. Davis will revolve around these two interpretative foci.

On the topic of biblical authority, I am interested in finding out why the Bible is necessary for illustrating the story that Dr. Davis wants to tell. I think one could argue that she could make a strong case for the dangerous way that humans exploit the earth without use of the biblical text. One of the most inspiring and sobering movies of the twenty-first century, *An Inconvenient Truth*, reminds us of how the power of moral persuasion can be used to raise consciousness around an environmental issue without strong references to religious motifs. In fact, much of the Bible, especially the interpretation of passages such as Gen 1:28, have done a great deal of harm to the earth at the expense of humanity. At their heart the biblical creation stories are strongly anthropocentric for better or for worse. Even if we find ourselves agreeing with the basic ideas of Dr. Davis's stimulating close reading of the Priestly creation story, we must also acknowledge that this cosmic liturgy reaches its climax, although not its conclusion, with the creation of humanity. The J-narrative, while more plot driven than P's account, also has the creation of humanity at the center of its constructed world. Moreover, while Dr. Davis goes a long way toward reinterpreting these texts and their vocabulary to create a reading that puts us in better touch with *hāʾădāmâ*, "the ground," I wonder if these texts have too much momentum in favor of earth exploitation. I do not want to argue this point too forcefully now, but I raise it as a topic for discussion. Does the biblical text and its language of "conquering" (*wĕkibšūhâ*) and "ruling over" (*rĕdû b-*) the earth lend itself too much toward a trajectory of human exploitation of nature?[3] The history of interpretation on this passage might suggest so.

I agree with Dr. Davis that much of the Priestly writer's intent in Gen 1:1–2:4a is for humans to grasp fully their own place in creation. More precisely this poem situates humans and creation into their ordered places under the sovereign rule of *ʾĔlōhîm*. Propriety in relation to the created order is certainly a biblical virtue for humanity. In fact, Dr. Davis's analysis can be taken a step further. One can infer from her interpretation that bad things happen when human beings do not practice such propriety. Later in the book of Genesis the human beings not only forget their proper place—that is, living in conjunction with the birds of the air and the fish of the sea by being fruitful and multiplying (cf. Gen 1:22 and 1:28) and filling (from the root, *mālēʾ*, "fill, be full") the earth—but later in the P account, human violence and corruption so fill (passive Niphal stem of *mālēʾ*) the land, that God decides to "decreate" the earth through a return of the watery chaos (Gen 6:11–13). P's description of the preflood scene corresponds nicely with Dr. Davis's interpretation of Gen 1:28 by pointing out the negative consequences of a life out of order. However, the stories in Gen 6 also suggest that these agrarian

Israelites can find themselves getting out of alignment with creation just as easily as twenty-first century urban North Americans. In fact, I find very compelling parallels between contemporary notions of earth exploitation and P's description of an earth (*hāʾāreṣ*) that is "corrupt" or "spoiled"[4] and filled with violence. With such a problematic characterization of humanity's relationship to the land one wonders if the biblical text requires more than a reinterpretation through agrarian eyes. Perhaps a feminist hermeneutics of suspicion is in order—an interpretative practice that both exposes the oppressive hierarchies in the text, while seeking for a more egalitarian reading of the biblical material. In this case the dominance exists not only between two human elements (male and female), but between the human and the humus, between the earthling and the earth.

My second observation centers on narratives and the construction of story. One of the most profound insights in Dr. Davis's paper emerges in conversation with her friends from the Land Institute. There is, as she puts it, "an unbreakable three-way connection among people, God, and land." When we disrupt the balance between *ʾādām* and *ʾădāmâ*, there is a rupture in the human-divine relationship. Similarly, as we find in Gen 3, when human beings rebel against the divine will, the earth will suffer consequences along with humanity. This insight properly ties human destiny to the fate of the earth and *vice versa*, providing us with a solid rationale for the marriage of agricultural studies and biblical theology. My question, however, remains: Which story informs this particular narrative about "the drama of eating"? Dr. Davis's interpretation of Gen 2–3 should sound very familiar to those within the Christian faith, since it is a brilliant rearticulation of "the Fall" story. In fact, she artfully weaves this language into her narrative when she says, "Humans and land together 'fell' into the world the Israelites knew." I, along with many other biblical scholars, have argued elsewhere that this traditional interpretation of Gen 2–3 renders certain aspects of the text problematic. Knowledge of good and evil—that is, complete knowledge, "good and evil" being an idiom that represents the total knowledge from beginning to end—is a necessary, if not painful, reality for human existence on the earth. Other creation myths from the ancient Near East also reflect this theme. In the Epic of Gilgamesh, for example, the primordial creature Enkidu initially communes with the animals while refusing civilization. After a sexual encounter with a woman Enkidu receives a wisdom that separates him from the animal realm, a carnal knowledge if you will. When he returns to join with the animals, they run away in fear. Enkidu has become human and in the process is painfully alienated from the wild beasts. His mind, however, is filled with a new "wisdom."[5] Genesis 3 tells a similar story in which the human beings become fully human through the painful acquisition of knowledge.

For interpretations that read this story as a "Fall," however, this necessary knowledge is bad, or at the very least wrongly acquired. Even within Dr. Davis's refocusing of this story through an agrarian lens, the idea of knowledge being bad seems out of place. Would not more knowledge help and not hurt when it comes to the use of environmental resources? Is not better knowledge the ground upon which forward thinking projects like the Land Institute is built? Even if this fruit of knowledge is taken and consumed, as described in the biblical text, is not such acquisition necessary to being a mature human being? Maybe the irony in this text reflects the pain of human existence, namely, that in acquiring the knowledge that is necessary for us to live, we simultaneously alienate ourselves from the land through consumption; and hence, we estrange our bodies from their very source (the ʾādām from the ʾădāmâ). Perhaps our hope lies outside of the garden, even as we long to return to our source. The Lord always seems to make provision for our self-alienated state (e.g., making coverings for our nakedness and shame). Moreover, the human species has this uncanny knack for survival. For even when God decreed death for the first human farmers (Gen 2:17), yet they continued to live, even in their alienated state outside of the garden. There is no punishment of death in this story—one of the great surprises and enigmas in this text. Perhaps it is in this omission that we can find hope.[6]

ENDNOTES

1. Fernando F. Segovia, "Toward a Hermeneutics of the Diaspora: A Hermeneutics of Otherness and Engagement," in *Reading from This Place. Volume I: Social Location and Biblical Interpretation in the United States* (ed. Fernando F. Segovia and Mary Ann Tolbert; Minneapolis: Fortress, 1995), 57.

2. I use the term "narrative" here intentionally. Hayden White's work has shown that even the most mundane forms of historical discourse reflect a strong narrativity. See Hayden White, *Tropics of Discourse: Essays in Cultural Criticism* (Baltimore: Johns Hopkins University Press, 1978); and *The Content of the Form: Narrative Discourse and Historical Representation* (Baltimore: Johns Hopkins University Press, 1987).

3. Dr. Davis rightly notes that the suffixed verb, *wĕkibšūhâ* ("conquer it"), evokes language representative of the conquest of Canaan. While it is true that the Priestly source does not include the violent expulsion of the Canaanite groups, it is instructive that P decides to use conquest language to describe humanity's relationship to the land. The next verb (*rĕdû*), when accompanied by the preposition *b-* usually connotes the subordination of one by another (Lev 26:17; 1 Kgs 5:4; Ezek 34:4; Neh 9:28). Hence, "rule over" is the more likely translation especially when in proximity to the preceding verb, "conquer." While the cognate languages suggest a more pastoral sense in this verb, it is clear from the biblical references that this verb can also connote oppressive rule.

4. The verb, *wattissāḥet*, has the connotation of being spoiled or marred.

5. See *Ancient Near Eastern Texts Relating to the Old Testament* (ed. J. B. Pritchard; Princeton: Princeton University Press, 1969), I.iv.29, p. 75.

6. I have argued elsewhere that survival is a key theme in Gen 2–3. See Frank M. Yamada, "Constructing Hybridity and Heterogeneity: Asian American Biblical Interpretation from a Third Generation Perspective," in *Ways of Being, Ways of Reading: Asian American Biblical Interpretation* (ed. Kah-Jin Jeffrey Kuan and Mary F. Foskett; St. Louis: Chalice, 2006),

164–177. A more complete exegesis of this passage is forthcoming in an essay entitled, "What Does Manzanar Have to Do with Eden?: A Japanese American Interpretation of Genesis 2–3" (*Semeia Studies* volume edited by Ferenando Segovia, Tat-siong Benny Liew, and Randall Bailey).

CHRISTIAN *COMMUNITAS* IN THE *MISSIO DEI*: LIVING FAITHFULLY IN THE TENSION BETWEEN CULTURAL OSMOSIS AND ALIENATION

PAUL DE NEUI

To the Sons and Daughters of Issachar who understand the times and know what Israel should do. (1 Chron 12:32)

There is a story by Kukrit Pramoj, former prime minister and leading Buddhist scholar from Thailand, based on the NT account of a man born blind whom he called Simon. The story describes the difficult life of blind young Simon, and how upon the death of his father life became desperate. Simon began to beg in the streets to support his widowed mother. One day a fruit vendor named Ruth took pity on him. She led him to the market where he was able to increase his income. Through Ruth's eyes and kind descriptions the world became full of color and beauty to him for the first time. Eventually they fell in love.

One day Ruth heard that a man named Jesus from Nazareth would be passing by. The miraculous reputation of this Jesus had preceded him so that when he came near Simon cried out, "Lord! Son of God! Please help me to see!" And he was healed.

Turning to find the first person he sought, healed Simon was disappointed to find that Ruth was nowhere to be found. Then what did he see? The filth of a poor Asian market, debris in muddy piles, dead bodies of animals lying unburied, emitting a stench never noticed before, crowds of people, faces bathed in sweat, vendors' fatigued faces, cruelty, malnourishment, and death.

Closing his eyes he retraced his way home, but the ancient, toothless woman who answered the door praising God for her son's healing repulsed him. Making his way to Ruth's home where she was hiding, Simon insisted that she show herself. At last she opened the door, but his joy turned to immediate fear and disgust. There stood his beloved Ruth so hideously deformed by a burn that he could not stand to look at her. Finally he saw Jesus crucified. Falling on his knees Simon cried, "Oh God, give me back my blindness!"[1]

I find Kukrit's story both jarring and revealing, and frankly I often need that. How quickly I am absorbed by my cultural environment of comfort and optimism and forget that for many people suffering is their daily reality of life. Culture is where the blind Simons of the world must somehow survive in the contradiction between the promises of a healing Jesus and the present cruelties of the human condition. As Gustavo Gutierrez said, "How do you tell the poor that God really loves them when everything in their life points in the other direction?"[2] As a Christ follower living in a broken world, I live in a tension between cultural absorption that blinds me from following God's priorities in the world and complete cultural separation from the world that makes me or the God I profess unintelligible to the culture in which God has placed me. In the words of Lucien Legrand, this is the tension of the "puzzling tangle of intercultural dependence and counterculture, of osmosis and protest."[3] I have chosen to call it the challenge of living faithfully in the tension between cultural osmosis and cultural alienation.

If nothing else, my years as a missionary taught me that God had plenty of work to do in my heart as I sought to partner with what God was already doing in the Buddhist culture of northeast Thailand. I found it impossible to live faithfully in the cultural tension between osmosis and alienation on my own or even as a missionary family. With our Thai sisters and brothers we had to become something known in anthropology as *communitas*, companions together sharing, not bread,[4] but rice and the mutual experience of God's grace at work in us as we sought to follow God's lead. The thesis of my paper is that through Christian *communitas* the church lives faithfully in the tension between cultural osmosis and alienation and is continually transformed to God through partnership with the *missio Dei* already at work in the culture wherein God has placed her.

THE *MISSIO DEI*

Christianity's engagement with culture, the theme of the symposium, is actually about participation in God's greater mission at work in and with all the world's cultures. As a missiologist, the starting point for theology and praxis is the *missio Dei*. This term, literally the sending of God, describes who God is, the one who sent the Son and then sent the Spirit and now sends the church to partner with the work that God continues to do in every corner of creation.[5] Mission is not something the church owns, but it is a role to which she is called by God, for God, and to God.

> Mission is *missio Dei*, which seeks to subsume into itself the *missiones ecclesiae*, the missionary programs of the church. It is not the church which "undertakes" mission; it is the *missio Dei* that constitutes the

> church. . . The *missio Dei* purifies the church. It sets it under the cross—the only place where it is ever safe. . . The *missio Dei* is God's activity, which embraces both the church and the world, and in which the church may be privileged to participate.[6]

As a missionary myself it was always comforting to realize that I did not bring God along with my physical and cultural baggage to my new host country. God was already there, and I was being asked to join God's bigger mission. Initially I considered myself a fairly important piece in this strategy. I was a seminary graduate with church experience and plenty of technical knowledge. However, entering into years of language and culture learning soon taught me that I had a long way to go. Eventually I learned that it was the *missio Dei* already at work that was calling people like Banpote Wetchgama when he recognized God in the sound of the Lao *kaen* and began to use for the worship of Jesus Christ this popular local instrument which had been used to call up evil spirits. Before that it was the *missio Dei* which compelled an elderly grandmother to rise up off the floor in the middle of a Bible discussion and caused her to dance to a Holy Spirit led inner music in a transformed expression of worship.[7] Even further back in Lao and Siamese history, it was the *missio Dei* that had planted within the oral Buddhist tradition the promise of *Pra See An*,[8] the savior to come, so that when the good news of Christ appeared it was not a foreign religion but the fulfillment of all that for which people had been waiting for centuries. God had been actively working within the cultural context before the missionary arrived, but God also chose human partners in bringing about a deeper transformation. This process of ongoing transformation was both in the receptors and in the missionary agents as they participated in this greater mission.

How the *missio Dei* operates is a great mystery. Initially it is the witness that "goes out into all the earth, with words to the ends of the world."[9] It is the myriad cultural lenses through which God's invisible qualities are clearly seen.[10] It encompasses the rising and falling of all the world's peoples and nations (πᾶν ἔθνος) so that all "would seek God and perhaps reach out and find God, though he is not far from any of us."[11] The *missio Dei* also involves human agents, some willing, some unknowing, and is ultimately clearly revealed in Jesus Christ.

The process of that calling and sending in the *missio Dei* always involves a change in the agent who participates. Sometimes this change is quite radical. It can be metaphysical as in a bush that burns but is not consumed[12] or supernatural as when a donkey is given human speech.[13] Christ referred to this when the Pharisees urged him to quiet the loud praising voices of his disciples, "I tell you if they keep quiet, the stones will cry out."[14] The *missio Dei* will continue. A deeper transformation occurs in the human agents who are sent by God in the wider mission. This is seen in the life of Abram when God sent him from all that was known in order to bless all peoples of the world and in the process brought about a work of faith in his life.[15] This transformation is evident in the life of Ruth whose filial piety drew her to the God of her less than missional mother-in-law.[16] Unwilling agents are left in a liminal phase. Will they take the next step and be agents of transformation while also receiving the transformation that God desires? Sarah laughed at the possibility; Esther needed three days of fasting to think it over; for Gideon two fleeces were required. God used a call, a storm, heathen sailors, a fish, a city, a vine, heat, shade, and a worm to invite Jonah to join the transforming process. God's question to him is also for us, "I care, shouldn't you?"

In the NT many examples could be cited of how God changed people in the process of participating in the *missio Dei*. The stories include common herdsmen, foreign spiritualists, uneducated fishermen, prostitutes, widows, corrupt government workers, religious leaders, and military officials. Jesus himself identified with this preparation process by going through baptism and a subsequent time of testing before entering into his mission. It was the transforming work of the *missio Dei* that sent a fearful Annanias to face a religious fanatic who had been breathing murderous threats against his people and, not only to call this former enemy "brother," but to pray for his physical healing and spiritual anointing.[17] How many missionaries are doing that today? At times the *missio Dei* also sent those from outside the community of faith to purify it and bring it back to God's direction and wider purpose. The *missio Dei* sent an unclean Gentile named Cornelius to direct the missionary Peter and ultimately brought about a transformation, not only in Peter, but in the theological understanding of the entire church of Jesus Christ. Many other examples could be given.[18] All of creation can be employed and sent by the triune God in *missio Dei* into the cultures of the world.[19]

CULTURE AND THE *MISSIO DEI*

For the human element of creation, culture is the arena of the *missio Dei*, and it is within this cultural arena of mission that theology is given birth, context, meaning, and life practice.[20] Culture is a human product that cannot be separated from humans, and God is not ashamed to enter incarnationally into culture fully and completely.[21] The Latin root *cultura* originally indicated the ordered tilling of the soil. Today the English word "culture" primarily refers to the "orderedness" of human existence. The variations of "orderedness" that social groupings produce express something of the creativity of God, each in its own way.

Culture is not an isolated or independent force that compels people to act in certain socially-accepted fashions. It is people that compel one another to act and speak and influence each other's thought patterns. Cultures can neither bind people together nor alienate people from each other without human agents.

> People who speak of a culture as if it were a pseudo-personal entity that goes around doing things to people, have let themselves fall into a kind of cultural determinism that implies little or no room for human choice. . . . Culture is not a person. It does not *do* anything. Only people do things. The fact that people ordinarily do what they do by following the cultural "tracks" laid down for them should not lead us to treat culture itself as something possessing a life of its own.[22]

It is common to hear the term culture used in combination with an ethnic or demographic adjective as in the cases of "Black culture," "Hispanic culture," "urban culture," "gay culture," "non-Western culture," and others. Sometimes religious words are attached to it that also indicate categories of humans such as "Muslim culture" or "Buddhist Culture." In these cases social groupings are being labeled, and the proper term should be "people." Everyone possesses and embodies some type of culture (or combination of cultures) even if they cannot identify it.

Paul Hiebert further defined culture as the learned behavior patterns, ideas, and products created by a group of people.[23] Mimi White summarized culture as "meanings and the making of them."[24] Once again, these are embodied in people. What occurs within the people of a particular society both individually and corporately holds significance for that culture. These items could also be termed worldview values. Culture could be defined as who I am without my ever having to think about it.

Identification of one's own culture may be an extremely difficult task, particularly for those who are of the dominant cultural group. These features are mutually understood by insiders but may be nearly impossible for those same insiders to perceive or define. One may be part of a dominant cultural structure and never recognize this until it is somehow threatened. This is when the deepest meanings held by that culture tend to surface. Kathryn Tanner writes that "a culture is definable *as a culture* only in distinction from others that it is not."[25] Only by looking at ourselves through the lens of another culture do we ever really get to see and even begin to understand our own cultural values and distinctiveness. Only exposure to the other allows us to see ourselves. Through the stories of the blind Simons of the world our own perspectives expand, and God uses such insights and experiences to build new understandings, both theological and cultural. This seems to be a missiological approach that God often uses to move people beyond themselves in his transforming process.

TWO SIDES OF CULTURE

Cultures have two sides. On one side the myriad of diverse human cultures represents the vastness of the creative triune God continually desiring to express itself for God's praise and glory in our world and in the heavenly realms.[26] Cultures include components that are true, noble, right, pure, lovely, admirable, excellent, and praiseworthy.[27] The evidence of these components can be tangible, social, physical, material, and even spiritual. John Calvin stated, "All the notable endowments that manifest themselves among unbelievers are gifts of God."[28] Craig Detweiler and Barry Taylor state, "God shines through even the most debased pop cultural products."[29] This is the *imago Dei* found in individuals, cultural groupings, and their collective products. All are part of the very good creation of God awaiting the final fulfillment.[30] Jacob Loewen wrote, "We may never see the full richness of God's revelation until we are able to participate in the multitude of different perspectives brought to it by the multitude of languages and cultures in the world."[31]

The opposite side of culture is also true. Just as human cultures reflect the *imago Dei*, they also contain the imprint of the fallenness of humanity. Culture and the worldview values behind them display "both the wisdom of God and the flaws of sin."[32] These flaws are generated and expressed individually, corporately, and globally. They can also be evidenced on levels external, visible, social, physical, material, and even spiritual. Human cultures strive with one another in a continual desire to express themselves for the sake of self-centered praise and glory. These attempts counterfeit the true created purpose of humanity by following the original temptation of self-deification.[33]

It was not because of the good in human culture nor even the redeemable remnant of *imago Dei* retained somewhere in human culture that caused God to desire to restore humanity. The starting point of the *missio Dei* is solely the initiation of a God who, in spite of the sinful fallen condition of all the world's cultures, continued to love the entire created order and precisely at that point of rejection decided to do something about it.[34]

MISSIO DEI AND THE TENSION OF FAITHFUL LIVING IN CULTURE

Generations of theologians, missiologists, and practitioners thinking about Christianity's engagement with culture have been influenced by H. Richard Niebuhr's seminal work *Christ in Culture*. All critiques of Christendom and modernist tendencies aside, one of the major omissions of Niebuhr and many of his critics is their ignoring the fact that the transformation of culture God desires is not somewhere out there but is first and foremost required in the life of those who claim to be Christ followers. David Bosch said it best, "The first missionary task of the church is not to change the world but to change herself."[35]

The reality of living in human culture is the ongoing pressure to conform. The pressure to conform comes from the people within the culture. Some of these pressures are good and maintain the welfare of the society; other pressures are not. Ultimate absorption into culture is subtle, a comfortably slow decline into osmosis.

Understandably, partnering with the *missio Dei* requires full incarnation with the culture, identifying with people, speaking their language, allowing the gospel to be understood and to address clearly deep, heartfelt values in ways that make response possible. The other extreme is to be completely alienated from one's culture to such an extent that the prophetic voice is unintelligible, so foreign it cannot elicit a response, or as the old saying goes, "so spiritually minded as to be of no earthly good."

Lucien Legrand's review of Scripture's teaching about the life of the called of God in relation to their cultural context details this tension very clearly.[36] God is at work in two seemingly contradictory ways in culture and calls his people to partner in this apparent tension. On one side God is fully committed to a complete identification with the human condition through incarnation, not for the sake of relevance, but in order that the other seemingly opposite position of raising a prophetic voice against the evils found in that same human culture may be clearly understood and responded to. It is a call to live in the tension which I have diagrammed below, dedicated to complete incarnation without absorption and faithfulness to the prophetic role without total alienation.

Model of Legrande's Cultural Tension

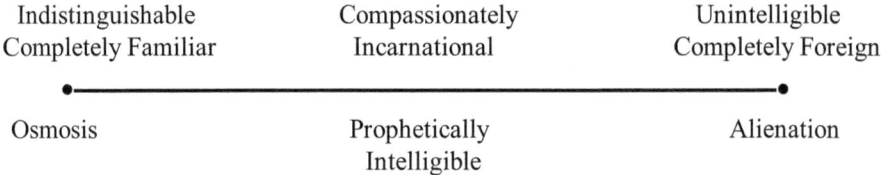

ABSORPTION THROUGH OSMOSIS

Statistics show that Christians basically do whatever the world does. Christians watch the same movies, buy the same kinds of cars, listen to the same music, and eat and drink the same as everyone else.[37] The divorce rate of Christians is no different from that of non-Christians and in some cases is higher.[38] Rather than saying that Christianity has an engagement with culture, perhaps we should say that Christianity has an incestuous relationship with culture since the culture is really an expression of ourselves. Attempts to jar Christians out of their comfortable position both intellectually and in their lifestyle include Mark Noll's *The Scandal of the Evangelical Mind*[39] and Ron Sider's more recent publication *The Scandal of the Evangelical Conscience*.[40]

Nearly every week we can find another article in the local paper or another headline story featuring a fallen religious leader, a popular media-promoted theme which apparently Christians also enjoy learning about. Even a figure as venerated as Mother Teresa is not exempt from this publicity as *Time* magazine's recent article detailing her private struggle of faith would indicate.[41] False examples of faith abound in the movies wherein the pastor, priest, or Christian spiritual leader is inevitably deeply flawed and often beyond redemption. The reality is that cultural osmosis deeply impacts and pressures all Christ followers but especially those of us who claim to be leaders and representatives of the church of Jesus Christ. It is a reality to which we must be honest in our personal confessions to each other and to the world.[42]

PROTEST AND ALIENATION

At the other end of the spectrum, while the community of Christian faith needs to be incarnational enough to be heard and not completely absorbed by cultural osmosis, how are we doing as Christ followers and as a church in raising the prophetic voice in our culture? Are there Christian voices speaking out against ungodly culture and dehumanizing injustices? Are these voices understood in ways that allow a response to the gospel, or are they instilling cultural alienation away from it?

Perhaps one of the most popular approaches to allow the voice of the gospel to be heard in the culture is through the attempt to disassociate oneself from the established church and to reject and revile the evils of the Christian past, particularly those under the rubric of Christendom. Craig Carter has done this in his appeal to rethink Niebuhr's positions:

> If you reject Christendom, you will sometimes appear left wing to your right-wing friends (or enemies) and you will often appear right wing to your left-wing friends (or enemies). When everyone has a problem with you, then you know that you are doing something right. . . . Our goal is to be indigestible to the world."[43]

While the emergent church movement may or may not be new in its various approaches, it is an attempt to live a faithful witness in a world that has many legitimate complaints with the church. It is an appeal to say to the culture, "Wait! Don't go! The gospel is not what you think it is!"

Since the origin of Christendom the military approach to opponents has had a certain appeal that some might attribute to God's commands to Moses and Joshua to conquer the land and claim it for God. Today the militant voice of Christians is raised against the sins of culture in a variety of forms. Peter Kreeft's *How to Win the Culture War: A Christian Battle Plan for a Society in Crisis* states, "This book will offend many people, for the same reason it will delight many others: because it is not only *about* a war—'a culture war,' a spiritual war, a jihad—but it is itself an *act* of war. . . . If nobody wants to crucify you, you're not doing your job. Or else your job isn't *his* work."⁴⁴ Kreeft goes on to say that the clock can and must be reversed since, "we invented it, we can break it, and we can fix it."⁴⁵ He calls for a return to the times of spiritual persecution that purified the church, "If God still loves his Church in America, he will soon make it small and poor and persecuted, just as he did to ancient Israel. If he loves us, he will cut the deadwood away, and we will bleed . . . for Christ's work is bloody. Christ's work is a blood transfusion. That is how salvation happens."⁴⁶

Christian youth movements are also engaged in the battle against culture. One example is Teen Mania Ministries (TMM), a mobilizing missionary sending agency whose mission is, "To provoke a young generation to passionately pursue Jesus Christ and to take His life-giving message to the ends of the earth!"⁴⁷ TMM has recently developed a project called BattleCry that fights against many social evils. Quoting from their website:

> A stealthy enemy has infiltrated our country and is preying upon the hearts and minds of thirty-three million American teens. Corporations, media conglomerates, and purveyors of popular culture have spent billions to seduce and enslave our youth. So far, the enemy is winning. But there is plenty we can do. We need to take action. We need to answer the Battle Cry.⁴⁸

Reporting upon the impact of a BattleCry visitation on his city, journalist Joe Garafoli of the *San Francisco Chronicle* reported:

> This battle is taken seriously. TMM has taken BattleCry to major cities where thousands of teens are encouraged to use their skills in "ruffling people's feathers" for God (Wu). At the San Francisco rally of 25,000 teens 44-year-old TMM founder Ron Luce challenged the sellout crowd of 25,000 mostly teenage youth, "Are you ready to go to battle for your generation?" he asked, and the young people roared "yes!" and some waved triangular red flags flown from long, medieval-looking poles. The battle lines are clearly drawn. "This is more than a culture clash," Luce said. "It's a culture war."⁴⁹

San Francisco's leadership was less than appreciative and issued citations against the group's visits in the future. Nevertheless, BattleCry returned the following summer. Some would find this approach on the extreme of alienation; however, it is popular among a certain conservative evangelical population. A CNN reporter describing the reactionary demonstrations and shouting matches labeled it, "the intersection of faith and the secular world." Afterwards one tearful young participant wanted to clarify a misconception, "Our war is not against people, it is against the evils of our culture."⁵⁰ Unfortunately this attempt to soften the blow becomes meaningless when culture is understood as what people themselves embody it to be. When, for example, homosexuality is the identifying characteristic of a highly profiled segment of society, to speak of loving the sinner and hating the sin is to speak a foreign language entirely.[51] BattleCry's attempt to speak out boldly for Christ through militant marching demonstrations is judged primarily by San Francisco culture as committing the unforgivable sin of intolerance and the raising up of a new generation of intolerant people. What may reinforce the zeal of the committed serves to widen the gap of cultural alienation.

One area in which Christians have attempted to avoid complete cultural alienation and allow the gospel to speak intelligently to the culture is through the arts. Here is the lonely desert of the present day prophet, often critiqued and "indigestible" by both church and culture. It is possible for Christian expressions of the arts to maintain the prophetic voice incarnationally with integrity and intelligence. William Romanowski urges the Christian artist to avoid a reactionary approach to culture, "Even if we are overrun with popular artworks that indulge evil, Christians should resist the temptation to try to balance them out with portraits of life on the bright side—a penchant that makes their own art bear little resemblance to reality."[52] The masks of false piety are quickly noticed by those who know them well. Just as the blind man didn't want to see the reality of the broken and dirty world around him, so Christians have sometimes been in denial of the reality of the pain and hurt inside and outside the church. At times the sanctuary-from-the-world mentality is actually less of a removal from other people as it is from honesty with self. Each of us continues to carry in our mortal selves both the image of God and the dishonesty that seeks to hide in shame from what we really are.

LIVING FAITHFULLY WITHIN THE TENSION

At the same time that we mark the rapid decline in the world around us, we are entrenched so deeply in our cultural matrix and comfort that we do not notice the changes that simultaneously occur in us. Western culture in particular values the idea of change and for many years has linked this with the concept of civilization to show progress and forward movement of our society. Ours is a pool of cultural products and ideas constantly being stirred and never allowed to settle. The challenge is to remain rooted and fluently speaking the language of the culture yet with eyes and values fixed upon the standards of Jesus.

How is it possible to live faithfully in the tension between cultural osmosis and cultural alienation? How can the Christian community continue to be salt and light in a culture that attempts to water it down and darken it? At this point I would like to turn to anthropology and look from a social science perspective at how cultures change and what sustains those changes on a secular level to see how this might also address ongoing spiritual and cultural transformation.[53]

How do cultures change? Harvie M. Conn describes cultures as incomplete structures that are in constant movement. Social reinforcement generally holds cultures together, but even among those labeled as high cultures there are still rough and restless edges on the cultural margins where social changes are most likely to occur.

Cultures are neither aggregates of accumulated traits nor seamless garments. There is a dynamic to human cultures that makes full integration incomplete; gaps and inconsistencies provide opportunities for change and modification, some rapid and some slow.[54]

In his study of the Ndembu people of Zambia, Victor Turner observed that groups experiencing healing rites became bonded into what he called *communitas*, a Latin term he borrowed to indicate those who have moved somewhere across the threshold or limen into a liminal phase that will move them toward a mutually achievable goal. *Communitas* is a bond of oneness beyond ordinary community, an actual communion together that does not destroy individuality but brings alive the full gifts of each participant. It is a leveling process wherein "he who is high must experience what it is like to be low,"[55] yet accomplished in a setting that is accepting, life-giving, and unifying.

> *Communitas* liberates individuals from conformity to general norms. It is the fount and origin of the gift of togetherness, and thus of the gifts of organization, and therefore of all structures of social behavior, and at the same time it is the critique of structure that is overly law-bound. . . . It is richly charged with feeling, mainly pleasurable. It has something magical about it. Those who experience *communitas* feel the presence of spiritual power.[56]

Communitas is a withdrawal from the larger society but continues to impact the larger society even after the conclusion of the liminal phase. The benefits of *communitas* include joy, healing, the gift of "seeing," mutual help, religious experience, the gift of knowledge, and long term ties with others. Changes are not only individual; they ultimately result in a "utopian blueprint for the reform of society."[57] According to Michael Frost, "Societies need the liminal experience of *communitas* because it pushes society forward, nurturing it with the freshness and vitality that come from the deeper communion that is experienced there. It is the liberation experienced in *communitas* that sows the seeds of cultural regeneration back in normal society."[58]

What is the significance of *communitas* for followers of Christ? How is this related to faithful living in the tension between cultural absorption and cultural alienation? *Communitas* occurs through mutual commitment to a task greater than the group itself. Let me illustrate Christian *communitas* with another story from Thailand, this from one of the poorest districts of one of the poorest provinces in the northeast of the country. It was here that God brought about a transforming movement toward Christ through a common mission to reach out to those touched by AIDS.

In one particular village, close to a temporary shelter for the HIV positive, was a small home gathering of Christ followers, none of whom had ever met anyone with AIDS before. A beautiful little girl under the age of two whose parents both had AIDS was completely rejected by her extended family. A woman in the Christian community decided to bring her home to adopt her. Through this demonstration of love the parents found the new life and hope that Christ offered them and were eager to learn more of the reality of this path. The adoptive mother, Mrs. Pon, invited the parents, while they were still living, to the local worship gathering in her village.

When Mrs. Pon brought the girl Jimlim home, the small collection of Christ followers of Lao Klang village entered a liminal phase. They were embarking on a mission that would change them socially, theologically, spiritually, and possibly even physically. Together they had to face some serious questions. Were they willing to pay the price of their decision to welcome those with AIDS into their fellowship? In a tradition that practiced the Lord's Supper using one ball of rice and one common cup, would they all soon become infected? What if someone were to bleed on the straw mat where they were sitting during the worship service and that night a church member were to sleep on top of it? Could they get AIDS through mosquito bites? More importantly, what would the larger community think? Should the children play together? Would they be allowed to attend the school? Could they allow those with AIDS to use the same village well? With no sewer system in Lao Klang, should the HIV positive be restricted from washing their clothes and their bodies within the perimeters of their neighborhood? Should they share or build separate outhouses for them? Eventually would they be allowed to hold a cremation for them in the local temple or not? Would they all eventually be driven out of the village completely?

Over a period of several months all of these questions and many others were addressed. The church realized that AIDS was not spread through saliva. A common cup was passed at communion. The HIV positive, well-experienced by now with social rejection, had already prepared separate cups in which to pour any drinks that were offered them. They asked that their food be placed in their own containers and thereby not infect the food of others. However, the Christ followers learned to dip fingers into the common rice basket and even to share the same common bowl of soup with separate spoons. Together they learned the limits of how far they could go. Those in the final stages of AIDS were too shamed by their sores and darkened skin to bathe in public with others and either bathed at night or at distant locations. AIDS orphans were enrolled in the same school. In reaction some parents pulled their children out, but others were more supportive. This small community of Christ followers became a model for what could be done to integrate the outcasts into the larger social community.

With time there was greater understanding that all of this was not done merely to be socially or morally just. If asked, none of the Christ followers would admit to being a hero, but all would admit they had been changed. When their new brothers and sisters died of AIDS all of the Christ followers came bringing wood to build the funeral pyres, even though blood relations would refuse to come to honor their own dead. As the flames rose they sang of the transformation that came to them in Christ Jesus, and it moved the whole society. They had gone through the task together to become truly *communitas*, and this included the missionaries. Together we were changed people who had changed society in one small corner of a poor province of Thailand.

CONNECTING CHRISTIAN *COMMUNITAS* WITH *MISSIO DEI*

Connecting with the *missio Dei*, partnering with a cause greater than oneself, and experiencing *communitas* would appear to be a natural fit for the church. Christian *communitas* and its byproduct of Christian community is at least an ideal, if not a reality in most churches. Would not the opportunity to partner in God's greater mission and to deepen relation with God, with each other, and the world be attractive? In his book *A World Waiting to Be Born* M. Scott Peck shares his experience when he developed the Foundation for Community Encouragement (FCE), an organization dedicated to promoting his version of genuine transformative community.

> When we began FCE, we assumed that the church would be a natural market for its services. Christians generally knew that the early church seemed to have had an extraordinary amount of community. . . . Many clergy and laypeople bemoaned the lack of community within their churches. . . . What organization could possibly be more interested in welcoming the presence of God into its midst?[59]

The results within the church were disappointing. Churches showed virtually no interest in building a deeper sense of commitment to each other or their surrounding culture. After analyzing possible reasons for this resistance, Peck concludes:

> Community requires a great deal of time and work. The workplace is the center of most people's lives. Next comes the family. Church, if it comes in at all, is usually a poor third or fourth. Most churchgoers simply do not have the time to "do" community at church. Nor do they want to do the painful work of emotionally stretching at church that community requires. The few who make attempts to actualize the church as a place

of the Kingdom of God on earth may find themselves silenced by the congregation with an enormously powerful, subtle effectiveness.[60]

Communitas, if it is experienced at all in churches, now occurs during short one to two week periods where we are taken out of our comfort zone and placed in a situation where we are supposed to do something. This is also known as the short term mission trip. The glowing reports that come back reflect the changes that have occurred in the lives of the sent. Youth complain that church is nothing like that and wonder why *communitas* cannot be a regular, rather than a once-in-a-lifetime, event.

According to Peck's research *communitas* does exist in Western culture, but not in the church. It is alive and well in the business world. "Here is where a single decision may cost [people] their employment, their livelihood. Here is where millions of dollars may be in play every day—sums of money a thousand times greater than their entire annual church budget. These decisions *count*."[61]

If the task is urgent enough, if it is truly life and death, then those involved will be willing to pay the price to experience and become *communitas*. Otherwise, we sit comfortably and allow the creeping influence of cultural osmosis to slowly do its work. Understanding the urgency of our participation with the *missio Dei* transforms our cultural blindness to compassionate incarnation and prophetic intelligibility.

ENDNOTES

1. Kukrit Pramoj, "The Hell Which Heaven Forgot," *Practical Anthropology* 13 (May–June, 1966): 129–139.
2. Gustavo Gutierrez, Nov 16, 2006. Open Forum at North Park Theological Seminary.
3. Lucien Legrand, *The Bible on Culture* (Maryknoll, N.Y.: Orbis, 2000), 16.
4. Companion originates from Latin roots *com*, "with," and *panis*, "bread," literally bread fellow or messmate.
5. David Bosch, *Transforming Mission* (Maryknoll, N.Y.: Orbis, 1991), 390.
6. Ibid., 391, 519.
7. Paul De Neui, "What Happened After Grandma Danced," in *All the World is Singing: Glorifying God through the Worship Music of the Nations* (Tyrone, Ga.: Authentic, 2006), 16–18.
8. Tongpan Phromedda, "Listening and Learning from Others: A New Model for Church Planting," in *Voices from Asia: Communicating Contextualization Through Story* (trans. Paul De Neui; unpublished manuscript), 23–25.
9. Ps 20:4.
10. Rom 1:20.
11. Acts 17:26–27.
12. Exod 3:1–10.
13. Num 22:21–31.
14. Luke 19:39–40.
15. Gen 12:1–5; Heb 11:8–10, 17–19.
16. Ruth 1:16–18.

17. Acts 9:10–19.
18. Job 33:14; Eccl 3:11; John 1:10.
19. Kevin Daugherty, "*Missio Dei:* The Trinity and Christian Missions," *Evangelical Review of Theology* 31 (2007): 151–168.
20. Martin Kähler wrote, "Mission is the mother of theology." *Schriften zur Christologie und Mission* (Munich: Chr. Kaiser, [1908], 1971), 189–190.
21. Heb 2:11.
22. Charles Kraft, *Worldview* (Pasadena, Calif.: Fuller Theological Seminary, unpublished manuscript, 2001).
23. Paul Hiebert, *Cultural Anthropology* (Grand Rapids: Baker, 1976), 25–33.
24. Mimi White, quoted in John Fiske, "British Cultural Studies and Television," in *What is Cultural Studies?* (ed. John Storey; London: Arnold, 1996), 115.
25. Kathryn Tanner, *Theories of Culture* (Minneapolis: Fortress, 1997), 35.
26. Rev 7:9–10, 15.
27. Phil 4:8.
28. John Calvin, *Institutes of the Christian Religion* (trans. John T. McNeill; Philadelphia: Westminster, 1960), 3.14.2.
29. Craig Detweiler and Barry Taylor, *A Matrix of Meanings: Finding God in Popular Culture* (Grand Rapids: Baker, 2003), 8.
30. Gen 1:31; Rom 8:22–23.
31. Jacob Loewen, "The Inspiration of Translation," in *Understanding and Translating the Bible* (ed. R. G. Bratcher et al.; New York: American Bible Society, 1974), 86–99.
32. Harvey Cox, "Culture," in *Evangelical Dictionary of World Missions* (ed. A. Scott Moreau; Grand Rapids: Baker, 2000), 255.
33. Gen 3:5.
34. Rom 5:8.
35. Bosch, 246.
36. Lucien Legrand, *The Bible on Culture* (Maryknoll, N.Y.: Orbis, 2002).
37. William D. Romanowski, *Eyes Wide Open: Looking for God in Popular Culture* (Grand Rapids: Brazos, 2001), 28.
38. "Compared with the rest of the population, conservative Protestants are *more* likely to divorce." Brad Wilcox, sociologist quoted in Ron Sider's *The Scandal of the Evangelical Conscience* (Grand Rapids: Baker, 2005), 19.
39. Mark Noll, *The Scandal of the Evangelical Mind* (Grand Rapids: Eerdmans, 1994).
40. See n. 38.
41. David Van Biema, "Her Agony," *Time* (September 3, 2007): 36–43.
42. See Donald Miller's ch. 11 on confession in *Blue Like Jazz* (Nashville: Thomas Nelson, 2003).
43. Craig Carter, *Rethinking Christ and Culture: A Post-Christendom Perspective* (Grand Rapids: Brazos, 2006), 202–203.
44. Peter Kreeft, *How to Win the Culture War* (Downers Grove, Ill.: InterVarsity, 2002), 11, 54.
45. Ibid., 10.
46. Ibid., 21.
47. "Our Mission," Teen Mania Ministries, http://www.teenmania.com/corporate/index.cfm. Accessed September 11, 2007.
48. Teen Mania Ministries at http://www.teenmania.com.
49. Joe Garafoli, "Evangelical Teens Rally in S.F.," *San Francisco Chronicle* (March 25, 2006), http://sfgate.com/cgi-bin/article.cgi?f=/c/a/2006/03/25/ MNG6OHU6RR1.DTL. Accessed August 17, 2007.

50. BattleCry on CNN, Part 2 of 2, Clip 6:06 (http://battlecry.com/pages/bconcnn.php). Accessed September 11, 2007.

51. See Kreeft's conversation with a gay Catholic in ch. 6, "The Fiercest Battle: Sex Wars," in *How to Win the Culture War*.

52. Romanowski, 134.

53. In this I am indebted to the work of Michael Frost found in his book *Exiles: Living Missionally in a Post-Christian Culture* (Peabody, Mass.: Henderson, 2006).

54. Harvie M. Conn, "Culture," in *Evangelical Dictionary of World Missions* (ed. A Scott Moreau; Grand Rapids: Baker, 2000), 253.

55. Victor Turner, *The Ritual Process: Structure and Anti-Structure* (Chicago: Aldine, 1969), 97.

56. Edith Turner, "Communitas," in *Encyclopedia of Religious Rites, Rituals, and Festivals* (ed. Salamone Frank; Oxford: Routledge, 2004), 98.

57. Turner, "Communitas," 98, 99.

58. Michael Frost, *Exiles: Living Missionally in a Post-Christian Culture* (Peabody, Mass.: Hendrickson), 110.

59. M. Scott Peck, *A World Waiting to Be Born: Civility Rediscovered* (New York: Bantam, 1993), 351.

60. Ibid., 352.

61. Ibid.

RESPONSE TO DE NEUI

LUIS R. RIVERA

This paper names a reality, identifies a problem, presents a diagnosis, and offers a remedy. The fundamental reality is the historical and theological fact that Christian churches always exist in and are part of larger cultural communities. There is no acultural church simply because believers are cultural beings and agents, shaped and informed by the cultural processes, activities, productions, and conflicts that take place in the communities and countries in which they live and to which they belong. The church is always part of a larger culture and is also a cultural reality. The church always finds itself culturally situated.

This is not only a sociological and anthropological reality but also a theological reality. Three theological arguments are evident in this regard: *missio Dei, imago Dei,* and the incarnation. The paper expresses the conviction that the God we trust and serve is a God present and active in all cultures. God is animating the emergence and transformation of cultural agents (both Christians and non-Christians) that create, develop, and transform their cultures. "Culture is the arena of the *missio Dei*," and the incarnation is the paradigm of God's presence and action in culture for the church to imitate. "God is not ashamed to enter incarnationally into culture fully and completely." Let me suggest that an earlier paper in this journal, Professor Johnston's paper on God's Spirit in the world for life and wisdom, and I would add justice, is a pnematological grounding for the *Missio Dei*.

The paper recognizes that human cultures are problematic and ambiguous. There is a positive and a negative side to all cultures. On the one hand, cultures are human productions that "include components that are true, noble, right, pure, lovely, admirable, excellent, and praiseworthy." This is the expression of the *imago Dei* "found in individuals, cultural groupings, and their collective products." On the other hand, human creatures are fallen and cultures manifest this dimension in their practice of self-deification which is expressed in "ungodly culture and dehumanizing injustices."

From the perspective of the paper God's presence and action in all societies and cultural groups around the world should alert Christians and make it possible for them to develop a committed, but also critical stance, toward cultures. Let me propose that we have implicitly recognized that we live in an empire, the United States of America. What happens to our understanding of our theme, Christianity's engagement with culture, when we begin to recognize that we are a church in and of a world empire? How do we assess these two dimensions of the American imperial culture?

The problem as defined by the paper is that the churches have adopted two inadequate stances and strategies that prevent them from being faithful partners in God's incarnational presence and prophetic mission in cultures. Either they engage in cultural absorption through osmosis which reduces their capacity to be prophetic or they engage in alienating protest which leads them to cultural alienation. Neither of these represents *missio Dei* at its best. The argument is: "The challenge is to remain rooted and fluently speaking the language of culture yet with eyes and values fixed upon the standards of Jesus."

Yet, how can churches avoid these extremes and follow God's way of incarnational compassionate presence and prophetically intelligible mission in culture? Prof. De Neui suggests that this is possible by living and practicing *communitas*, that is, a communal way of living in groups that take critical distance (not separation or segregation) from the dominant forms and traditional practices of human groupings in cultures to practice alternative lifestyles with deep bonds of relationships where people are gathered and united in common purposes, affirming their dignity and gifts, and meeting their profound needs through mutual help, friendship, long term ties, and religious experience. *Communitas* is one of the ways by and through which cultural transformation takes place. Secular and religious forms of *communitas* make possible new transforming options and creative ways in and for cultures.

Overall I like this proposal, but I wish to address three aspects of it: the understanding of culture, the view of the incarnation, and the criteria for *communitas* as a strategy for cultural change. In these comments I am complementing rather than replacing what the paper presents. I find the understanding of culture a bit irenic insofar as there is no clear discussion about the conflictive dynamics of cultural production in relation to agendas and structures of power in any society. I think Prof. De Neui gives a hint of this when he talks about "ungodly culture and dehumanizing injustices" in cultures.

But, cultures are also the product of people and groups in competition for power and conflictive relationships. People define and organize human life and communities in terms of ideologies, power relationships, and economic and political structures that define their behavior patterns, ideas, products, systems, relations, traditions, institutions, etc. Cultures are also transformed by power struggles. The paper relates the beautiful and moving story of a congregation in Thailand as an example of transforming *communitas*. I would say that the African

American and Anglo churches that engaged in militant pacifism in the civil rights movement in this country are also models of Christian *communitas* at the service of *missio Dei*. What other strategies and models are possible for the church to become compassionately incarnate and prophetically engaged in transforming themselves and the cultures?

I want to affirm the understanding of *missio Dei* as both embracing and critically engaged in and with cultures, but this requires a reexamination of God's incarnational and prophetic revelation in Jesus of Nazareth. For many Latino/as and Latin American theologians God's incarnation took place in a marginal, mestizo, Galilean, and most likely poor Jew who went about practicing and preaching an egalitarian and inclusive *communitas* with the last, the least, and the lost as an expression of a compassionate, graceful, forgiving, just, and liberating God in the midst of a violent empire and colonial order of his time. He lived, died and was raised not as the leader of a holy war from heaven, but as a faithful, defiant, and militant pacifist martyr or witness who resisted evil and mediated the present and coming kingdom of God in the company of the poor, the marginalized, the oppressed, the impure, and the sinner.

What are the Christologies and Pneumatologies that can lead churches to live faithfully in embracing in respectful and transforming ways the ambiguous human cultures for the glory of God and the well-being and common good of humanity? The treatments in Prof. Metzger's paper of the God-on-the-gallows and in Prof. Johnston's understanding of the Holy Spirit's presence among all people give us some good clues.

Finally, what are some of the practices and criteria that can help churches become *communitas* for *missio Dei*? The ministry of the church in Thailand suggests a version of what liberationist Christians have called the preferential option for the poor. Prof. Metzger's reference to Rev. John Perkins and the work of Christian Community Development Association with its principles of relocation, reconciliation, and redistribution is another example of Christian *communitas*. Churches need to be connected, attentive, responsive, and serving the material, political, cultural, and spiritual needs, aspirations, and struggles of the last, least, and lost among all people and Christians. This is not the only requirement but a central one for understanding and practicing Christian *diakonia* and *agapē* as a task and mark of the church. What other practices and criteria can we identify in order to become a Christian *communitas* with incarnational prophetic presence and prophetic incarnational living among the rich, ambiguous, conflictive, and changing cultures of the world in which God is present and active?

THE BIBLICAL THEOLOGICAL CONTRIBUTION OF PANDITA RAMABAI: A NEGLECTED PIONEER INDIAN CHRISTIAN FEMINIST THEOLOGIAN

RAJKUMAR BOAZ JOHNSON

In 1986 my wife Sarita and I experienced a life-changing experience when we took a train ride to Ramabai Mukti Mission. The mission is about thirty-six miles from Pune. We were teaching at Union Biblical Seminary, Pune, India, one of the largest seminaries in India. We thought this would be a good way to get away from the hustle and bustle of academic life. Little did we know that this would be a life-altering experience.

The train ride itself was not very eventful. The train had the usually packed carriages. The people traveling with us were like millions of people who take the train ride in India every day. We got off at the Kedgaon station and took a long bullock cart ride to Ramabai Mukti Mission.

The very sight of Ramabai Mukti Mission was like entering a sacred domain. We were escorted by the head sister of the mission from one dormitory to the next. With tears in our eyes we saw hundreds of women: older women seventy, sixty, or fifty years old; younger women in their thirties or twenties; teenagers; little girls; and baby girls. Under ordinary circumstances this would not have been such a moving experience, but these were no ordinary women. These were women who had been rescued. They had been rescued from child prostitution, from temple prostitution, from forced child marriage to a man who may have been twenty to thirty years older than the little one. They had been rescued from the pains of *sati*, widow burning. They had been rescued from female infanticide . . . the stories went on and on. It was as if all the woman-refuse of India were gathered in one place. Yet, the foundation stone of Ramabai Mukti Mission which was laid in 1889 told a different story. It read, "The foundation of this building was laid in Christ . . . that our daughters may be as corner-stones, polished after the similitude of a palace. (Psalm 144:12)." These were royalty. It all began with the vision of one woman, Pandita Ramabai.

Ramabai's impact on India was so great that in 1989, a hundred years after the founding of Ramabai Mukti Mission, the government of India, even though led by the Hindu party, could not help but acknowledge her legacy. The government issued a commemorative stamp to honor the life and legacy of Pandita Ramabai. The official brochure with the stamp reads as follows:

> Pandita Ramabai (1858–1920): Pandita Ramabai, the youngest daughter of Anant Shastri, was a social reformer, a champion for the emancipation of women, and a pioneer in education. Left totally alone by the time she was 23, Ramabai acquired a great reputation as a Sanskrit scholar. Deeply impressed by her prowess, the Sanskrit scholars of Calcutta University conferred on her the titles of "Saraswati" and "Pandita." She rebelled against the caste system and married a shudra advocate, but was widowed at 23, having a baby girl. In 1882, she established the Arya Mahila Samaj for the cause of women's education in Pune and different parts of Western India. This led to the formation of the Sharda Sadan in 1889—which school completes a hundred years this year—a school which blossomed into an umbrella organization called Pandita Ramabai Mukti Mission, 40 miles outside Pune. In 1896, during a severe famine Ramabai toured to villages of Maharashtra with a caravan of bullock carts and rescued thousands of out-caste children, child widows, orphans and other destitute women and brought them to the shelter of Mukti and Sharada Sadan. A learned woman knowing seven languages, she translated the Bible into her mother tongue—Marathi—from the original Hebrew and Greek. Her work continues today, a memorial to her life and path.

The above quote from an official Government of India publication makes it clear that Pandita Ramabai made a very holistic impact on Indian society.

THE CONTEXT OF THE DEVELOPMENT OF RAMABAI'S THEOLOGY

Two issues that Ramabai confronted at a very early age in her life were gender bias against women in Hindu society and racial bias against the *Shudras*, the untouchable caste. These two issues form the background of the development of her biblical theology and her work. Ramabai was born in 1858, the daughter of a Maratha Chitpavan Brahman, a member of the purest of the highest caste. At that time in the history of India people of this caste never associated with people of any other caste. They considered themselves to be the purest of the pure priestly caste. Any association with people from other castes would make them unclean. There was an additional problem though. Ramabai was a girl. Women, even those who came from the highest caste, were regarded as being much lower than men, even men of the lowest castes. Much later in her life, after detailed study of Hindu texts, Ramabai would write,

> There were two things on which all those books, the Dharma Shastras, the sacred epics, the Puranas . . . were agreed: women of high and low caste, as a class, were bad, very bad, worse than demons, and that they could not get Moksha (salvation) as men. The only hope of their getting this much-desired liberation from Karma and its results, that is, countless millions of births and deaths and untold suffering, was the worship of their husbands. The husband is said to be the woman's god; there is no other god for her. This god may be the worst sinner and a great criminal; still HE IS HER GOD, and she must worship him. She can have no hope of getting admission into Svarga, (heaven), the abode of the gods, without his pleasure; and if she pleases him in all things, she will have the privilege of going to Svarga as his slave, there to serve him and be one of his wives among the thousands of the Svarga harlots who are presented to him by the gods in exchange for his wife's merit. . . . The woman is allowed to go into higher existence thus far but to attain Moksha or liberation, she must perform such great religious acts as will obtain for her the merit by which she will be reincarnated as a high caste man, in order to study Vedas and the Vedanta, and thereby get the knowledge of the true Brahma and be amalgamated in it.[1]

Commenting on the important issue of race and caste, she continued,

> The same rules are applicable to the Shudras, the untouchables. The Shudras must not study the Veda and must not perform the same religious act which a Brahman has a right to perform. The Shudra who hears the Veda repeated must be punished by having his ears filled with liquefied lead. . . . His only hope of getting liberation is in serving the three high castes as their lifelong slave.[2]

Most Indian women at her time just succumbed to what society required them to be. Ramabai, however, contrary to the norm, set about the task of studying the Hindu texts. Her father, a rebel of sorts, had initiated her into the study of Sanskrit, the language of Hindu priests. She became a diligent student of the language and later studied the Hindu texts in great detail. In the Hindu texts she found that there really was no hope for women. This led her to the study of ideologies beyond Hinduism. In the course of her search she was exposed to the gospel of Jesus Christ. She wrote that quite accidentally, "I had found a little pamphlet in my library. I do not know how it came there, but I picked it up and began to read it with great interest. It was St. Luke's Gospel in the Bengali language."[3] The story of Jesus' dealings with women in particular grabbed her attention. Throughout the text, whenever women encountered Jesus, he elevated their status. He offered them spiritual salvation. He offered them emotional and social salvation. Of course, this was a great contrast to the place of women in Hindu texts. She started reading the rest of the Bible. In Genesis she came to realize that men and women were created equal in the image of God. The reading of the Bible gave her a completely new understanding of the place of women in society.

Ramabai's solution to the problem of racial and caste discrimination was very bold, yet simple. She just decided to marry a gentleman from the lowest caste, the Shudra caste. This was an unthinkable act with immense ramifications. Ramabai was a woman, but at least she was a woman who belonged to the highest caste. When she married a man from the lowest caste, her stature in society plunged to the lowest level. She was now a "lowest caste woman" in the eyes of Hindu society. She was well aware of the fact that in Hindu society, "They are looked upon as being very like the lower species of animals, such as pigs; their very shadow and the sound of their voices are defiling."[4]

Unfortunately, her husband died of cholera, two years into their marriage. Hindu society would have interpreted this as a curse on her, but Ramabai kept on confronting the ills of society. She moved from Calcutta in Eastern India to Poona in Western India, closer to Bombay. The life of a widow in the India of her time was very hard. Most widows had to disassociate themselves from society, lest their curse would descend on people with whom they associated. Most widows just lived lonesome lives on the banks of rivers like the holy Ganges, hoping for some sort of reprieve in their next lives. Ramabai, again contrary to the norm, decided to engage deeply in the study of the Bible and society. She sought to understand the solutions that Jesus offered to Indian society of her time.

RAMABAI'S CONFRONTATION WITH PROSTITUTION, SLAVERY, AND FEMALE INFANTICIDE

The next stage in the development of Ramabai's thought took place during a visit to England in 1883. During this time she was exposed to the crucial work of the Sisters of Wantage. These Sisters were deeply involved in the emancipation of prostitutes from slavery to cruel urban gangs. Many of these prostitutes belonged to lower-class families. They were forced to sell themselves into sexual slavery due to class distinction. Ramabai found that the work of the Sisters of Wantage was bathed in the teaching of Jesus regarding women. The work of the Sisters had a deep impact on Ramabai. All the while she was thinking of the complexity of issues which women faced in India. This work among the orphans, widows, and prostitutes became the model of Ramabai's work and words in India. Of this crucial life-changing experience she wrote,

> The Sisters there took me to see the rescue work carried on by them. I met several of the women who had once been in their Rescue Home, but who had so completely changed, and were so filled with the love of Christ and compassion for suffering humanity. . . . Here for the first time in my life I came to know that something should be done to reclaim

the so-called fallen women, and that Christians, whom Hindus considered outcastes and cruel, were kind to these unfortunate women, degraded in the eyes of society . . . I had never heard or seen anything of the kind done for this class of women by the Hindus in my own country. I had not heard anyone speaking kindly of them, nor seen any one making any effort to turn them from the evil path they had chosen in their folly. The Hindu Shastras do not deal kindly with these women. The law of the Hindu commands that the king shall cause the fallen women to be eaten by dogs in the outskirts of the town. They are considered the greatest sinners, and not worthy of compassion. After my visit to the Homes at Fulham, where I saw the work of mercy carried on by the Sisters of the Cross, I began to think that there was a real difference between Hinduism and Christianity. I asked the Sisters who instructed me to tell me what it was that made the Christians care for and reclaim the "fallen" women. She read the story of Christ meeting the Samaritan woman, and His wonderful discourse on the nature of true worship, and explained it to me. She spoke of the Infinite Love of Christ for sinners. He did not despise them but came to save them. I had never read or heard anything like this in the religious books of the Hindus; I realized, after reading the 4th Chapter of St. John's Gospel, that Christ was truly the Divine Saviour He claimed to be, and no one but He could transform and uplift the downtrodden womanhood of India and of every land. Thus my heart was drawn to the religion of Christ. I was intellectually convinced of its truth on reading a book written by Father Nehemiah Goreh and was baptized in the Church of England in the latter part of 1883, while living with the Sisters at Wantage.[5]

Ramabai gained a new vision for her life after her encounter with Christ during these years. In several books and booklets she has written extensively of her mystical communion with Christ, for example:

I have come to know the Lord Jesus Christ as my personal Saviour and have the joy of sweet communion with Him. My life is full of joy, "For the Lord JEHOVAH is my strength and my song; He also is become my salvation." Now I know what the Prophet means by saying, "Therefore with joy shall ye draw water out of the wells of salvation." I can scarcely contain the joy and keep it to myself. I feel like the Samaritan woman who "left her waterpot, and went her way into the city, and saith to the men, Come, see a man, which told me all things that ever I did: is not this the Christ?"[6]

THE MUKTI MISSION

On her return to India Ramabai began the process of developing her biblical theology and her work at Mukti. First, there was the horrible practice of female infanticide. Girls were a great liability among all the castes. Parents had to pay huge sums of money in dowry to get their daughters married. Parents went into immense debt as a result of this practice. Boys, on the contrary, were a great asset. They brought in huge sums of money into the family when they got married. As a result, female infanticide was very common. A second issue was the practice of *Temple Dasis* (or prostitute priestesses). This was an alternative for parents to female infanticide. Girls would be just devoted to certain temples as soon as they got their first period. These *dasis* would become the property of the temple priestly hierarchy. It was a form of spiritual-sexual slavery. An alternative form of this sexual slavery was called *nautch* girls. A third challenge Ramabai faced was forced marriages of little girls to men from the same caste, who could be thirty years older than them. They could be the third or fourth wife of the rich, high caste man. This was a more humane alternative to female infanticide or temple prostitution. They did not have to pay a high dowry. Yet, it was abhorrent nonetheless. The fourth challenge that Ramabai faced was the practice of Sati, the practice of a widow being forced to jump into the funeral pyre of her husband during the cremation of his body. Those that refused to jump into the funeral pyre were shamefully ostracized from society.

Ramabai's answer was the Mukti Ashram, the temple of salvation. This became the fertile ground of the development of Ramabai's Indian Christian theology. After the initial intense opposition, slowly but surely, instead of killing their female babies, parents began bringing their female babies and leaving them at the door of Mukti. Instead of giving into pressure and jumping into the funeral pyre of their husbands, young brides, some as young as thirteen years old, began running to Mukti for refuge. Ramabai and her group of sisters began going from one place to another, rescuing young women from temple prostitution and *nautch* slavery. When young women who brought "insufficient" dowry were threatened with death, they fled to Mukti. In the early twentieth century, as a result of Ramabai's work, there was a huge spiritual awakening in western India. Hindus, Muslims, and nominal Christians began experiencing the transforming power of God.

During these years of the Great Awakening in India, in addition to an incredibly busy life, Ramabai did a lot of writing. She translated the Bible from Hebrew, Aramaic, and Greek into Marathi, her native language. She wrote numerous theological and devotional works. She composed some of the most profound devotional songs. This material gives us insight into Ramabai's brilliant theological mind.

It is the thesis of this paper that Ramabai's work was influenced greatly by her biblical and theological formulations. Her understanding for the transformation of Indian society was influenced by her interpretation of the Bible and its application to the context of India. Her words and works are a stellar example of how the Bible and Christ confront and transform culture.

Unfortunately, a cursory reading of works on Asian and Indian Christian theologies finds no mention of Pandita Ramabai as a theologian. There is much which has been written on the works of Indian Christian theologians like Brahmobandhab Upadhyaya, A. J. Appaswamy, Vengal Chakkarai, P. Chenchiah, and P. D. Devanandam, to name a few. In more recent times much emphasis has been placed on the works of Dalit theologians like M. E. Prabhakar and A. P. Nirmal. One wonders whether there is a gender bias![7]

A SKELETAL OVERVIEW OF INDIAN CHRISTIAN THEOLOGIES

Indian Christian theologies have taken five forms:

1. Jnana theologies and theological hermeneutics: Brahmabandhab Upadhyaya attempted to express his Christian theology within the framework of Sankara's Advaita Vedanta. He used Jnana Marga, the Hinduism of the Way of Knowledge, to express his theological propositions.
2. Bhakti theologies and Bhakti theological hermeneutics: A. J. Appaswamy used *bhakti Marga*. He used Ramanuja's *Vishishta Advaita* to express his theological propositions.
3. Karma theologies and Karma theological hermeneutics: M. M. Thomas used the framework of *Karma Marga* to formulate his Christian theology.
4. Western theological models have been used by many others to express their theological thoughts. These theologies are of the kind influenced by Western missionaries or theologians like Hendrik Kraemer.
5. Dalit theologies: Dalit theologies began emerging in the 1980s and the 1990s. These were primarily influenced by the liberation theologies of Latin America.

These theologies may be divided into two categories: theologies which are formed on the basis of Hindu Upanishads, Vedas, and Puranas; and theologies which use as their framework Western philosophical models. For the purpose of this paper I would like to pay closer attention to Jnana theologies and Dalit theologies. I will show that Pandita Ramabai provides a better model in comparison to these two kinds of theologies.

THEOLOGIES BASED ON THE UPANISHADS

Indian Christian theologies were solely proposed by those Christians who came from high caste backgrounds. They tended to dwell almost entirely on Vedantic ontological understanding for their theological formulations. Good examples are Brahmobandhav Upadhayay (1861–1907) and his close friend Keshub Chandra Sen. Upadhyay was also a close friend of Swami Vivekananda who single-handedly made Hinduism a household term in Western society after his speech in 1893 at the World Parliament of Religions in Chicago.

Keshub Chandra Sen came up with a theology of God based on the Vedantic concept of *Sat Cit Ananda*. He explains the concept of *Brahman*, in the form of a triangle:

> The Apex of the triangle is the Supreme Brahman of the Vedas . . . in his own glory. From him comes down the Son in a direct line, an emanation from divinity, into Jesus. Thus God touches one end of the humanity, and then running all along the base permeates the world, and then by the power of the Holy Spirit drags up the degenerate humanity to himself.[8]

Similarly, Upadhyay also sought to come up with a Hindu-Christian theology of God. He wrote:

> His eternal self-knowledge or logos is to be conceived as identical with the divine nature and yet distinct from the Supreme Being in as far as by comprehending himself generates his logos. God, knowing himself by producing or generating his own image and word, is called Father; and God as known by himself by his inward generation of the word is called the Word or the Son.[9]

Upadhayaya also sought to explain Christology in Hindu categories. For example, he wrote:

> According to the Vedas, human nature is composed of five sheaths, *kosas*. . . . These five sheaths are presided over by personality (*ahmpratyayi*) which knows itself. This knowing individual is but a reflected spark of the supreme reason (*kutastha-chaitanya*) who abides in everyman as the prime source of life. Similarly, the time incarnate Divinity (the Logos, the Christ) is also composed of five sheaths. But, he is presided over by the person of the Logos, *Cit* himself and not by any created personality (*aham*). In the God-man, *Cit*, the five sheaths, or *kosas*, are presided directly by the Logos-God.[10]

We will note that Ramabai takes an entirely different approach to her development of Indian Christian theology. She believed that a genuine Indian Christian theology must be based on rigorous biblical theology and Pre-Vedic Indian philosophy. Vedantic philosophy, according to her, is inimical to the development of a good Indian Christian theology.

DALIT THEOLOGIES

The Dalits are the untouchables of India, *atishudras*. The Hindu brahmanical texts define these people as lower than human beings. Dalit intellectuals have realized that the consciousness of their people was shaped by Vedic and puranic myths. It served the interests of the dominant castes and classes. A consciousness based on ancient history had to be formed to strengthen their existential identity.

Two examples of Hindu texts show how their identity was shaped:

> When they divided the *Purusha*, into how many parts did they arrange him? What was his mouth? What were his arms? What are his thighs and feet called? The *Brahmin* was his mouth, his arms were made the *rajanya* (warriors), his two thighs *Vaishyas* (traders and agriculturists), and from his feet the *shudras* (servant class) were born. (The *Rig Veda* X. 90:12)

> But the Shudra, whether bought or unbought, he may compel to do the work of a slave; for he was created by the self-existent (*svyanbhu*) to be the slave of the Brahmin. (*Manu Dharma Shastra* VIII, 413–414)

According to Dalit theologians like James Massey, there are 200 million Dalits. If one includes the other backward classes or the *shudras*, then the number would rise to more than 700 million. This is seventy-five percent of the population, and seventy-five percent of the Christian church is Dalit. Only very recently have the Dalits begun to have their voice heard. In fits and starts Dalit theology began taking shape in the 1980s and the 1990s, but unfortunately it was heavily influenced by the liberation theologies of Latin America and took on a decidedly Marxist orientation. Dalit theologians expressed discontinuity with traditional Indian Christian theology, which has been articulated mainly by upper-caste theologians.

Arvind Nirmal, one of the pioneers of Dalit theologies, expresses it best. He suggests that the core of Dalit theology will be formed from the existential experience of the Dalits.

> It will be produced on their own dalit experiences, their own sufferings, their own aspirations, their own hopes. It will narrate the story of their pathos and their socio-economic injustices they have been subjected to throughout their history. . . . This also will mean that a Christian dalit theology will be a counter theology.[11]

Maria Arul Raja, another prominent Dalit theologian, claims that the Dalit theology must take as its basis "the wretched condition violently imposed on the

Dalits [which] forces them to seek an immediate apocalyptic intervention from the unseen God." This desire for an "apocalyptic intervention" must form the basis of Dalit theology. "The method of the Dalit reading of the Bible is oriented towards concrete historical commitment transforming the present reality into a new liberative one."[12] The method of interpretation is liberation and praxis oriented.

In this paper I argue that these theologies are not genuine Indian Christian theologies which are based on an Indian hermeneutic of the Bible. They either seek to express Christian theologies in the framework of Upanishadic thought or in the framework of some other philosophical thought, e.g., a Marxist framework. They do not seem to interact with the biblical text seriously to come up with an original biblical theology for India.

Pandita Ramabai sought to come up with a genuine Indian Christian theology which took the message of the Bible seriously for her context, a subaltern context. She came up with a genuine biblical and subaltern theology, a theology which came from the pen of a Hindu-Christian woman who had set aside her caste to marry an outcaste. She came up with a genuine Indian Christian, feminist theology, a genuine Dalit theology, and the core of her theology may be found in her translation of the Bible into Marathi.

RAMABAI'S DEVELOPMENT INTO A GENUINE INDIAN CHRISTIAN BIBLICAL THEOLOGIAN

In a valuable contribution, *The Bible and the Third World*, R. S. Sigarthirajah gave a little attention to Pandita Ramabai, woefully little in my estimation. The book covers wide ground. In the first two sections he treats the pre-colonial period in India, China, and Africa and the colonial period during the British and French colonization of Asian and African areas, where he also discusses biblical interpreters like Olaudah Equiano, William Apess, and K. N. Banerjea. He calls this the period of colonial embrace of the Bible, and here he devotes a few pages to Pandita Ramabai.[13] The third section of the book is devoted to postcolonial reclamations. He suggests Ramabai's contribution to biblical interpretation may be termed "textual management." It seems, though, that a closer look at the works of Ramabai leads one to the understanding that she engaged in extensive thought in breaking new ground towards a genuinely Indian Christian biblical theology. Sugirtharajah may have underestimated the work of Ramabai in terming it merely as "textual management."

Another person who paid close attention to Ramabai's work in recent times is Meera Kosambi, who heads the center for women's research at S. N. D. T. University, Bombay. In 1995 she published a volume entitled *Pandita Ramabai's Feminist and Christian Conversions: Focus on Stree Dharma Neeti*.[14] In 2000 she published a valuable volume entitled *Pandita Ramabai Through her Own Words:*

Selected Works.[15] In these writings Kosambi shows how Ramabai's thought was influenced by the dual concerns of the state of women and the state of untouchables in Hindu society. Unfortunately, Kosambi comes to the conclusion that Ramabai's feminist ideology was fully formed in *Stree Dharma Neeti*, which is not the case. Kosambi would have done well to pay attention to Ramabai as a biblical theologian who spoke to the needs of women's concerns and untouchable concerns from her theological formulations.

It seems clear to me that Ramabai's formation as a Christian and a biblical theologian were influenced by these dual concerns as Kosambi suggests, but I have come to the conclusion that her ideas were in a very initial stage of development in *Stree Dharma Neeti*. She became a mature feminist thinker when she translated the Bible and became an original, Indian Christian, feminist theologian. In the following brief sketch, I propose that Ramabai's development into a biblical feminist theologian was a gradual process.

The first verifiable stage of Ramabai's development as a theologian may be seen in her writings from 1878. As a young woman of twenty she was proclaimed to be the first Hindu woman *Pandita* in Calcutta. Calcutta was the hub of a renaissance movement called the Brahmo Samaj. When the professors at Calcutta University conversed with Ramabai and realized her immense knowledge of Sanskrit, she was inducted into the hall of priests. She was proclaimed to be a *Pandita* (expert in Hindu texts) and *Saraswati* (goddess of learning).

This was an unthinkable move in Indian society. It may be crucial to note that the Brahma Samaj movement, which was responsible for this induction into the elite club, was a movement which sought to free Hindus from Hinduism. This movement was profoundly influenced by the Christian missionary educationists of Serampore.

During this induction into the hall of Pundithood, Ramabai wrote,

> Oh you learned men of honour, you have showered upon me flowers of praise, but I am not worthy of this honour; neither am I a Pandita. Qualities as large as the mountains have been attributed to me although I am but an atom amongst you great men. Truly, I am neither a *Saraswati* nor a *Sharada* but I consider myself to be a devotee in the temple of your august assembly.[16]

The second stage in her development as a philosopher/theologian may be seen in her first book *Stree Dharma Neeti*, which she wrote in 1882.[17] This was a part of a quest for answers to the problem of women and outcastes in India, but it seems clear that it was an unfulfilled quest. *Stree Dharma Neeti* seeks to establish the "code of conduct" for Hindu women. However, it seems like she could not find the basis of freeing women from suppression and denigration in Hinduism. She came to the conclusion that "education," "westernization" within Indian boundaries, should form the basis of the modern code of conduct for women.

In the book she developed ten principles which would empower women in India. These ten principles are steadfastness, endurance, self-control, not committing thefts, cleanliness, prudence, learning, truthfulness, and not getting angry. The "foundation" of this *Stree Dharma Neeti* is "self-reliance." She wrote, "The foundation is self-reliance, that is relying on oneself. Now we [Indian women] must not look to others for our advancement. Every woman must exert herself courageously for her own advancement, as self-reliantly as possible."[18]

The third stage may be seen in her second book, *The High Caste Hindu Woman*, which she published in 1887 and which reveals that she realized that the principles she has developed in 1882 in *Stree Dharma Neeti* were a lost cause.[19] These principles were really developed in Hindu texts for men, not for women. *The High Caste Hindu Woman* suggests a note of deep despair in her voice. It begins the next major stage in the development in her thought. She is more incisive about Hindu texts. She realized that as long as Indian women are subjected to the codes of conduct expected of them in the Hindu texts, they will never be free. This began a quest for a text which would become the grounds of female liberation in India. Secularization of the codes of Manu would not cut it. In my opinion this is what fuelled her biblical theology. It became the heart of her quest for a biblical theology for the Indian woman.

She wrote in *The High Caste Woman*, "A Brahman of a High clan will marry ten, eleven, twenty. . . . The illustrious Brahman need not bother with the care and support of many wives, for the parents pledge themselves to maintain the daughter all her life."[20] She observed regarding female infanticide,

> Opium is generally used to keep the crying child quiet, and a small pill of this drug is sufficient to accomplish the cruel task; a skillful pressure upon the neck, which is known as "putting nail to the throat" answers the purpose. There are several other nameless methods that may be employed in sacrificing the innocents upon the unholy altar of the caste and clan system.[21]

Therefore, she deemed it

> of first importance to prepare the way for the spread of the gospel by throwing open the locked doors of Indian zenanas, which cannot be done safely without giving suitable education to the women, whereby they will be able to bear the dazzling light of the outer world and the perilous blasts of social persecution . . . millions of heart-rending cries are daily rising from within the stony walls of Indian zenana; thousands of child widows are dying annually without a ray of hope to cheer their hearts. . . . will you not, all who read this book, think of these, my countrywomen, and rise by a common impulse to free them from life-long slavery?[22]

The translation of the Bible forms the fourth stage of her development as an Indian Christian, feminist theologian. This is clear in many writings. In the little book called *My Testimony*, which she wrote many years later, she wrote, "I realized, after reading the 4th Chapter of St. John's Gospel, that Christ was truly the Divine Saviour He claimed to be, and no one but He could transform and uplift the downtrodden womanhood of India."[23] It is clear to me that, if Ramabai had had time after the translation work was completed, she would have explored these themes more in her writings. However, she died an untimely death, and one is left with the task of discovering her Indian Christian, feminist theology from her translation of the Bible.

In the philosophy of translation which she developed I will show that Ramabai sought to keep the Marathi translation of the Bible free from any influence of Hindu philosophical thought. She was especially conscious of terms which denigrate women and untouchables. In her mind, if Hindu words, themes, and philosophical thought find their way into the Bible, they will perpetuate female slavery of the sort that Hindu texts prescribe. In the quest for the language to express her biblical theology, she found refuge in pre-Vedic language. This pre-Vedic language found in vernacular languages was relatively untouched by Hindu texts. This pre-Vedic language offered Ramabai an expression of the thoughts of the subaltern women and untouchables.

THE BASIS OF RAMABAI'S INDIAN CHRISTIAN HERMENEUTICS: A HERMEUTICS OF THE INDIAN WOMAN AND SHUDRA

Ramabai's hermeneutics was far removed from Western methodologies. One text from the Hebrew Bible became the primary motto of Ramabai's life: "The spirit of the Lord GOD is upon me; because the LORD hath anointed me to bring good tidings unto the humble; He hath sent me to bind up the broken-hearted, to proclaim liberty to the captives, and the opening of the eyes to them that are bound" (Isa 61:1). According to Ramabai the gospel for India found its central focus in this text. According to Luke this, of course, was the central theme of the message of Jesus (Luke 4:18).

Ramabai's works at Mukti and as a theologian were all tied to this central theme. She translated the word *'ănāwîm* with the Marathi *din*, a term which refers to the *Dalits*. She viewed the Hindu women as the *bharg hirdyacha lokas,* the severely wounded ones who need deep holistic medical treatment. These are the ones who are captives to the laws of Manu and societal captivity. Therefore they needed liberty and healing. Ramabai's biblical interpretation and theological formulation were motivated by the deep desire for personal and social transformation, the transformation of the subaltern—the women, and the outcastes.

Ramabai also realized that the liberty of the Hindu woman could not be found through modernistic, biblical methodology which was brought into India by Western missionaries and teachers. She expressed the opinion that modernistic methodologies of reading the Bible and forming theology merely distract from true Indian, freeing encounters with the text. She wrote, "We must draw a clear line and know how far we should go with them,"[24] i.e., with modernistic methodologies and the resultant theologies. Modernistic methodologies produce theologies which are far removed from genuine biblical theology. She reasoned that they engender Western formulations of thought rather than genuine Indian Christian theologies.

It may be observed that the interpretive methodology adopted by Ramabai ironically might be very similar to that adopted by the rabbis of late antiquity, which Michael Fishbane calls inner-biblical intertextuality.

She suggested that the historico-critical methods are modernistic in their approach to the biblical text. These diachronic approaches do not enable the Hindu woman or the Dalit reader to encounter the text of the Bible. They distract from "the simple Gospel to our people."[25] It also seems clear that Ramabai regarded modernistic text-centered approaches as invalid for the development of true Indian Christian theology. Would she have had a similar reaction to today's synchronic approaches? Perhaps! A close reading of Ramabai's methodology would suggest that she might think that these approaches do not enable the Indian woman or Dalit to view his/her existential situation in the light of the historical reality behind the text. She would regard reader-oriented approaches similarly as being very modernistic in their methodology. Reader-oriented methodologies make the historical *Sitz-im-Leben* behind the text irrelevant. They also undermine the narrative integrity of the text. In doing so they undermine the narrative integrity of the Hindu woman and the shudra.

Ramabai's biblical interpretation seeks to understand inner-biblical intertextuality and then transfer that intertextuality to the realm of the "new text," i.e., the woman and the shudra in their present situation and in their history. Inner-biblical intertextuality, as it is seen in the works and translation of Ramabai, seeks to express and incorporate the intertextuality which is contained in the Bible in its own context. This is very different from modernistic post-critical, deconstructionist readings of the Bible. In the latter the *receptor* text obliterates the context and the meaning of the *conceptor* text through the process of deconstruction. The codes and conventions of the *receptor* text destroy the codes and conventions of the *conceptor* text. Consequently the new receptor community must destroy the codes and conventions of the conceptor communities of the biblical text. Ramabai, quite in contrast to this interpretive methodology, sought to affirm the codes and conventions of the conceptor communities of the Bible. It seems very clear that in developing her methodology of biblical translation she clearly saw that the codes and conventions of the conceptor biblical communities were directly proportional to the codes and conventions of women and shudras in India. This forms the grounds for the liberation of the Indian woman and the Shudra.

Ramabai's title for her biblical translation project is a poignant example of this. She entitled her Bible translation *Wonderful Testimonies* (*pĕlā'ôt 'ēdôt*). This became the nuclear theme of her development of a biblical theology. She took Ps 119 to be the formative mega theme for the formulation of a biblical theology for the Indian context. She viewed each event in the Bible as an inner-biblical development, a reinterpretation and reapplication. The exodus event, a wonderful testimony, is reinterpreted in the inner-biblical text of the Hebrew Bible. The Hebrew Bible contains a series of wonderful testimonies (*pĕlā'ôt 'ēdôt*) which take on various shades of meaning. At each step the earlier wonderful testimonies are foreshadows of later ones. The Gospels then take the shape of the Jesus event, another wonderful testimony. Ramabai suggested that this is how her Bible translation must be read. The biblical wonderful testimonies must be seen in continuity with the existential situation of the Indian woman and shudra. When one uses the text of the Bible in this sort of a hermeneutic, then the "liberty" of the Indian woman and outcaste will be seen as a continuation of the wonderful testimonies, the salvation testimonials of the biblical texts. This is indeed why she called her life story *My Testimony, Adi*.

In the thought of Ramabai this method of interpretation results in the formation of a "new text," i.e., a "new identity." This is the Mukti text, the Mukti identity, the Mukti community. The oppressed women and shudras of India are in continuity with the biblical tradition and interpret their current context through the formation of the new text, the Mukti text. It is crucial to underscore that this is not merely a modernistic "reader-oriented" method. Ramabai viewed the original text, the wonderful testimonies, very seriously as formulating the "new text."

This philosophy of hermeneutics may also be seen in the title she gave to her original translation of the Bible into Marathi. She decided to go with the Jewish canonical order *Torah, Nevi'im,* and *Ketuvim*. This is a canonical understanding of hermeneutics, which reminds one of scholars like Brevard Childs. The canonical order of the Bible as present in the Masoretic Text became the basis of her development of the wonderful testimonies. Pandita Ramabai came to the opinion that this canonical order bodes well for the development of an Indian Christian, feminist theology. The worship songs she wrote give a clear example of this progression of these wonderful testimonies. They generally contain the canonical order, moving from the exodus event, to the Prophets, the Psalms, and the Christ event. The refrain was the Mukti event. The Mukti Ashram was a continuation of God's wonderful testimonies. This must be seen as a crucial aspect of Pandita Ramabai's feminist and existential biblical theology.

RAMABAI'S PHILOSOPHY OF TRANSLATION: A WINDOW TO HER THOUGHT

In a letter written at Christmas, 1908, Ramabai revealed her philosophy of Bible translation. She wrote:

> At the beginning of the year 1905, a Band [*sangathan*] was formed of some of the Mukti people . . . there were about seventy of us. . . . Early in that year, I heard the call of the Holy Spirit to give my time and strength to the preparing of a work which would enable the Christian *stree sangathan,* women teachers being trained, to understand the Holy Scriptures in their original languages . . . . it seems right that the work be prepared in the English language also, that the labour of years may not be lost, but that the English speaking Christian people of other parts of India, may be helped to prepare similar works in their own vernaculars to aid the Bible-readers of their own provinces."[26]

It is interesting to note that Ramabai saw her work of the translation of the Bible into Marathi and other vernaculars on par with the translators of the Septuagint. It was "seventy young women" whom she trained, who translated the Bible into the vernaculars, which is quite a contrast to the practice in Hinduism where women were not supposed to touch a holy text. She intentionally put these young girls on an equal footing with rabbis who translated the Hebrew Bible into Greek.

Ramabai set aside substantial amounts of time for this task. Quite in keeping with Indian fashion she found it necessary to apologize for the amount of time she took to translate the Bible. She wrote, "I had to give up all personal correspondence, all public speaking, and traveling for the last four years in order to devote all my strength and time to this work. My good friends, you must have thought me very neglectful and unfaithful or devoid of deep gratitude as I am not writing long letters to you."[27]

In a circular letter which was written in January, 1909, Ramabai laid out the main "principles" of her translation:

> 1. Vocabularies of both Hebrew and Greek, with grammatical analysis of words occurring in each verse of the Bible.
> 2. Interlinear and comparative word for word translations in the words of some of the great English and American versions.
> 3. Interlinear and simple literal translations in some of the vernaculars of India.
> 4. A brief Bible Commentary in the words of the Holy Scripture.[28]

These four principles of translation show a deep appreciation of how translation work and indigenous biblical hermeneutics are closely tied together. I would explain her "principles" this way:

1. The work of translation must be based on careful grammatical and syntactical analysis of the Hebrew and Greek text of the Bible.
2. The work of translation must make careful comparison with contemporary scholarship present in good Western translations of the Bible.
3. The work of translation must not be based on Sanskrit, the language of Hinduism, but rather on pre-Vedic language found in the vernaculars of India.
4. The common people of India, the people on the margins, must be provided with straightforward commentaries which speak to their existential situation.

Pandita stuck to these four principles throughout her tedious work of translating the Bible. Her translation work is perhaps the earliest and best example of pure and simple Indian Christian, feminist, biblical theology.

Principles One and Two. Ramabai's adherence to the first two principles may be seen in the following three aspects of her translation method. First, she made sure that she trained young women in the language and grammar of the original languages of the Bible. These women were infants, child widows, and temple prostitutes she had rescued. They were generally not from the high castes of Hindu society. These were indeed the *'ănāwîm*. This was a bold move to make in the light of the people with whom she was dealing. Her supporters were predominantly Western missionaries who were more interested in her work at Mukti, the saving of girls from temple prostitution and other desperate situations. She, on the other hand, realized that if her work were to continue, it had to be based on the message of the Prophets and the Torah. This was the text which would form the groundwork for the liberty of the Hindu woman and the shudra. This was the text which would form the groundwork of the new *Stree Dharma Neeti,* the code of the liberated woman.

Second, Ramabai was a great scholar of Sanskrit and had taught Sanskrit at various universities. She took tremendous care in faithful analysis and presentation of Hebrew, Aramaic, and Greek grammar and thought. She had a deep knowledge and appreciation for seven Indian languages, which made the job of translation into these languages quite an interesting project. She took pains to teach the liberated women of Mukti these languages so that this would become the basis of them remaining free.

Third, clearly Ramabai sought to pay careful attention to what the interpreters and translators of her time were saying about the text. She read Western theologians quite widely and gave careful consideration to the most important translations of her time, the Authorised Version, the English Revised Version, and the American Revised Version. At the same time, as will become clear in the following analysis, she moved away from the translations when the canonical context required it, when she had a clear understanding that the perspective of the author may have been different, or when she realized that a particular translation would not make sense to her Indian readership.

Principle Three. With reference to the third principle, namely use of the vernacular Indian languages, Ramabai sought to take into careful account the philosophical baggage behind the use of specific words. On the whole she avoided Sanskrit words which gave the Hindu readers a meaning which may be diametrically opposed to biblical theology or was inimical to the liberty of women and Dalits. Several examples demonstrate this.

First, *putra* is a word which is used to describe the "sonship" of Jesus Christ in several Indian translations. Ramabai suggested that the Hindu reader would equate the gospel with *Karma Marga*. She quotes from *Manushastra* IX:137, 138, "through a son (*putra*) one conquers the worlds, through a son's son, he obtains immortality . . . because a son (*putra*) delivers (*trayte*) his father from hell (*put*), he therefore is the *putra*, a deliverer from the *put*." This terminology was akin to using philosophical language which would propagate the same denigration of women as is found in Hinduism. Therefore, she carefully avoided these kinds of terms. She had learned her lessons in the writing of *Stree Dharma Neeti* and *The High Caste Hindu Woman*.

Unlike theologians such as Keshub Chandra Sen and Brahmabandab Upadhyaya, who used Upanishadic terminology to express their theologies, Ramabai used terms which came from the pre-Aryan period, which found their way into the vernacular languages. In this case she sought to use the word *mulga* instead of *putra*. The word *mulga* means "son" without the Upanishadic and Vedic sexist connotations. Therefore, one is able to give it a meaning in keeping with biblical theology.

Second, Ramabai took issue with the Marathi translation of Gen 1:1, *prarambh devane akash vprithvi hee uthpan keli*. She suggested that the phrase *devane . . . uthpan keli* gives the Marathi reader the sense that the universe was produced from the same substance as the *Nirguna Brahman*, which united with *Maya* to produce the egg. In the thought of the Vedas the universe and the divine *Brahman* are one substance, yet are nothing, *shunyata*. She suggested that this does not give a correct view of biblical theology of God or creation. In biblical theology God is removed from creation. He is transcendent. The old Marathi translation gave a sense of the immanence of the divine in creation. Ramabai suggested that the Hindu Brahmins, who assisted in the translations of the Bible, used Hindu terms which propagated the denigration of women and the Shudras. Ramabai suggested in strong language that a good translation must provide a ground for biblical theology which is truly biblical and far removed from Hindu philosophical baggage. It should not give the impression that God and creation are seamlessly of the same substance.

With regard to the concept of creation in Gen 1:1, instead of the old Marathi translation for "to create," Ramabai sought to make use of pre-Vedic words like *assanyanth anli*, which express the idea of a creation which is removed from the Other, God. The old Marathi translation, which was derived from Sanskrit, gives the idea that the universe and the Creator emerge from the same substance. Hindu terminology made creation and the Creator indistinguishable. She thought that creation and God must be separated from each other to express good biblical theology. In this text as well Ramabai sought to use pre-Vedic thought which resembled the biblical understanding of reality and the ultimate Reality.

Third, in her translation of the names of God she chose either to stick with a transliteration of the Hebrew and Greek or she chose pre-Vedic terms. In the case of the Tetragrammaton, YHWH, she chose to use the word *Yehovah* and then sought to define the word in biblical categories. The word Brahman, for example, would take on two meanings, *Saguna Brahman,* i.e., the Brahman full of attributes; or *Nirguna Brahman,* i.e., the Brahman without attributes. In either case, it is only the Brahmin man, the priestly man, who could aspire to merge with the *Brahman*. The Brahmin woman could never aspire to enter into a relationship with *Saguna Brahman*. Ramabai regarded this as an antiwoman and antishudra theology of God. Therefore, she avoided it completely and chose to stick with the transliteration of the name of God, YHWH. This word, she suggested, comes from the root of being. Therefore, it is conducive both for men and women. In doing so she is able to express ideas in profoundly biblical categories.

In the case of the word ʾĕlōhîm she chose to go with the Latin *Deus* or with the translation *Deva*. Older Marathi translations chose the word *Ishvara* or *Paramishvara*. Ramabai contended that these names of God also suggest a very Hindu, man-oriented definition of God.

These two words are good illustrations of how Ramabai sought scrupulously to avoid terms with Hindu presuppositions attached to them. She thought these presuppositions would continue to keep Indian women under the subjection of man.

Fourth, Ramabai's third principle may be seen with words for repentance and salvation. The Marathi translation reads *Pshchathap kara* in rendering "Repent, for the kingdom of heaven is at hand" (Matt 3:2). Ramabai felt these words give the reader the wrong understanding of "repentance" and suggest according to *Manu* XI, 230 that the act of feeling sorry for one's sins "afterwards" sanctifies the person.[29] Ramabai thought this does not give the reader a biblical understanding and instead of the word *pshchathap* chose the pre-Sanskrit term *palta kara*, which expressed better for her the biblical force of the Hebrew *šûb* and the Greek *metanoeō*. May this be regarded as a feminist reading, as well? The laws of Manu generally gave the Brahmin man the easy way out with the word *pschathap*. In contrast, the women and the untouchables have to face angry gods and goddesses which carries with it the baggage of penal substitution. Ramabai sought to circumvent this problem with the use of the words *palta kara*. This introduces the idea of a loving God who seeks Brahmins, Kshatriyas, Vyashyas, Shudras, Outcastes, and women. Everyone may return to him because he is a loving God. By using a simple non-Vedic term Ramabai sought to underline that the biblical philosophy of "repentance" is a radical personal and societal change.

Ramabai's third principle forms a good model for today's Dalit Christian theologians. Unfortunately, much of Dalit Christian theology is built around philosophical thought which is foreign to India, such as Marxist thought. In contrast, she sought to elevate the language of the Dalits, a language which is disdained by the high caste Hindus (and Christians), by using it in the very text of the Bible. She sought to avoid language which denigrates the subaltern in various ways and instead used language which freed them and raised them to the level of the rest of Hindu society. In the process she came up with a new theological jargon which is built on pre-Hindu Dalit language and philosophy.

Principle Four. Ramabai thought that the best biblical theology for indigenous thought can be produced by the simple text of the Bible. Many of her disputes with Anglican clergy revolved around Western theology which was being imposed on the Indian people. She wrote, for example, "I believe in the Word of God only and in the testimony of His Prophets. I am a disciple of Christ—though one of the least."[30]

In a letter to Sister Geraldine, whom she called Ajeebai, she wrote, "Indian people are touched by the simplicity of Christ's teaching. Take away the outward shows of your words and grand ceremonies and teach simply the words of Christ as they fell from His lips, without making any comments and you will see the power they have of enchanting the people's hearts."[31] She thought the most profound theology must be written in the simplest language, the language of the subaltern, the language of Indian women and Dalits. She felt complex language was a tool of oppression. Simple vernacular Dalit language, on the other hand, was the source of freedom and liberty.

In reading Pandita Ramabai's writings it becomes clear that her understanding of the theology of the Scriptures was influenced in many ways by a deep sense of feminine Indian mysticism. She was very keen to provide Indians with an opportunity to have what she called a "Word-Seed" encounter. She viewed her relation with Christ in terms of a mystical "Word-Seed" encounter. In 1908, while she was working on the Bible translation project, she wrote, "the Word-Seed, faithfully and prayerfully sown, does surely bear fruit."[32] The Word-Seed encounter is freeing and in her estimation would free Indian women from the bondage which Hinduism brings.

Pandita Ramabai was taken by the Prophets and the Gospels because they directly addressed the needs of women in India. In *The Cry of Indian Women*, written at the beginning of her Word encounter with Christ, she wrote:

> I think that the condition of women in India is not better than that of animals in hell . . . if a female child happens to be born to anyone, there is a feeling of sadness . . . the indignities to which widows are subjected in India is indescribable. All people look on them with disgust. People seem to think that it is their fault because of which their husbands have died. . . . They believe it to be inauspicious to see the face of a widow.[33]

She claimed that the Word-Seed encounter freed Indian women, female children, and Indian widows.

RAMABAI'S BIBLICAL HERMENEUTICS IN TEXTS OF THE PSALMS

I was not able to get a copy of the whole *Wonderful Testimonies*, Ramabai's interlinear translation of the whole Bible. This text is available for use only in Cambridge University's archives. I was able to procure a copy of פִּלְאוֹת עֵדְוֹת, *Wonderful Testimonies—The Book of Psalms*.[34] An analysis of the larger work must wait for a book length treatment at a later time.

The following observations from some Psalm texts will provide further examples of Ramabai's profound work as an original, Indian, biblical, feminist theologian.

In Ps 1:1 she chose to translate ʾašrê hāʾîš with the words *sukhi to purush*. In doing so she decided to go against the Authorized Version, the Revised Standard Version, and the British Revised Version. The Marathi words do not convey the idea of blessedness. Rather they convey the idea of holistic happiness—spiritual, emotional, and physical. This was indeed Ramabai's dream of Mukti. It was the place of *sukhi*, for all those women who were rescued from terrible situations. The Mukti society was the new liberated society.

Ramabai viewed Ps 1 as the foundation of the new liberated Christian community. In the Psalms and in the rest of her translation it is interesting to observe that Ramabai sees the *Torah* as a new book of laws, *Niyamshastra*. This word is used intentionally to draw a contrast with the laws of Manu. Her first two books *Stree Dharma Neeti* and *The High Caste Hindu Woman* form the framework against which she develops her theological positions in her translation of the Bible. This is the new liberating *Niyamshastra*, which is the diametric opposite of the laws of Manu.

The High Caste Hindu Woman is full of assertions regarding the state of women, female infants, and widows in the *Manushastra*. These laws became the basis of the state of women in Indian society. Ramabai quoted from the *Manushastra,* "Though destitute of virtue, or seeking pleasure elsewhere, or devoid of good qualities, yet a husband must be constantly worshipped as a God by a faithful wife . . . a faithful wife, who desires to dwell after death with her husband, must never do anything that might displease him who took her hand, whether he be dead or alive" (*Manushastra* V, 147–156).[35] The Code of Vishnu adds, "A woman after the death of her husband should either lead a virtuous life or ascend the funeral pile of her husband" (*Vishnu* xx.2).[36]

Ramabai viewed the Torah quite in contrast to this as a *Shastra* which elevates the status of women in society and raises them to the place of *sukhi*, holistic happiness.

Psalm 2 in Ramabai's estimation is a messianic Psalm. In contrast to the Authorized Version, the Revised Version, and the Revised English Version, she decided to transliterate the word *māšîaḥ*. This word has no Sanskrit or pre-Vedic antecedents. Ramabai preferred that it remain in transliterated form so that Indians would be able to shape its meaning according to a biblical theology. She was also aware that this was an Arabic/Urdu term, which would address the needs of a Muslim readership.

This messiah is a kingly figure, who was set out as a libation offering from the foundation of the world, according to her choice of words in Ps 2:6: *majha raja sthapla ahe*. This is, of course, quite in contrast to the situation of Hindu women in the Vedas. In the use of these words Ramabai sought to talk in terms of a secure place for Indian women who acknowledge this messianic figure. Women may receive *sukhi* place, a place of happiness and freedom, because this is the will of God from the foundation of the world. From a canonical perspective of "wonderful testimonies" this *māšîaḥ* finds his crucial definition in the work of the messiah in the Gospels.

Ramabai's choice of the names of God in Pss 1–3 is quite telling. She chose to let the Tetragrammaton be transliterated as *Yehovah*. In Ps 2:4 for ʾ*ădōnāi* she chose the word *Prabhu*. Similarly, for the word ʾ*ĕlōhîm* she chose the word *Deva*. Both of these words have their origin in pre-Aryan, pre-Vedic roots. In an explanatory note she suggested that this word ought to be understood as the description of "Triune God." However, she made it clear that this is not the Trinity in the sense of Brahmobandab Upaddhyaya's *Sat Cit Ananda*, nor is it classical Hinduism's *Brahma*, the creator, *Vishnu*, the preserver, and *Shiva*, the destroyer. This is the Triune God of Christianity.[37]

In a letter written and published in *Mukti Prayer Bell* (4.3, November 1909), Ramabai wrote:

> There are many words of this kind which clearly refer to Hindu thought, and not Christian. These words should not be allowed to remain in the vernacular translations of the Bible . . . the words *Ishvar* or *Parameshvar* are proper names of *Mahadeva*, one of the Hindu Triade, and do not denote the Supreme God. The words Jehovah, and Jah revealed by God as His proper names, are translated by the word *Parameshvar* in Marathi; and why the words *Yehovah and Yah* were not

transliterated instead of allowing a mistranslation to take their place is not explained. The word *Parameshvar* does not express the meaning of the name Jehovah as revealed in (Exodus 3:14), Revelation 1:4, namely, "Which is, and Which was, and Which is to come.[38]

It seems quite clear that Ramabai took issue with the use of Hindu terminology made in Indian Christian theologies. Her opinion seems to be that the use of this kind of terminology just makes the narration of biblical theology more complicated to the Indian mind. It gives the Indian mind an unbiblical idea of God. She took similar issue with other theologians who use Hindu names for God. She wrote, "These and other such words as *Bhav, Bhavasagar, Bhagwan, Tribhuvan,* etc. are correctly used by different schools of Hinduism. However, when Indian Christian theologians use them, it destroys the biblical theology of God."[39]

Again it is clear that Ramabai sought to avoid terms of divinity which were intended to subject women and the untouchables to a very demeaning state. *Ishvar, Parameshvar, Bhav, Bhasagar, Bhagwan*, etc. were Brahamanic terms. The theologies of God which emerged from these names of the divine were completely out of reach for women and shudras. For this reason Ramabai preferred to transliterate the Hebrew names for God. For example, she considered that the name *Yahweh*, the "one who is, who was, and who is to come," would give women and untouchables a great amount of encouragement and power. This God does not change according to the whims and fancies of the brahamanical texts which brought the women and shudras under the subjection of the Brahmins. This God is a being who elevates the status of the subaltern.

Throughout the Psalms, and indeed the whole Hebrew Bible and NT, Ramabai chose to translate the word *šāmayim* with the word *Akash*. This is the word she used in Gen 1:1: *Pra-rambhi Devane Akashe Ani Prithvi hi asthithvath anli*. Her translation of Ps 19:1 reads, *Akashe Devacha mehima vernithath*—"the heavens declare the glory of God." The literal translation of Ramabai's Marathi would be the "skies." This translation is in contrast to other Indian translations which use the word *swarg*. She wrote:

> The word *swarg* denotes the abode of the gods where Indra, the king of the Hindu gods is supposed to reign. The place is described to be full of sensual pleasure, where a man goes to enjoy the pleasure brought by *apavarga*, merit. He is supposed to be fortunate, and lives a life of unmixed pleasure, enjoying the company of hundreds and thousands of celestial harlots called *apsaras*. After all this *karma* is spent, he is cast down to the earth, and is reincarnated in some good high-caste family. Where he has all the chances of reattaining *swarga* by his *apavarga*. (This is also the state of) *Nirvana*, which is attained by the *janana*, knowledge of *Brahaman, Bhagawatgita* 9:20, 21.[40]

It seems clear that Ramabai has again avoided antifeminine terms. The term *swarg* suggests a man-oriented heaven. Women are denigrated to the role of those who ingratiate the sexual desires and needs of men. This was the kind of situation from which she had rescued the temple prostitutes who became an essential part of the Mukti Ashram. These young ladies were taken by high caste Hindus into the temple precincts, as soon as they got their first period. They were then trained to become temple priestesses, who gave men sexual/spiritual pleasures. This also became the picture of the Hindu *swarga*. Therefore, Ramabai very vigorously sought the disuse of terms like *swarga*. Instead, she sought the simple use of pre-Vedic oriented vernacular, which simply presented the place of afterlife, heaven, as the place of the presence of God.

CONCLUSION

This paper makes it clear that students of Indian Christian theology have done grave injustice to the discipline by neglecting a profound Pandita. Ramabai undoubtedly took an entirely different approach to her development of Indian Christian theology. Ramabai came to the conclusion that the most authentic Indian Christian theology is neither Jnana, nor Bhakti, nor Karma theology. She removed herself from the methodology adopted by high-caste men theologians. Vedantic philosophy, according to her, was inimical to the development of a good Indian Christian theology. She also distanced herself from theology which is derived from colonial Western philosophical models. She came to the conclusion that the most authentic Indian Christian theology must be derived from non-Vedic, non-Aryan, non-Western thought. She demonstrates that her theology is much more effective and authentic than the theological formulations of contemporary Dalit theologians.

Ramabai's theology of the text of the Bible is authentically biblical and Indian. It is *pĕlāʾôt ʿēdôt*, the wonderful testimonies of the biblical world, which were experienced by the prophets and the apostles, seamlessly woven into the *pĕlāʾôt ʿēdôt* of her recipient community. The recipient *Mukti* community's wonderful testimonies are modeled after the biblical ones. This is what transforms the recipient community. This was an authentic Word-Seed encounter which transforms society from the inside out.

Ramabai used theological terminology which is intentionally nonracial and nonsubversive. It is theological terminology which seeks to bring about true freedom in the Indian context. She shunned any terminology which took people back into racial or caste discrimination.

Ramabai was also very concerned that her theological proposals be authentically biblical and authentically Indian. Her translation of the Bible modeled this very well. It became the ground of an authentic Indian Christian theology of God, humanity, creation, salvation, etc. It touched all aspects of theologizing and should become the ground of generations of authentic Indian Christian theologies.

Constantly and consistently Ramabai was conscious of the fact that words have a profound impact on society and especially on the state of women in society. She was well aware of the fact that Indian translations of the Bible were done by high-caste Hindu men. Ramabai's solution was to use terms which were non-Hindu so that the Bible would never be used as a tool of the demeaning of women in Indian society. For this reason I call her the first genuine Indian Christian, feminist theologian.

Her goal was to provide several generations of Indian readers of the Bible, especially the subaltern, unique opportunities of "Word-Seed" encounters. It is a translation which is genuinely Indian-feminist and genuinely biblical. It is a product of the highest Indian Christian theology. It is theology which liberates the Indian women and untouchables.

Through her invaluable translation of the Bible she came up with a biblical theology which, I propose, must become the paradigm of a genuine Indian Christian feminism and a genuine Dalit theology.

ENDNOTES

1. Pandita Ramabai, *A Testimony: Of Our Inexhaustible Treasure* (Kedgaon, Ma.: Mukti, 1907), p. 6.
2. Pandita Ramabai, *A Testimony*, 7.
3. Ibid., 9.
4. Ibid., 8.
5. Ibid., 10.
6. Ibid., 12.
7. Classical texts like Robin Boyd, *An Introduction to Indian Christian Theology* (Delhi: ISPCK, 1969, 1975, reprinted 2005); or Sunand Sumithra, *Christian Theologies from an Indian Perspective* (Bangalore: Theological Book Trust, 1990) make no mention of Pandita Ramabai. Most up to date compendiums like R. S. Sugirtharajah and Cecil Hargreaves, *Readings in Indian Christian Theology* (TEF Study Guide 29; London: SPCK, 1993) make no mention of Ramabai. Influential journals like *Religion and Society* published by the Christian Institute for the Study of Religion and Society, Bangalore; *Dharma Deepika: A South Asian Journal of Missiological Research* make no mention of Pandita Ramabai. M. M. Thomas in *Towards an Indian Christian Theology: Life and Thought of Some Pioneers* (Tiruvalla: Christa Sahitya Samithi, 1998) gives Ramabai a paltry three pages. However, he merely covers her work at Mukti, not her works as a biblical theologian.
8. K. C. Sen, *Lectures in India*, p. 16.
9. *Sophia Monthly* 2 (April, 1895): 11.
10. *Sophia: A Weekly Review of Politics, Sociology, Literature, and Comparative Theology* 1 (June 23, 1900): 8.
11. Arvind Nirmal, "Towards a Christian Dalit Theology," in *A Reader in Dalit Theology* (Madras: Gurukul, 1990), 59.
12. Maria Arul Rajah, "Towards a Dalit Reading of the Bible: Some Hermeneutical Reflections," *Jeevadhara* 26 (1996): 31.
13. R. S. Sugirtharajah, *The Bible and the Third World: Pre-Colonial, Colonial, and Post-Colonial Encounters* (Cambridge: Cambridge University Press, 2001), 97–105.

14. Meera Kosambi, *Pandita Ramabai's Feminist and Christian Conversions: Focus on Stree Dharma Neeti* (RCWS Gender Series; Bombay: Research Center for Women's Studies, 1995).

15. Meera Kosambi, *Pandita Rambai Through Her Own Words: Selected Works* (Oxford: Oxford University Press, 2000).

16. *Pandita Ramabai: Introduced by Shamsundar Adhav* (Confessing the Faith in India Series 13; Madras: Christian Literature Society, 1979), 32.

17. Pandita Ramabai, *Stree Dharma Neeti* (Code of Conduct for Women) (Poona, 1882).

18. Kosambi, *Pandita Rambai's Feminist and Christian Conversions*, 65. The third chapter is Kosambi's English translation of *Stree Dharma Neeti*.

19. Pandita Ramabai, *The High Caste Hindu Woman* (Philadelphia: Jas Rodgers, 1887).

20. Ibid., 13.

21. Ibid., 14.

22. Ibid., 118–119.

23. Pandita Ramabai, *My Testimony*, 10.

24. *Pandita Ramabai: Introduced by Shamsundar Adhav*, 214.

25. Ibid., 215.

26. Ibid., 197.

27. Ibid., 199. (Correspondence, Christmas, 1908).

28. (second circular letter, January 1909) origin?

29. *Pandita Ramabai: Introduced by Shamsundar Adhav,* 207.

30. A. B. Shah, ed., *Letters and Correspondence of Pandita Ramabai* (Bombay: Maharashtra State Board for Literature, 1977).

31. Ibid., 24.

32. Kosambi, *Pandita Ramabai Through Her Own Words: Selected Works,* 327.

33. Ibid., 109, 112.

34. פִּלְאוֹת עֵדֹוֹת, *Wonderful Testimonies—The Book of Psalms* (Kedgaon: Mukti, 1910).

35. Ramabai, *High Caste Hindu Woman,* 33.

36. Ibid., 41.

37. פִּלְאוֹת עֵדֹוֹת, *Wonderful Testimonies*, 2.

38. *Pandita Ramabai: Introduced by Shamsundar Adhav,* 210.

39. Ibid., 212.

40. Ibid., 211.

RESPONSE TO JOHNSON

AMANDA BECKENSTEIN MBUVI

I want to engage Professor Johnson's paper from the perspective of the body. In their own ways, both feminists and postcolonialists are known for devoting special attention to the body. Feminists (as well as womanists and mujeristas, etc.) observe that the devaluation of the body corresponds in so many ways to the devaluation of women. Postcolonialists also engage a continuing history in which people have been categorized on the basis of their physical features. Moreover, they highlight the unacknowledged role of politics and experience both in scholarship and in theology. Those defined as different are constantly made aware of their status, while those who constitute the mainstream enjoy the luxury of being simply a person or a Christian, with no qualifying adjectives. Yet, as Professor Johnson reminds us, those categories are not absolutes. One may be privileged in some respects and marginalized in others, and one may choose to become downwardly mobile, as did Pandita Ramabai, who married away her high-caste status. I am not particularly familiar with India and I do not claim to fully understand the complexity of its multilayered society. Nevertheless, the dual dynamics that Ramabai negotiated, within India and between India and the West, seem to me important for understanding the theological richness of her work.

Context influences us all. One could hardly do justice to Dietrich Bonhoeffer without considering Nazi Germany, and yet the study of Bonhoeffer generally takes place under the auspices of Christian theology, not German theology. His works are immediately and rightly understood to be relevant to all Christians, not just Germans and germanophiles. The discrepancy between the reception of Bonhoeffer and that of Ramabai could probably be traced to many causes, but it ultimately comes down to the body.

The question of why we should care is important for understanding the discourse surrounding a woman who defied the traditional fault lines that continue to separate concerns with gender from concerns with race, class, and colonialism and from concerns with a life-transforming, gospel-oriented theology, consigning each to a separate camp. (Katie Cannon tells the story of being at a conference in which people were given the rather perplexing instruction to gather into groups, with the African-Americans in one corner and the women in another.) Perhaps as a matter of strategy, perhaps as a matter of sin, marginalized groups often prefer to address only those with greater power than themselves and do not make a point of engaging other excluded voices. In this way they challenge their own marginalization, but they do not challenge marginalization as such. At the same time, many white Western feminists ignore someone like Ramabai because, focused on gender oppression, they often do not want to consider the privileges they enjoy by virtue of their race, social class, or nationality. They prefer the dichotomy in which one belongs simply and unequivocally to either the (righteous) oppressed or the (evil) privileged. They do not recognize that the same tendencies they condemn in men are also present in themselves.

I suspect that these cleavages underlie Sugirtharajah's reference to Ramabai's work as "textual management" and Professor Johnson's distaste for that designation. Professor Johnson speaks as a committed Christian addressing committed Christians (with varying attitudes toward liberation), while Sugirtharajah's intended audience more likely consists of committed liberationists (with varying attitudes toward the Bible and Christianity). For Christians, "textual management" might have the ring of heresy, suggesting something less than authoritative biblical interpretation, but for liberationists, it simply points to one among many strategies for dealing with legacies of oppression. Many postcolonial thinkers take an interest in the Bible and/or Christianity simply as an aspect of experience that some have engaged to great effect. However, for those like Professor Johnson and myself who refuse to separate a concern for the poor and oppressed from a passion for the life-transforming gospel of Jesus Christ, it is not enough that a response to oppression be strategic, although strategy is important. We also want to know why it should be identified with Christianity because we recognize that the gospel demands and nurtures a concern for the poor and we do not want to see that aspect of Christ's message and work—or those who proclaim it—regarded as less than authoritative for all Christians. It is precisely this reconciliation with Christian tradition that some liberation-oriented biblical scholars and theologians resist because they are convinced that the tradition itself is bankrupt, and with good reason. After all, the words and especially the actions of privileged Christians have done little to suggest that the gospel really is good news for the poor, and much to suggest that it is not.

I want to conclude this response with a discussion of two bodies, the body of Purusha and the body of Christ. Explaining the context in which a Dalit identity is shaped, Professor Johnson quotes the *Rig Veda*:

> When they divided the *Purusha*, into how many parts did they arrange him? What was his mouth? What were his arms? What are his thighs and feet called? The Brahmin was his mouth, his arms were made the rajanya (warriors), his two thighs Vaishyas (traders and agriculturists), and from his feet the shudras (servant class) were born. (The *Rig Veda* X. 90:12)

This vision of the body depicts a social hierarchy in which different groups vary in both purpose and dignity. Strikingly, speaking is reserved for only a few. First Corinthians 12 offers a very different conceptualization of the body. Here the body is one and has many members, all equally valuable even though they have different functions, and the members that seem less honorable are not demeaned thereby but are shown greater honor. Distinctions and dissension are not allowed, and all care for each other and experience together whatever happens, whether suffering or rejoicing.

In context this passage describes the importance of the variety of spiritual gifts to the church, but it is not too much of a stretch to understand it as offering a broader vision of diversity within the church. It is this vision that Pandita Ramabai enacted among the young women with whom she ministered by training them in biblical linguistics so that they might do the work of translation. It is this vision that the Western missionaries betrayed by disregarding that work in favor of Ramabai's rescue work. Like so many of us, they assumed that speaking belongs only to a few. Although they opposed the women's exploitation, by not taking their translation work seriously they also treated them as bodies, nothing more. I appreciate Professor Johnson's bringing Pandita Ramabai to our attention, and I hope that she may remind us to live out Christ's radical vision of community that is as shocking to the twenty-first-century United States as it was to her India.

MISSIONARY ACTS, THINGS FALL APART: MODELING MISSION IN ACTS 17:15–34 AND A CONCERN FOR DIALOGUE IN CHINUA ACHEBE'S *Things Fall Apart*[1]

ANDREW M. MBUVI

> The white man is very clever. He came quietly and peaceably with his religion. We were amused at his foolishness and allowed him to stay. Now he has won our brothers, and our clan can no longer act like one. He has put a knife on the things that held us together and we have fallen apart. (Obierika in *Things Fall Apart,* p. 176)

In a conversation with one of my former professors during my doctoral studies, I wondered aloud why "the dialogue model of mission" employed by Paul in Acts 17:15–34 never seems to have been formally adopted in the Western church in relation to eighteenth and nineteenth-century missions in Africa and other former colonies. His answer, which seemed to make sense then, was that the mission to Athens was a failed mission since, as he put it, "Do you see any of Paul's letters written to the church in Athens?"

Nonetheless, the more I reflected on this answer the more unconvinced I became of its premise, and the more holes appeared in its logic and argument. Did Paul write to every church he planted? Do we have all the letters that Paul wrote to churches? These and other questions bothered me and I decided that the answer I received was untenable. In fact, earlier Acts 17:11–12 says that the Bereans received Paul and his message enthusiastically and many believed, both Jews and Greeks. Yet, we do not know of a letter by Paul to the church in Berea, do we?

Contrary to my professor's declaration of Athens as a failed mission, I maintain that it was rather that another model of mission had triumphed over the Athens dialogue model in the post-Enlightenment, Western Christian mindset—the "great commission" model (Matt 28:28–31). Largely orchestrated by the supposed "father of modern missions," William Carey (1761–1834), the concept of the "great commission" is driven by evangelicalism's pursuit of the mandate to "make disciples" as an eschatological precondition for the Second Coming.

The "great commission model" is driven by a certain triumphalistic millennialism and a conviction that *knowledge* (information/education /enlightenment?) is ultimately what brings conversion, but it leaves little room for dialogue. That is why schools in the colonies were built so as to educate the people to be able to read the Bible for themselves. In this respect it failed to realize that there are other aspects (e.g., aesthetics or affect) that may have a greater propensity in communication for a particular people. Paying greater attention to this may have averted some of the major *faux pas* of the European missionary endeavors in Africa. The impact on Africa was enormous as waves of missionaries landed in colonies to preach (conquer with?) the gospel, spurred on by such texts as Hab 2:14 ("For the earth will be filled with the knowledge of the glory of the Lord, as the waters cover the sea"; cf. also Isa 11:9). These missionaries were aided by the political fortunes of the European explorations/exploitation, political powers, the economic boom provided largely by colonies with their native workers and slaves in the new world, and the ability for faster maritime travels.

Paul's efforts were quite different. He perceived a deep-seated hunger for the divine in the Athenians that manifested itself in the idols on display within the city. Instead of faulting the spiritual expression in idols, he saw the spiritual hunger that lay beneath and addressed it: "Men of Athens! I see that in every way you are very religious" (Acts 17:21). Paul also seems to have been genuinely impressed by their spirituality, especially after he had been rejected several times by his own Jewish community in various cities (Acts 17:13). We see here a fairly different Paul than the typical firebrand that we are accustomed to in the epistles, one willing to engage in dialogue with non-Jews. In fact, Paul was even willing to adopt and adapt their sayings of wisdom: "For 'in [God] we live and move and have our being'; as even some of your poets have said, 'For we are indeed his offspring'" (Acts 17:28).

The possibility of dialogue exists only if one believes that the other has something worthwhile to offer. Otherwise, instead of a subject-to-subject relationship you have a subject-to-object relationship. Once the other is dubbed a "savage," "heathen," "primitive," "of the devil," "godless," etc., then there is no space for dialogue. This language, well articulated in such works as Daniel Defoe's *Robinson Crusoe*, was applied to the African (who lived/lives in the *dark continent*) by Euro-American colonizers, missionaries, and explorers, precluding any possibility of dialogue with the African subject.[2] In essence the declaration was, "You are to listen to us, we have *truth*, you have falsity, and without us you are doomed to perdition."

In one of the most celebrated writings of modern Western literature, Joseph Conrad's *Heart of Darkness*, Africans are portrayed as savage, shadow, brute, part of nature, simply to be pitied and treated humanely much like one would with animals. Like a dog the African could be trained to do simple tasks like drive the steamboat, and that ever so poorly. Note the starkness of his language.

> We penetrated deeper and deeper into the heart of darkness. It was very quiet there. At night sometimes the roll of drums behind the curtain of trees would run up the river and remain sustained faintly, as if hovering in the air high over our heads, till the first break of day. Whether it meant war, peace, or prayer we could not tell. . . . We were wanderers on *prehistoric earth*, on an earth that wore the aspect of an unknown planet. We could have fancied ourselves the first of men taking possession of an *accursed inheritance, to be subdued* at the cost of profound anguish and of excessive toil. But suddenly, as we struggled round a bend, there would be a glimpse of rush walls, of peaked grass-roofs, a burst of yells, a whirl of *black limbs*, a *mass of hands* clapping, of *feet stamping*, of *bodies swaying*, of eyes rolling under the droop of heavy and motionless foliage. . . . The *prehistoric man* was cursing us, praying to us, welcoming us—who could tell? . . . [we were] wondering and secretly appalled, as sane men would be before an enthusiastic outbreak in a madhouse. . . . We were accustomed to look upon the shackled form of a conquered *monster*, but there—there you could look at a thing monstrous and free. The earth seemed unearthly. It was unearthly, and the men were—No, they were not inhuman. Well, you know, that was the worst of it—this suspicion of their not being inhuman. It would come slowly to one. They howled and leaped, and spun, and made the *horrid faces*; but what thrilled you was just the thought of their humanity—like yours—the thought of your *remote kinship* with this wild and passionate uproar. . . . And between whiles I had to look after the *savage* who was fireman. He was an improved *specimen*. He could fire up a vertical boiler. He was there below me, and upon my word, *to look at him was as edifying as seeing a dog in a parody of breeches and a feather hat walking on his hind-legs*. A few months of training had done for that really fine chap.[3]

This is the best that Marlow, the narrator in *Heart of Darkness,* could muster in terms of description of the African—appendages, masks, prehistoric creatures, dogs. It is partially in response to this portrayal of the African that Chinua Achebe wrote his novels.[4]

Achebe saw the African novelist as a teacher—an evangelist, if you will—whose role it is to tell the African story from the point of view of the African as a corrective to the outsiders such as Conrad who have told *our* story.[5] He wrote:

> Here, then, is an adequate revolution for me to espouse—to help my society regain its belief in itself and put away the complexes of the years of the denigration and self-abasement. And it is essentially a question of education, in the best sense of that word. Here, I think, my aims and the deepest aspirations of my society meet. For no thinking African can escape the pain of the wound in our soul. . . . The writer cannot expect to be excused from the task of re-education and regeneration that must be done. In fact he should march right in front . . . I for one would not

> wish to be excused. I would be quite satisfied if my novels (especially the ones set in the past) did no more than teach my readers that their past—with all its imperfections—was not one long night of savagery from which the first Europeans acting on God's behalf delivered them. Perhaps what I write is applied art as distinct from pure. But who cares? Art is important but so is education of the kind I have in mind. And I don't see that the two need be mutually exclusive.[6]

Bernard McGrane remarks on the nature of the missional Christianity that emerged post-Enlightenment while reflecting on Defoe's *Robinson Crusoe*:

> The *truth* of the savages, the cannibals, is that either God allows them or condemns them to *live in falseness*, to live a cruel, barbarous, unholy life. In the Enlightenment . . . the *truth* of the non-European Other is that he *manifests the false*, he makes manifest true ignorance and error, true unenlightenment. . . . The principle function and sign of the truth of Christianity is that it explains the falsity of the Other's difference.[7]

This is a form of Christianity that was not disposed towards dialogue with the other since it had already determined the other to possess not an ounce of *truth*.[8]

In the novel *Things Fall Apart* Reverend James Smith, the new missionary in Umuofia, "saw the world in black and white. And black was evil" (p. 184). His equation of the African religion with the Canaanite worship of Ba'al meant that the concept of God in Africa could never be equitable with that of the biblical deity of Israel, YHWH/ʾĒl/ʾĔlōhîm. Any hopes of reconciling the African ontology with Judeo-Christian ontology in the manner that Paul does with the Athenian religion are dashed by such categorization. This is the core of what McGrane perceives to have been the essential manifestation of post-Enlightenment Christianity.

When cultures are so incongruent, how does one read Scripture? How does one strange culture take the Bible, itself a product of various strange cultures, to another strange culture? What is involved in this sort of border crossing that demands transformation for both the border crosser/stranger/foreigner and the native? Culture has authority that is not ultimately theological but is more difficult to pinpoint. Yet, it so shapes thought, life, experience, and their interpretations to the extent that it cannot be ignored even when not fully fathomed. Culture is infused in the whole expression of personhood that the German word *Weltanschauung* ("worldview") comes closest in articulating the sense of culture within a given group of people.

Even this expression is limited since it fails to acknowledge that there are multiple worldviews that govern the different communities. There is no single monolithic "African culture" but a multiplicity of communities each with distinct and shared cultural traits. Even within one tribal or ethnic group, there are variations. The people of Umuofia are Igbo and so are the people of Mbanta or

Mbaino (all these are names of towns or villages in the novel). Despite their shared language (with its distinct dialects), distinctive aspects of their lives distinguish one village from the other. The African novel, especially the colonial and postcolonial products, seek to reclaim or reconstruct the African past and the encounter with Christianity as a corrective to portrayals of such encounters by Westerners.

THE ENGAGEMENT OF AFRICAN NOVELS WITH THE BIBLE

My conviction is that the authors of African novels describing Christianity's engagement with Africa do not merely give *descriptive* commentary on society but seek to give a very *proactive* and *prescriptive* interpretation of society.[9]

Achebe's story is as much informed and shaped by biblical narratives as it is African. This is in alignment with Simon Gikandi's apt summation of the authorial intent of the African novel: "The text is not mere content or form: it is the process of form recreating reality in terms set by authorial consciousness, constituting a world which might resemble the external reality, but is also the novelist's own universe."[10] It is an idealized world in which the aspirations of the author can be "realized" while at the same time engaging the challenges of real life situations.

When the African novelist engages matters religious, it is usually with an intention of analytical interpretation of the religious elements alongside other cultural aspects. Congruently, the African readership of these writings have typically not been leisure readers but serious consumers of the content with the expectation of learning, transformation, and reformation of social life.

Most educated Africans would have read these novels as part of their high school English curriculum requirement. Read in community, i.e., loudly in class over a number of weeks, such novels foster a strong sense of identity formation within the student body that goes beyond simply lessons in English grammar.[11] Their rhetoric has an earnestness that hopes to convince and convict. For this reason their use in literature classes across the African continent has shaped, and continues to shape, modes of thinking about matters African and otherwise.

Many of the earlier generation of African novelists were the product of colonial education with an emphasis on a Europeanized Christianity from which a considerable number seem to have turned away. While not completely abandoning Christianity, there was a compulsion to assert a clear sense of the need either for rejection of Christianity altogether or a rehabilitation of it in light of African religious ethos. For instance Ngugi wa Thiong'o's *A Grain of Wheat* seeks to find a middle ground where African religious experience is integrated into Christianity to form an expression of African Christianity.[12] (Obviously his title is drawn directly from John 12:24: "I tell you the truth, unless a kernel of wheat falls to the ground and dies, it remains only a single seed. But if it dies, it produces many seeds.") Mongo Beti's *Le Pauvre Christ de Bomba* (*Poor Christ of Bomba*) satirically questions the role of the Roman Catholic Church in rural Cameroon in promoting a perception of sexuality foreign not only to the European and African alike, but also devoid of any biblical mandate.[13]

The typical African novel is a political document steeped in a literary response to society's ills and particularly those of colonialism and its aftermath, including the failures of postcolonial African political leaderships. The end result was very often reprisals against these authors by their own governments, which led to their being ostracized or forced into exile. The examples are myriad: Mongo Beti was exiled thirty-two years from his native Cameroon for his novels which implied complicity of the African leaders in the colonial process.[14] Bessie Head was denied reentry into her homeland of South Africa and forced into exile in Botswana, but denied citizenship in Botswana for the better part of two decades. Ngugi wa Thiong'o of Kenya was detained without trial and eventually forced into exile, first in Britain and later in the United States. Nobel Laureate Wole Soyinka, forced into exile for his writings and political activism, was eventually allowed to return to Nigeria only after a change in the government.

These examples are sufficient to make clear that the typical African novelist is not only politically engaged but is also essentially committed to his/her works, fully aware of the dangers that accompany them. It is obvious then that the typical African novelist sees him/herself more as a teacher of society than a mere entertainer. Even such comedic writings as Soyinka's *The Road* or Ferdinand Oyono's *Une Vie de Boy* are laced with stinging political and social indictments.[15]

While they have been analyzed for such aspects as use of Greek structure, hardly anyone reads these novels as commentaries on the Bible. This is what this paper attempts to do. These writings do not simply narrate, *they seek to persuade*. They do not simply intend to entertain but to educate and to challenge the reader to a way of understanding the events related.

A BIBLICAL SCHOLAR VENTURES AN EXEGESIS OF AN AFRICAN NOVEL

I want to venture into reading, or more appropriately exegeting, perhaps the most widely read African novel, Chinua Achebe's *Things Fall Apart*.[16] I do this primarily from the vantage point of a biblical scholar to ferret out what and how biblical and Christian encounters engage, reconstitute, and prod the African culture in the novel, and vice versa. I hope to show that this novel is, to a certain degree, an interpretive response to certain readings of the Bible in contention or in dialogue with some other interpretations of the Bible.

Such a claim is bolstered by the realization that the very title of the book *Things Fall Apart* is from W. B. Yeats's poem entitled "The Second Coming" in reference to the return of Christ.[17] If the "first coming" was to herald "peace and goodwill to all people" (Luke 2:14) and the "second coming" is to portend judgment, then in a sense all that the people of Umuofia have gotten is a "second coming," and not the first. Okonkwo, the protagonist of *Things Fall Apart*, is a respected person in his village of Umuofia ("children of the forest") as a result of his great achievements, but whose impudence and stubbornness make him unable to adjust to the changes taking place and lead to his self-destruction.

The author, christened Albert Chinualumogu Achebe in honor of prince Albert of England[18] (later abbreviated as a *nom de plume* to Chinua Achebe), was born to a Christian family with an evangelist father. Achebe's Christian mother, however, retained the tradition of Igbo storytelling in the home, and Achebe loved these occasions. Achebe's uncle and at least one other neighbor maintained images of his personal *chi* (his personal god) in his home, and this fascinated the young Achebe, who occasionally snuck in to partake of the religious meals and ceremonies.

The novel begins with a wrestling match scene which becomes a primary metaphor in the rest of the story. There is wrestling with new ideas, new cultures, new government, waning of old lifestyles, and the challenge of Christianity to the Igbo religion. Having won all "wrestling" encounters in his life, Okonkwo, unlike Jacob who wrestled with the divine and prevailed in Gen 32:24–25, wrestles Christianity (and his *chi*) and loses.[19] The community wrestles the advance of Western Christianity, education, and colonialism and loses.

The triumph of the missionaries is inadvertent and at the expense of Igbo religious belief, when they were assigned the Evil Forest as the place to build their church in Mbanta (p. 150). After the expected days elapsed and none of the missionaries died as the villagers expected, the first few converts emerged. It was not conviction of Christian doctrine that led to conversion but recognition of the need to alter their conception of the divine in light of the new happenings. If you will, a shifting of allegiance occurred. On other occasions it was the melody of the songs as sung by the Christians that have the capacity to "pluck at the heart of an Igbo person." Nwoye, Okonkwo's first born son, was also converted to Christianity. Okonkwo already loathed Nwoye because his son's laziness reminded him of his father, whose laziness drove his own desire to succeed, but his son's conversion epitomized the battle within Africans in their first encounter with the Western Christianity embodied in the missionaries.

The aesthetics of dialogue are such a crucial part of the Igbo culture that failure to comprehend this facet amounts to failure to understand an Igbo. Beauty of speech ("Proverbs are the palm-oil with which words are eaten"), the appreciation of song (singing that plucks at an Igbo's heart, p. 146), poetry (Nwoye's captivation by Christian hymns, p. 147), casting away of newborn twins into the evil forest (p. 151), and love of wrestling matches, all reflect a certain view of life that an outsider may well fail to appreciate as commensurate with the ethos of this society. Furthermore, prayer is so central to the religious expression among the Igbo that every visit is associated with the breaking of a kola nut accompanied by prayer for health and blessing—"he who brings kola, brings life."

Rather than Conrad's chaotic inscrutable vision of a dark, brooding, and menacing Africa, Achebe unveils a vivacious society complete with order and structure, with its strengths and weaknesses, with public and private institutions, and with joys and pains. In other words, a complex society such as any that one would encounter anywhere in the world had such a person "eyes" to behold it. Such things as warfare were not simply engaged in at any person's whim but would be the final result of a failed series of negotiations, and only at the divine behest of the "Oracle of the Hills and the Caves."[20] (In this conception of the divine, does one hear overtones of YHWH the divine warrior, who also is God of the mountain, as is the Oracle of the Hills and Caves?) This sounds quite a bit like the stories of Israel in the OT where warfare would only be sanctioned by the deity (Exodus, Joshua, and 1 and 2 Samuel) and, similarly, when the human character disobeyed there were negative results.[21]

Rather than the African being barbarous, it is the action of British soldiers which is horrific and perturbing, for in retaliation for the death of a single white man they atrociously slaughter and virtually annihilate the Abame clan. Even the intertribal wars resulted in a dozen deaths or so in Igbo land. Even the Umuofia spirits who came to avenge the "killing" of one of them by a Christian convert were not rambunctious but calmly informed Rev. Smith that he would not be harmed and they simply destroyed the church building (pp. 190–191). This is not the picture that emerges from Conrad's writing.

Biblical Allusions and Inferences: Miscellaneous Texts. In contrast to Okonkwo's inflexibility, the laws and customs of the Igbo community are portrayed as flexible and malleable in old man Ezeudu's story: "My father told me that he had been told that in the past a man who broke the peace was dragged on the ground through the village until he died. But after a while this custom was stopped because it spoiled the peace which it was meant to preserve" (p. 31). The potential to assimilate Christian values in a profound manner exists in the Igbo culture, if only those who were bringing Christianity were not blind to it.

There is no clear indication that the "Week of Peace" is reminiscent of the biblical Day of Atonement or that the Feast of New Yam (pp. 36f.) partly envisions the festival of Harvest (Pentecost) in reverse (planting rather than harvesting) or is simply like a Sabbath Week when no work was done (p. 31), but the parallels are intriguing.[22]

The tongues of fire displayed when the "ancestral spirits of the clan were abroad" echo those that appeared at Pentecost in Acts 2 (p. 88), while the explanation of the formation of the nine villages on the premises of the nine sons of the "father of the clan" sound uncannily similar to the story of Jacob and the tribes of Israel in Genesis. The ubiquity of the number "seven" or the eighth day of circumcision in the novel seem closely parallel to the Bible.[23]

It is interesting that the Europeans are not hinted at in the novel until the eighth chapter and only fully introduced in chapter fifteen, well after Achebe has left the reader awash with the fascination of the Igbo culture and allowing for the clear sense this is an irruption into the Igbo society. In contrast with the picture of the African as an irrational murderous brute that horrifies the European in the writings of Conrad and Marlow, the killing of the first white man to venture into Igbo land in the Abame village is clearly explained in terms of the community's religious conviction of an evil omen—the "Oracle of the Hills and Caves" having prophesied the coming of the white man that "would break their clan and spread destruction among them" (p. 138).

It is difficult to claim *untruth* in the Oracle's prophecy. Encounter with Christianity and Western culture resulted in a permanent transformation of life in Umuofia, as it did in the rest of Africa, and not always for the best. One may venture to say that the picture of Umuofia is one of an Igbo land with things already falling apart well before the arrival of the white European on the scene in chapter eight. Indeed, for Achebe, it is only because the things are already falling apart that the white man is able to penetrate into the community and subjugate it. However, the picture of war, peace, and pestilences thus painted is one in which cyclical events of time simply reflect the ever present reality of the world rather than being eschatological signifiers (Matt 24:6f.; Mark 13:7f.; Luke 21:9f.).

Ikemefuna and the Akedah (Abraham's sacrifice of Isaac in Gen 22). In a neighboring village of Mbaino, a daughter of Umuofia (Udo's wife) was killed. The people of Umuofia decide to ask for the usual reparation following such cases: a young virgin (as replacement of the dead wife) and a son of one of the Mbaino killers (to be disposed of in accordance with the Oracle's wishes). The lad, Ikemefuna, ended up in Okonkwo's custody over three years and Okonkwo grew fond of the boy even more than his own son Nwoye, whom Okonkwo considered lazy and an unfortunate reminder of his own father whom he loathed.

In the event that the "Oracle of the Hills and the Caves" determined that the boy must die, the parallels with the *Akedah* emerge, where Abraham is asked by God to sacrifice his son Isaac and alludes to the NT sacrificial death of Jesus by God the Father.[24] Needless to say, Ikemefuna was not Okonkwo's son, but to Okonkwo, Ikemefuna was the "son" that Nwoye was not, and he even called Okonkwo "father" (p. 28). Warned not to participate in the sacrificial killing of Ikemefuna, Okonkwo's own fear of cowardice and sheer stubbornness led him to spill the blood of the young one. ("Okonkwo never showed any emotion openly, unless it be the emotion of anger. To show affection was a sign of weakness; the only thing worth demonstrating was strength" [p. 28]). Commenting on the *Akedah* connection here, David Hoegberg surmises:

> The two stories side by side show the different ways in which divine authority can be textualized as either absolute or limited depending on how a narrative is structured. The biblical text presents God's judgment as unquestionably right and Abraham's faith as laudable, whereas in Achebe's story such faith is neither demanded nor particularly useful.... Achebe's use of an alien text, then, provides an implicit criticism of the Igbo rejection of the alien without holding the Western example up as better; in short, it is Achebe's act of inclusion with critical scrutiny, not Abraham's act of obedience, that is most important here.[25]

Against the advice of the elder, Okonkwo slew Ikemefuna, bringing upon himself the wrath of Ani, the goddess of the earth, the judge of morality in the clan. This act led Nwoye to reject his father and the clan gods and turn to Christianity.[26] It was not simply the knowledge of the Christian message which Nwoye had heard on numerous occasions in the market but a deep felt hatred of his father that turned him away from his Igbo gods. There was more to conversion than simply mental conviction; for Nwoye, Christianity seemed to answer the nagging problem of killing of twins and the death of Ikemefuna, his "brother."[27]

One can contrast this with the notion of mission and evangelism in relation to European and American missionaries in Africa. Ikemefuna, an enemy's child, is fully integrated ("wholly absorbed," p. 54) into the family of his "enemies" so much so that he becomes one of the family. There is no intent to deceive. This is what makes Okonkwo's part in his death that much more tragic. Not only was Ikemefuna transformed so that his initial fear dissipated and he became endeared to Okonkwo's family, Okonkwo and his family were transformed by their encounter with Ikemefuna. Nwoye was transformed into a responsible and hardworking young man (p. 54), the little children were mesmerized by Ikemefuna's storytelling, the wives had compassion on him, and even Okonkwo developed a fondness for the boy, partly for making Nwoye, his effeminate son, act more mature and manly.

An individual's action had direct correlation to the fortunes or misfortunes of the community. For example, proper respect for the dead resulted in peaceful coexistence with their spirits (p. 32). As in the biblical world, the spiritual and the physical worlds in African conception intersect, and the border line between them is porous, allowing for movement between them (cf. 1 Sam 28:7f.). One's actions in the physical realm/world have direct correlation or effect in the spiritual realm. Okonkwo's breaking of the "Week of Peace" drew the wrath of the goddess Ani's priest and could portend a poor harvest as divine judgment on the community: "[Priest Ezeani] brought down his staff heavily on the floor. 'You have committed a great evil.... The evil you have done can ruin the whole clan.'" God must be appeased with a sacrifice (p. 30). Is this parallel to the sin of Achan that threatened divine destruction of the Israelites for the sin of one person (cf. Josh 7:1–29)?

Okonkwo's struggles to adjust to the changes bear resemblance to the breakup of community's cohesiveness in light of colonialism and Christianity. Suddenly brother rose against brother, a thing unheard of in the community's past. Achebe does not seem to suggest that change was unnecessary or all negative, but that the type of upheaval caused by the colonial encounter would forever change Umuofia even in aspects that would have otherwise not needed change. Elements of the society that would have served as an entry point for dialogue and constructive engagement were completely missed by the Europeans whose vision of the colony was that of "*The Pacification of the Primitive Tribes*" that ends the novel (p. 207).

Provision for a place of escape for one who had committed inadvertent killing like Okonkwo echoes the biblical "cities of refuge" in Israel. Unlike Okonkwo's predetermined seven-year exile, in Num 35:25–32 the period of exile to the city of refuge in Israel was indeterminate and lasted until the death of the high priest. In both communities the purpose was to avert divine judgment on innocent blood. Failure by the Christian converts and the white governors to perceive the wisdom in this and its biblical parallels led to the conviction of murder and the hanging of Oduche (p. 177).

Like the biblical exile which usually involves divine judgment on a wayward and sinful Israel, Okonkwo's exile was for his failure to heed to the warnings of the elder and the Oracle. His exile however was not into the hands of enemies or bondage, which Okonkwo might have preferred, but to his mother's community which must have felt worse than bondage to Okonkwo. For one who compared weakness to women, he had to endure the embarrassment of finding refuge among his mother's community. It is no wonder he committed suicide in the end.

In the matter of Christians' reluctance to accept *osus* (outcasts) in their church, the people told Mr. Kiaga the evangelist, "You do not understand. . . . You are our teacher, and you can teach us the things of the new faith. But this is a matter which we *know*." "An *osu* was a person dedicated to a god, a thing set apart—a taboo forever, and his children after him. He could neither marry nor be married by the free born. He was in fact an outcast living in a special area of the village, close to the Great Shrine" (p. 156). One cannot fail to see the parallels with biblical Nazirites like Samson who, like the *osu*, were dedicated to the deity as "a thing set apart" and like the *osu* "a razor was taboo" to him (Judg 13:5).

Engaging Biblical Texts. The radical stance of the European missionaries was also reflected in the first Igbo converts whose enthusiasm drove them to denigrate the traditions and religion of their fathers. Mr. Kiaga, having fully imbibed the essence of post-Enlightenment Christianity, unaware of his own place in the equation, now parrots: "The heathen speak nothing but *falsehood*. Only the word of our God is true" (p. 157). Enoch, a son of the priest of the snake cult (p.

178) and now a Christian convert, is rumored to have killed the sacred python and displayed too much zeal in his confronting and unmasking the African god ("killing" the spirit/*egwugwu*), which led to the burning of the church in Umuofia.

Mr. Kiaga's interpretation of Luke 14:26 ("If any one comes to me and does not hate his own father and mother and wife and children and brothers and sisters, yes, and even his own life, he cannot be my disciple") was literal, as Okonkwo's son became a Christian largely for literally hating his father (p. 152). In a culture that so greatly values community, this literal reading was decried and countered for the youth of the Mbanta by the sage counsel of the elder Uchendu, who lamented concerning Christianity, "An abominable religion has settled among you. A man can now leave his father and his brothers. . . . I fear for you. I fear for the clan" (p. 167).

In Mr. Brown and Rev. Smith, Achebe idealizes the dialogical nature of mission by providing, not just two contrasting personalities with two contrasting approaches to mission, but also two contrasting phases of Christian expression. A subtle contrast may even exist between the titles of *Mr.* Brown and *Rev.* Smith, perhaps indicating the difference between the establishment missionary's biases and cultural superiority complex (Smith) and the nonconformist (Brown) willing to see beyond his own sense of convictions and basing his teaching on 1 Cor 6:12 and 10:23 ("All things are lawful, but not all things are helpful"; "All things are lawful, but not all things build up.")

Another dialogical encounter happens in the conversation between Mr. Brown and the old man Akunna. In many respects, however, even Mr. Brown fails to emulate the essential focus of Paul's Athenian encounter when he focused instead on the *falsehood* of the smaller gods/idols that Akunna explained are created by Chukwu—creator of heaven and earth (pp. 179–180). He still remained the product of the same post-Enlightenment thinking. Akunna's answers clearly exemplify a well-thought-out Igbo ontology that is able to integrate the Christian faith to the Igbo culture, but Mr. Brown's lack of sensibility to these signals and motifs kept moving the conversation to trivial matters. For example, in an effort to denounce any aspect of divine dependence by the biblical God, Mr. Brown inexplicably told Akunna not to think of God as "a person." Yet he turns around and says to Akunna that God is a "loving Father" (p. 180).

Engaging Biblical Theology. The Igbo's failure to grasp complex doctrines like the Holy Trinity and Holy Communion is cited as "evidence" of their lesser intelligence by the missionaries. Okonkwo's conundrum of why God does not have a wife if he has a son, is simply brushed away as failure to comprehend the Holy Trinity—like anybody ever understood it! Okonkwo's response is that the Trinity sounds as much like madness as that of the Igbo's worshipping many gods (p. 158). Ogbuefi Ogonna, a man of title in Umuofia, had converted to Christianity and during Holy Communion thought that it was just a more sacred version of the tribal eating and drinking feast. Therefore, he carried his drinking-horn with him, only to be disappointed (p. 174). This could also be perceived as a subtle critique of the formulation of Holy Communion into less than what it was for Christ and his disciples—a feast indeed! The tiny cup and wafer have replaced the proper biblical feast that ought to accompany the Lord's Supper, eroding the communal aspect which is the foundation of Christianity.

CONCLUSION

Achebe rightfully perceives that there is no stereotype of missionaries as there should be no stereotype of African/Igbo peoples and communities. Foreignness is not only limited to the white man but is also reflected in other Africans from a different part of the country (p. 174).

For Achebe, together with the church came colonialism. While distinct, they are not necessarily separate—both were tied to the white man. Indeed, religion, trade, and government were inseparable. The law established was foreign to the Igbo, which resulted in cases being judged in ignorance (p. 174). The imposition of the British law was not unlike the "imposition" of a Western form of Christianity that deemed itself superior to any African custom or religion.

But, one wonders whether this is Achebe's ideal portrayed or the reality of history. Critics would say that Achebe has simply established an idealistic linear and direct link of history from a glorious past to a glorious future, which was interrupted by the barbarism of colonialism, and that not much of the glorious past can be verified.[28] Theologically, I perceive more missed opportunities of theological depth for the Igbo community by the failure of the initial Christian encounters to make the resultant Christian expression more authentically Igbo, and perhaps even more biblical! The end result has been a largely Western form of Christianity that in many ways failed to impact the very core of the Igbo (and African) communities. Paul deferred to the Athenian religion; the typical Western missionary did not defer to the African religious expression.

Possible conclusions include the following. One, I have overstated my case and seen more biblical parallels and imageries than are warranted. Would this mean Achebe's (re)construction of African culture is not legitimate? Two, Achebe knowingly uses Christian knowledge to reconstruct an Igbo past. Three, Achebe highlights in Igbo tradition elements that lend themselves comparatively to biblical parallels. This would be an apologetic endeavor by Achebe that seeks to show that what is found in Christianity can be found in Igbo religion. Four, Achebe may have been totally oblivious to these biblical motifs and connections and simply wrote a story that was trying to be faithful to the reality of the Igbo community's first encounter with Christianity.

In essential agreement with Hoegberg, I see in *Things Fall Apart* an intertextuality that blurs the boundary between the Igbo and the biblical world/text.[29] The novel is a deliberate engagement of the biblical text providing both an interpretation and an intricate intertextual reorientation of the biblical narratives. An infusion of African components into biblical narratives bolsters both a critique of the biblical material and provides an appraisal of their positive elements in the Igbo culture.

BACK TO PAUL IN ATHENS

Paul's assessment of the Athenian religion suggests a perspective that willfully engages the religious world and convictions of the other with the aim of mutual edification. Paul did not give an outright condemnation of Athenian religion as one for heathens and idol worshippers, the very accusation some Western missionaries openly made against some African communities. Instead, he spoke to their sense of godliness and spirituality. He decided not to fault the expression of the faith but instead to engage the deeper aspect of belief that was already in place. Paul recognized the need for dialogue and a certain level of mutual edification in ultimately sharing the gospel with the Athenians.

Contrary to this Pauline stance, the impression one has from such missionaries as Rev. Smith in the novel is that many a missionary to Africa carried the assumption that no vestige of *truth* could be found in the African communities. Mr. Brown, the congenial gentleman who respected the Igbo culture, was an exception, but even he could not extricate himself from the confines of a mindset that sought to *impose* rather than *dialogue*. Okonkwo's friend Obierika, bemoans this reality: "How can [the white man understand our customs] when he does not even speak our tongue? But he says that our customs are bad; and our own brothers who have taken up his religion also say that our customs are bad" (p. 176).[30]

Further still, the long conversations between Mr. Brown and the old man Akunna disclose Achebe's subtle intertextuality that has the "ignorant" native being the one with a more biblical understanding. Paul's claim that there was the creator of heaven and earth (Acts 17:24) finds its counterpart in Akunna's statement: "You say that there is one supreme God who made heaven and earth. . . . We also believe in Him and we call Him Chukwu. He made all the world and the other gods" (p. 179). The Athenians had the "Unknown God"; the Igbo have Chukwu. It is not Mr. Brown that comes out sounding like Paul in Athens but the old man Akunna.

Paul's initial encounter in Athens resulted in an invitation to return for further dialogue, but this was only after the subject of resurrection had struck at the chord of Athenian curiosity and thirst for new ideas (Acts 17:32). It is essentially their penchant for such "outrageous" teachings, which had been rejected elsewhere, that allows the conversation with Paul to continue. Yet, in no small measure, it was also Paul's affirmative use of their own cultural expressions ("For 'In him we live and move and have our being.' As some of your own poets have said, 'We are his offspring,'"Acts 17:28) that eliminates any antagonism with the more judgmental aspects of Paul's speech (Acts 17:30–31). The end result, we are told, is that some believed and followed Paul.

While the novel *Things Fall Apart* ends on a somber note with the disheartening suicide of the protagonist Okonkwo, who failed to adjust to the transformation of his Igbo culture following its encounter with Western culture, there seems to be more hope for the larger community. If old man Ezeudu is right, the community is able to weave into its religion and culture elements from Western Christianity perceived as beneficial without losing its identity.[31]

ENDNOTES

1. Chinua Achebe, *Things Fall Apart* (New York: Astor-Honor, 1959). Thanks is expressed for Velda Love's response to this paper which made it clear that the implications of this study can be wider than I would have envisioned.

2. Daniel Defoe, *Robinson Crusoe* (London: E. Midwater, 1718). These misconstruals hark as far back as the classical times with initial fantasies being replaced by new ones following voyages further south into the African continent. Cf. Dorothy Hammond and Alter Jablow, *The Africa That Never Was* (Prospect Heights, Ill.: Waveland, 1992).

3. Joseph Conrad, *Heart of Darkness* (New York: Barnes and Noble, 2003[1899]), 91–92. Italics mine.

4. See Chinua Achebe, "The Chancellor's Lecture Series 1974–75," *Massachusetts Review* 18.4 (1977): 782-792, subsequently published as part of a collection of essays under the title "An Image of Africa: Racism in Conrad's Heart of Darkness" in *Hopes and Impediments* (New York: Anchor, 1998), 1-20.

5. See also Joyce Cary, *Mister Johnson* (London: Victor Gollancz, 1939). See Chinua Achebe's 1998 "McMillan-Stewart Lectures" at Harvard University later published as *Home and Exile* (New York: Anchor, 2000).

6. Chinua Achebe, "The Novelist as Teacher," in *Hopes and Impediment* (New York: Anchor, 1988), 44–46.

7. Bernard McGrane, *Beyond Anthropology: Society and the Other* (New York: Columbia University Press, 1989), 52–53. Italics his.

8. Hammond and Jablow, *The Africa That Never Was*, 13–14: "The British colonial officials, missionaries, traders, settlers and even tourists used the same expressions and behaved in accordance with the preconceptions and biases of the popular tradition."

9. See Andrew M. Mbuvi, "The African Novel: An Unlikely Resource for a Socially Engaged Biblical Interpretation?" *SBL Forum* (May 2006), available at http://sbl-site.org/Article.aspx?ArticleId=527. This paper was originally given at the 2005 annual meeting of the Society of Biblical Literature.

10. Simon Gikandi, *Reading the African Novel* (London; Nairobi; Portsmouth, N. H.: James Curry, EAEP, Heinemann, 1987), x.

11. David Jefferess, "Postcolonialism's Ethical (Re)Turn: An Interview with Simon Gikandi," *Postcolonial Text* 2.1 (2006): "I want to go back and rethink what that work was, because in the postcolonial moment in which I emerged books were not read for pleasure. Pleasure was, perhaps, there, but books were seen as performing very important work and those themes in which books perform work are quite evident in almost all African literature at the moment of writing, and the moment of the word, of the scriptural economy, so as to say. So I am interested in how the novel is asked to perform a kind of social mission and to reform social lives, both during colonialism and after." This article is available at http://journals.sfu.ca/pocol/index.php/pct/article/view/464/165.

12. Ngugi wa Thiong'o, *A Grain of Wheat* (London: Heinemann, 1967).

13. Mongo Beti, *Le Pauvre Christ de Bomba* (Paris: Laffont, 1956).

14. Mongo Beti, *The Story of the Madman* (CARAF Books; Virginia: The University Press of Virginia, 2001), 164. Originally published as *Histoire du fou* (Paris: Julliard, 1994).

15. See Wole Soyinka, *The Road* (London: Oxford University Press, 1965) and Ferdinand Oyono, *Une vie de boy* (Paris: Presses Pocket, 1956). Achebe ("What Has Literature Got To Do With It?" in *Hopes and Impediments*, 167) commented, "But we must not see the role of literature only in terms of providing latent support for things as they are, for it does also offer the kinetic energy necessary for social transition and change."

16. See n. 1. This book has been translated into over thirty different languages, and over three million copies have been sold. While originally published by Heinemann in 1958, for pagination purposes the edition used here is Doubleday's Anchor edition first printed in 1994.

17. W. B. Yeats, "The Second Coming," in *The Dial* (November 1920) and in *Michael Robartes and the Dancer* (Dundrum: Cuala, 1921).

18. Chinua Achebe, "Named For Victoria, Queen of England," in *The Post-Colonial Studies Reader* (ed. Gareth Griffiths, Helen Tiffin, and Bill Ashcroft; New York: Routledge, 1995), 190–193.

19. In the description of Okonkwo's wrestling match with Amalinze the cat, reference is made to the hero who wrestled the spirit of the gods for seven days and seven nights. In this description one envisions Jacob's wrestling with the divine being in Gen 32, while the number seven resonates with its special value as the number of perfection in the Bible. In a sense, Okonkwo, who wrestles and wins his battles in life, cannot wrestle Christianity and eventually loses the battle by committing suicide.

20. "And in fairness to Umuofia it should be noted that it never went to war unless its case was clear and just and was accepted as such by its Oracle—the Oracle of the Hills and the Caves" (pp. 11–12).

21. A good example is the story of the conquest of Canaan where the rout of Israel by tiny Ai is attributed to failure to consult with the deity (Josh 6–7). Israel was defeated by the small town of Ai following its disobedience to God's warning not to go to war, even after they had achieved a great victory over a bigger Jericho since the latter was divinely sanctioned and the former was not.

22. The New Yam festival began the "new year" (p. 36). It is unclear what "year" means here. Is it Achebe's conception of a twelve-month year and as such a superimposition of a calendar year on a community that had no calendrical dating?

23. Seven drummers "possessed by the spirit of the drum," seven years of locusts, a naming ceremony happens seven market weeks after birth, and circumcision on the eighth day.

24. David Hoegberg, "Principle and Practice: The Logic of Cultural Violence in Achebe's *Things Fall Apart*," *College Literature* 26.1 (1999): 69-79, 73: "For Achebe, blind obedience to the god, whether by Okonkwo or the other elders, is not necessarily the wisest course, as it is for Abraham. Remember that Obierika, the 'man who thought about things'

(Achebe, 1959, 117), is the one elder who stays away from the killing even though he has no fatherly tie to the boy (1959, 64)."

25. Ibid.

26. C. L. Innes, *Chinua Achebe* (Cambridge: Cambridge University Press, 1990), 29.

27. Hoegberg, "Principle," 69–79.

28. V. Y. Mudimbe and B. Jewsiewicki, eds., *History Making in Africa* (Middletown, Conn.: Wesleyan University, 1993).

29. Hoegberg, "Principle," 69–79.

30. However, this needs to be balanced with the understanding that the earliest and most important works of translation of the Bible into African languages were done by European missionaries.

31. Indeed, one may surmise that this may be considered to be the case, as Africa today is hailed as home to the largest and fastest growing church in the world (whatever that means!). Missionary work is spearheaded by African missionaries whose sensibility to dialogue shapes their form and content of mission.

RESPONSE TO MBUVI

VELDA LOVE

When the Good News is used as a tool of oppression, things fall apart. Professor Andrew Mbuvi's Kenyan roots, theological training, and personal experience in Africa and in the United States lends a valuable voice to the conversation about Christianity and culture because of the long history of colonization. He raises critical issues about the history and legacy of colonization and the continuing impact of missionary endeavors in Africa.

I want to raise some questions and consider why Chinua Achebe's novel is pivotal in understanding why "things fall apart."[1]

1. Were the missionaries agents of imperialism?
2. Why did the missionary effort "fall apart" in both theory and practice in Africa?
3. What is it like to be an exile in your own country?

Insight into African religion is crucial for addressing these questions. John Mbiti, an Anglican priest who taught theology and religion for many years at Makerere University in Uganda, provides a general overview in his book *Introduction to African Religion*.[2] For the African, religion is woven into the fabric of life. Those not familiar with African religion wrongly label various aspects of its practices. Mbiti offers some helpful correctives.

1. African Religion is wrongly called ancestor worship—Africans do not worship their departed relatives. The departed relatives are believed to continue to live and to show interest in their surviving families. Families may show their belief by building shrines for the departed and placing bits of food or drink there or on the graves, and sometimes mentioning them in prayers.
2. African Religion is wrongly called superstition—a superstition is a readiness to believe and fear something without proper grounds. In African Religion much more than beliefs are involved. These beliefs are based on deep reflections and long experience.

3. African Religion is wrongly called animism or paganism. Animism means the system of belief and practices based on the idea that objects and natural phenomena are inhabited by spirits or souls. It is true that African peoples in their traditional setting acknowledge the existence of spirits, and that some of the spirits are thought to inhabit objects like trees, ponds, and rocks. It has to be seen in the context of the African view of the world in which God is considered to be supreme, and He has under him spirits and men. To say that there are spirits in the world does not mean that people's religion is only about these spirits. Christianity and Islam also acknowledge the existence of spirits, but neither of them is animism. Paganism or pagan is sometimes used as a derogatory word to describe Africans who are not followers of either Christianity or Islam. Yet there are many people in Europe and America who do not follow either of these world religions, and are often wholly irreligious, but they are never called pagans. Africans who follow African Religion are deeply religious people and it is wrong and foolish, therefore, to speak of them as pagans, or to regard their religion as paganism. Some of the world religions like Christianity and Islam have founders who started them. This is not the case with African Religion. It evolved slowly through many centuries, as people responded to the situations in their life and reflected upon their experiences.[3]

Given the complexity of encountering new cultures, one cannot successfully share the good news of the gospel without first learning who the people are, what their customs and traditions have been, and how they view religion and experience God and the world. What is the story of a people with a history and purpose? Dr. Mbuvi uses Chinua Achebe's novel as a source for understanding and a foundation for how the "dialogue model of mission" would have been useful when encountering the people of Igbo. It is clear from Achebe's novel that missional activity is approached by Europeans who operate out of an assumption of cultural, intellectual, religious, and moral superiority.

An additional question we may ask is whether Western Christianity was a disguise for instituting colonialism and white rule based on an assumption of cultural superiority. When a group of people assume their ways of being and thinking are dominant, they have developed an attitude that makes them believe they are superior. That feeling of superiority implies that others who operate differently are inferior. The group believes its race, gender, knowledge, scholarship, religious beliefs, and government are superior and have authority over others. When Christian missionaries began immigrating to Africa from Europe, they were under the assumption that their methods of evangelism were superior, and, therefore, Africans were inferior. This assumption of European superiority was birthed during the Enlightenment period of industrialization and absolute monarchy in England, Scotland, and Spain. The expression "enlightened absolutism" came from this era. Because absolutism is about one's perceptions of what truth is for them, their country, their church, and their people, absolute truth is the contention that in a particular domain of thought all statements in that domain are either absolutely true or absolutely false.[4] Mbuvi highlights this belief by quoting Bernard McGrane, who in reflecting on Defoe's *Robinson Crusoe* describes the nature of the missional Christianity that emerged in the post-Enlightenment period: "The truth of the savages, the cannibals, is that either God allows them or condemns them to live falseness, to live in a cruel, barbarous, unholy life. In the Enlightenment . . . the truth of the non-European Other is that he manifests the false, he makes manifest true ignorance and error, true unenlightenment."[5] Mbuvi correctly observes that this is a form of Christianity not disposed towards dialogue with the other since it had already determined the other to possess not an ounce of truth.

Defoe offers his readers an arrogant and incorrect portrayal of Africans. An assumption of superiority is not a thing of the past. In this present age we experience the same kind of assumptions based on race, gender, religion, age, and other aspects of life that create difference. Shortly after Sept. 11, 2001, Madeline Bunting wrote, "The U.S. founding recipe of Puritanism and enlightenment bequeathed a profound sense of being morally good. This superiority, once allied to economic and technological power, underpinned the world excesses of colonialism . . ."[6] To emphasize this point she quoted a statement made by Silvio Berlusconi (former prime minister to Italy) on the superiority of Western civilization and the conflict between Islam and Christianity. He stated, "Their values, or many of them, contradict ours. We think ours are better."[7]

Achebe spent an incredible amount of time in his novel allowing us to encounter the village in Umuofia, Okonkwo (a member of the Igbo clan), family obligations, and religious practices, some of which may resemble Christian traditions. In chapter after chapter we are invited into the lives of the people who inhabit the village. We witness the internal struggles of African village life, its customs, and its traditions, which are strange to the outside world. The Igbo recognize the changes taking place among them, evidenced in the elder's dialogue about what is and is no longer necessary to observe. Achebe deliberately detailed who the *ndichie* (the elders) were, what the *Egwugwu* (an ancestral spirit from the underworld) and other Igbo spirits mean to the people, and how offenses are judged and settled. But it is Okonkwo who captures our attention, a man embroiled in internal struggle. He is both a metaphor and an example of one who operates out of an attitude and mode of absolutism. Achebe's narrative approach and *Weltanshuung* invite us into the Igbo village where we also learn about their belief in a supreme creator, *Chukwu*, who made all things.

Achebe has created a "dialogue model of mission," as Prof. Mbuvi has made clear in explaining Paul's mission to Athens in Acts 17:15–34. Although Paul was distressed to see Athens full of idols, he did not see the people merely as heathens. He was just overwhelmed by the customs in which they chose to worship—idolatry. Even though overwhelmed by the idolatry, Paul observed that the people are religious: "Athenians, I see how extremely religious you are in every way. For as I went through the city and looked carefully at the objects of your worship, I found among them an altar with the inscription, 'To an unknown god.'" This observation of the 'unknown god' gives Paul an opportunity to proclaim the Christian message. The God who made the world and everything in it, he who is Lord of heaven and earth . . ." (Acts 17:22–25; see also Gen 1:1; and Ps 24:1). Additionally Paul quoted Greek poets to make his point. His understanding of mission work was never related to commerce, conquest, or colonialism. He was clear about his role as a witness, a teacher, and a proclaimer of the good news of Jesus Christ. Paul's evangelism met with conflict; he and his colleagues faced hostility, death threats, jail, and persecution from his own and from those he sought to convert. However, Paul treated the cultures he encountered as human; he never demonized them, destroyed their sense of dignity, denigrated their sense of worth, or tried to change their identity.

I embrace Mbuvi's understanding of Achebe's rationale for a dialogue model of mission, as opposed to the ways in which missions has been used to colonize people. Instead of one dominant culture model, for Christians there is a compelling alternative for our coexistence on an increasingly crowded planet. Madeline Bunting points to the premise of the political philosopher Bhikhu Parekh: "The grandeur and depth of human life is too great to be captured in one culture. That each culture nurtures and develops some dimension of being human, but in that process it misses out on others, and that progress will always come from dialogue between cultures. We are all prisoners of subjectivity . . . and that is true of all of us individually and collectively, so we need others to expose our blindnesses and to increase our understanding of our humanity."[8]

My own encounter with Christianity at times has been a challenge as it relates to assumptions of superiority. As an African American woman I have lived with the tension of being labeled a "minority." Society, including the Christian church, perpetuates its use of words that categorize people of color (those of non-European heritage) to a subordinate lower class on every level: social, educational, intellectual, and religious. African Americans are considered people of color whose ethnic and race difference places us beneath Europeans and European Americans who are labeled the "majority" or "dominant culture." As long as I can remember, my encounter with the Christian church has never been one that directly or indirectly challenged the labels or names created for us. As African Americans we are members of God's church, yet because of white supremacy we are expected to answer to and incorporate these labels into our understanding of who we are as creations of God. But, as I study the Old and New Testaments, the Christian faith, and the good news, they indicate that *all* are worthy of being called *very good*. I am part of humanity and the body of Christ, and as an African American woman, considered equal to God's other *very good* creation—man. Therefore, I propose as of today that we, the Christian church, no longer adhere to terms, labels, and categories that are used as tools of oppression, separating us as believers and denying us the power of God to proclaim the good news to all persons of every race and culture. In order to impact all people and the Christian church in particular as God intended, our dialogue should no longer include terms that create political and anthropological divisions such as "minority," "subcultures," or "subordinate," for we are one in the body of Christ. I also propose we will no longer adhere to an assumption of superiority and white supremacy ideology because no group of people legitimately is a dominant culture. We are the multitude from every nation, tribe, people, and language. When we live into this reality, then the good news of the gospel will truly be good news for all of humanity.

ENDNOTES

1. Chinua Achebe, *Things Fall Apart* (New York: Anchor, 1994).
2. John S. Mbiti, *Introduction to African Religion* (2d ed.; Oxford: Heinemann, 1975).
3. Ibid., 16.
4. Enlightened absolutism is also known as benevolent or enlightened despotism.
5. Bernard McGrane, *Beyond Anthropology: Society and the Other* (New York: Columbia University Press, 1989), 52–53.
6. Madeline Bunting, "The West's Arrogant Assumption of Its Superiority is as Dangerous as Any Other Form of Fundamentalism," *The Guardian of London* (8 October, 2001), available at http://commondreams.org/views01/1008-01.htm, accessed Sept. 28, 2007.
7. Ibid.
8. Ibid., 2.

GLOBAL CULTURAL TRAFFIC, CHRISTIAN MISSION, AND BIBLICAL INTERPRETATION: REREADING LUKE 10:1–12 THROUGH THE EYES OF AN INDIAN MISSION RECIPIENT

SATHIANATHAN CLARKE

"For, in fact, the kingdom of God is (neither among nor within but) between you."[1]

"At every meal that we eat together, freedom is invited to sit down. The chair remains vacant, but the place is set."[2]

"Then people will come from east and west, from north and south, and will eat in the kingdom of God. Indeed, some are last who will be first, and some are first who will be last." (Luke 13:29–30)

The twenty-first century continues to witness the shrinking of our globe. Of course, the size of the world has remained the same, but every person and every locality has become so interrelated that access across the many continents has become relatively easy. Thus, it is customary to talk of our human life together in terms of one common global family. The economic implications of unfettered market exchange and movement of goods and capital in such a flat world are widely known.[3] Globalization also has profound cultural effects in our modern world. J. Tomlinson depicts the interconnection succinctly: "Globalization lies at the heart of modern culture; cultural practices lie at the heart of globalization."[4] We are becoming increasingly conscious of the complex networks that facilitate the amazing interchange of cultural objects around the world. As A. Appadurai rightly reminds us, "These objects include ideas and ideologies, people and goods, images and messages, technologies and techniques."[5] To some extent such interchange of "objects in motion" is the outcome of short term (tourist, mission, and business trips) and long term (immigration and sustained employment) movement of peoples from one geographical location to another. To a large degree though, such cultural traffic gets around the entire world via gateways of the internet, cables of television providers, and airwaves of radio stations.

The exchange of religious information often piggybacks on the expansive and interpenetrative cultural interflow made possible within this modern, complex, far-reaching, and efficient communication system. Notionally one may argue that this communication empire flattens the world into one level cultural playing field. Realistically though there can be no doubt that some parts of the world have much more control over others when it comes to the process and content of what gets circulated as religious and cultural information. Thus, while globalization has provided for international networks of interconnectivity to enhance free flow of cultural "objects in motion," at the same time such traffic is controlled by the economic and political "world of structures."[6] There are many ways in which one can analyze the inequity built into the flow of cultural traffic. Cultural and religious ideas need economic capital to aid uninhibited and effective circulation. Thus, Western media tends to penetrate the rest of the world much more forcefully and dexterously than the other way around. Also, cultural and religious emissaries require travel packages and permits to enable movement of embodied theological beliefs and social practices. Procuring visas for short term interreligious and intercultural exposures are easier when traveling from developed nations to the rest of the world than when people wish to travel from developing nations to any other country in the world. Travel to most developing nations from countries in the South or East is expensive, cumbersome, and problematic. Global cultural traffic is structurally predisposed to flow much more copiously from developing Western locations towards less developed non-Western sites. The developing nations thus become more vulnerable to being saturated with the cultural and religious beliefs and practices of the United States and Europe. This sponginess of developing nations must be interpreted within the less penetrable world that characterizes the developed nations.

Let me situate this discussion within the more familiar and manageable context of cross-cultural exchange between India and the United States of America. As an Indian living in the United States I am struck by the relative ease with which Western Christians can gain access into the inner interreligious and multicultural world of Indian communities. On June 15, 2007, I was at an event that screened a video documenting a group of sincere and fervent American Christians on a very short "mission trip" to India. There were many moving and gracious encounters between these Western Christians and different segments of local Indian communities. However, one encounter has stayed with me. It brought together the interlinking of culture, the Bible, and mission in a strange way. Let me narrate this encounter as best as I remember.

The camera zoomed in on a supposed mission event. The visiting Americans got off the minivan in which they were traveling and made their way toward the local people that had gathered outside their homes. Both sides in this encounter had very little idea about the other. Without wasting much time the

Americans got straight to the point. They did not appear too interested in whom they were approaching, what questions these Indians might have for them, or what their situation in life might be. They were bursting with information that they needed to deposit in the community: Jesus loved them all, he was the God that saves all human beings, and the Bible testified to this divine revelation. They settled upon a middle-aged gentleman. They held a Bible to him and told him about the truth of Jesus Christ that was contained in it. All of this was done in English. The local gentleman spoke to them in Tamil, my native language, which enabled me to follow both the missionary's communication in English and the respondent's articulation in Tamil. The man said that he did read the Bible even though he was a Hindu. The American did not know what was being said to him, and the native translator did not share this fact. Perhaps he did not want to ruin the American's elated presumption that he was the bearer of wholly new good news! He had come with this gospel and wanted to give it to the local Indian. Once the missive was orally communicated the swift emissary went on to ask if he could pray with the gentleman. A courteous nod permitted the American to offer an English prayer in the power of the Holy Spirit and though the name of Jesus. The parting gift was a promise to get a Bible to him, quite ignorant that this Hindu gentleman had already informed him that he was reading the Bible, presumably in Tamil. The team got back into the minivan and left as quickly as they came. They were filled with joy that they had preached the good news to an eager non-Christian who could now very well be on the salvation path. While the characteristic porosity of the local South Indian community reemerged visibly in this encounter, I was also struck by the not-so-Western mannerism of these Americans. Quite unlike what they would have done in any downtown American city, they confidently entered into the private world of another society to entreat them to accept their religious views and prayed for them in public.

Although somewhat of a generalization, since I have only lived in three cosmopolitan cities on the east coast of the United States during a period of about twelve years, I have concluded that urban Western living can be distinguished from my own Indian situation by the solid fences erected around its inhabitance. It is anticipated that such invisible borders will protect the sacredness of primary relationships of families and communal associations from infringement by the rest of society. Great awareness for preserving individual and familial space makes it difficult to permeate the inner provinces of communities in the United States. Ask any lonely foreigner who mistakes the American greeting "Hi, how're you doing?" as a God-sent word of deep concern and sincerely stops the greeter to explain the rough time she is experiencing through the week. It took me some time to realize that this was only a rhetorical question. I have now finally learnt not to repeat the cultural mistake of taking such ritual, public greeting as a personal inquiry into my real, private world. One is not expected to fuse the private and the public in the

United States. I recall a mild reprimand that I received from my Senior Warden at an Episcopal church on the outskirts of Boston in which I served as an Interim Priest in the 1990s. Just as I would do in India I was persuasively inviting myself into the homes of newcomers to pray with them and get to know them as members of my church family. One newcomer approached the Senior Warden for help with this unsolicited pastoral advance! She pleaded for distinct boundaries that would protect the separation between church and home. The Warden, who had much affection and respect for me, approached me with warmth and wisdom. He gently suggested that it would be better for me to wait for an invitation from the families in the parish before I offered pastoral home visits. I backed off from entering the private world of my parish members. They won the right to guard their own private space, and I became increasingly confined to the preassigned public space of the church and the parish hall.

The human desire to relate with the world family in more intimate ways is both a human necessity and Christian obligation. The invitation to Christian mission is a good example inasmuch as it stirs us toward engendering a life of well-being, health, and wholesomeness (salvation) in the world. Whether conceived of as local or global, mission is understood as a sending forth to engage and permeate the world of concrete communities, often quite different from one's own, with the new life gifted by Jesus Christ. Christian mission, as I understand it, involves Christ sending forth the church in the power of the Holy Spirit both to scatter and gather up the reign of God in the real world of economic, political, cultural, and religious similarities and differences. Two aspects of mission are relevant to our discussion concerning this self-expending and world-saturating Christian vocation. First, the dismantling of the self-protecting propensity of the church becomes the fulcrum for the life-promoting mission of God's reign. Bevans and Schroeder put this forcefully: "The point of the Church is not the Church. The Church can only be the Church if it is poised toward the kingdom. . . . The Church is missionary by its very nature."[7] Second, the complex world of distinct peoples and communities is already a domain in which the Triune God is operational because of God's overflowing love for all of creation. The church thus participates in, rather than initiates, Christian mission. D. Bosch must be credited for systematizing this new way of missional thinking more than twenty-five years ago. He states, "[M]ission is not primarily an activity of the Church, but an attribute of God. God is a missionary God. . . . Mission is thereby seen as a movement from God to the world. . . . To participate in mission is to participate in the movement of God's love toward people, since God is the fountain of sending love."[8] J. A. Kirk discernibly invokes the language of travel when asserting that "going and being in the heart of the world is the essence of mission." He urges that "Christians are to travel *into* the heart of the world, being at the points of suffering and need, and *towards* God's new creation."[9]

Although not the only model of cross-cultural mission, the temptation to ride economic and cultural privilege in order to propagate one's own faith in alien lands has a long and colorful history. There is now, I believe, a reasonably reliable consensus that calculated connivance with aggressive and exploitative imperial powers is a spurious and inexcusable method of religious expansion. A healthy debate persists regarding which Christian missions can be rightly accused of such unchristian, expansionist tactics. Yet, there is hardly any mission scholar in academic circles who is willing to defend the position that such violent and coercive methods can be justified in our resolve to fulfill the exhortation of Christ spoken in the form of a parable in which the master says to the slaves, "Go out into the roads and lanes, and *compel* people to come in, so that my house may be filled" (Luke 14:23). At a somewhat more widespread though subtle level, one must also be aware of the numerous strategies of cross-cultural mission that quite unconsciously gain mileage from the power embedded in one's own geographical and socio-economic location. In the global world of cultural traffic in which we find ourselves I would submit that any form of Christian mission that does not interrogate the power dimensions that facilitate the cultural and religious encounter between the self and the other becomes susceptible to covertly furthering colonial objectives.

We have analyzed our twenty-first-century world as characterized by a comprehensive, complex, and efficient system of global cultural traffic. We have also noted that this global cultural and religious communication system manifests tendencies of boundary fluidity among certain Indian communities and border calcification among some communities in the United States of America. Further, we noted a certain asymmetry in the influence of this communication arrangement. The economic and technical capital of the developed countries breed communication inequity so as to allow religious and cultural beliefs and practices to flow more copiously from the west/north to the east/south rather than the other way around. Both in terms of intercultural exchange among locations and peoples in different parts of the world and with regard to moving from the confines of the Western church community into the public lives of secular society or privatized homes, Christian mission involves moving outward toward the whole of life in the world. If Christian mission involves crossing church boundaries to accompany the movement of God into the real world of all peoples within the totality of their life, the issue of reimagining the role and objective of our mission vocations becomes pertinent and crucial. In the biblical interpretation that follows I shall address the matter of how the north/west can passionately, though responsibly, be involved in cross-cultural mission in our present global context that was just delineated.

Luke's narrative of the mission of the seventy (or seventy-two)[10] contained in Luke 10:1–12 may throw light on this matter of cross-cultural scattering and gathering up of the reign of God made available in the good news of Jesus Christ.

Even if it does not anticipate present-day international or transcontinental challenges of mission, it can be made to offer suggestions for cross-cultural, probably even interreligious, mission encounters. The Indian hues that embellish this biblical interpretation will be striking. Also, I admit to honoring a prior commitment to reread this text from the point of view of the recipients of mission rather than the Christian missioner, but there can be no denying that what I have imbibed from studying, ministering, and living in the United States will also influence my interpretation of this Lukan account.[11]

FROM SECURE LOCATION TO MISSION DISPLACEMENT

Christian mission is Jesus' invitation to be caught up in God's centrifugal (from Latin *centrum*, "center," and *fugere*, "to flee") dynamic that moves outward into countless regions of the world and variegated spheres of people's lives. It means going anywhere and everywhere that "Jesus himself intended to go" (Luke 10:1) for the sake of actualizing and announcing the proximity of the reign of God. It is important to highlight that "Jesus confirms their [the disciples] role as active brokers of the reign of God,"[12] which sprouts and spreads in conformity with the movement of God. It may be necessary to interrogate the suggestion that this passage marks a fundamental shift in Jesus' mission plan from one that was labyrinthine, diffuse, and need-specific to one that is linear, predesigned, and rule-governed. According to this view, the appointing and sending of this delegation of the seventy signifies a decisive change in the course of Jesus' mission from a peripatetic and circuitous mission ("I must proclaim the good news of the kingdom to other cities also; for I was sent for this purpose," Luke 4:43) to one that is much more linear and goal-directed ("his face was set toward Jerusalem," Luke 9:53). However, even a cursory study of Jesus' travel after this passage in Luke 10 makes one aware that Jesus' itinerary develops through a process of mediation between the external needs of local communities and his internal allegiance to embrace the way of the cross that would lead to his death outside of Jerusalem. James L. Resseguie has recently argued, in line with Karl Ludwig Schmidt (1919), that "although Jesus journeys to Jerusalem he never really makes any progress.... Thus, Luke's journey [even from Luke 9:51 onward] is not simply a pilgrimage from Galilee to Jerusalem."[13]

In the light of the crisscrossing flow of intercultural traffic in our own world, I too would want to interpret this mission journey by the seventy, not so much as a linear and single goal-directed expedition with Jesus on a predetermined path, but one undertaken on behalf of Jesus for the sake of the reign of God wherever this may need to be manifested. There is a certain freedom for the emissaries that can be read into this dispersal when Jesus says, "Go on *your* way" (Luke 10:3a). In fact, even while the passage communicates unambiguously that

Jesus sent his emissaries "ahead of him . . . to every place and town where he himself intended to go" (Luke 10:1b), we are led to conclude from their joyous return to Jesus at the end of this mission that he did not follow through on his intention. The emissaries had become the inlet of the reign of God on behalf of Jesus. For us, it means going on our way anywhere and everywhere that Jesus intends to go. There is no doubt a countercultural vector to this suggestion of mission vocation. The widely circulated U.S. mantra to buy into stability and security through procuring good real estate is simple and appealing: "location, location, location." Jesus' call to mission suggests a reversal to the objective of the world: displacement, redeployment, relocation. Crossan makes this connection vividly: "Itinerant radicalism means that one's itinerancy or even vagrancy is a programmatic part of one's radical message."[14] Jesus invites us into the dynamics of God's movement outward into the interiority of people's lives. This may require a willingness to move from the privilege of secure location and reliable routing to the hazard of displacement and redeployment for actualizing and announcing the reign of God anywhere and everywhere.

BOUNDARY CROSSERS RISK HOSTILITY AND ACCEPT VULNERABILITY

Christian mission, inasmuch as it involves crossing of boundaries, can entail conflict, even hostility: "I am sending you out like lambs into the midst of wolves" (Luke 10:3). In the context of global cultural traffic patterns we might point out that such resistance for gracious entry into local communities may come as much from our Western neighbors as from communities that live in regions far away. No doubt, this passage must be seen within the overall context of Luke's emphasis on the inevitability of persecution of Jesus and his disciples. Jesus and his emissaries find themselves in a "persecutional interlock," within a cycle of rejection, hostility, and persecution as they go public with the mission of God.[15] Such impending hostility is not to be a deterrent but rather part of the challenge of mission. For many Indians the language of lambs and wolves is problematic when referring to Christian mission. It serves to bolster the mistaken idea that foreign Christian missioners are always sheep and the peoples that inhabit the regions where they arrive are mostly wolves. While sometimes this may have been the case, we are aware through a critical study of mission history that there were other times in which Christian missioners were the wolves gone wild among vulnerable sheep. Particularly when they came with the protection of colonial explorers and rulers, Christian missioners aggressively and assertively entered into many communities as fearlessly as wolves. Once in the mission field such culture wolves also attacked religion and hungered for economic gain.

Yet, if one reads this passage creatively, one can make the argument that Jesus was referring to his disciples as lambs because he assumed that they would travel nonviolently into communities that may have had access to weapons of missioner destruction (WMDs!). It is fair to assume that there can be both sheep and wolves among both the missioners and the recipients of mission. While we can posit that all complex systems of exchange have a mix of wolves, sheep, and sheep-wolves, this biblical passage may help us discern facets that make the missioners sheep rather than wolf. In obedience to Jesus they are to "carry no purse, no bag, no sandals." This is the vulnerability that identifies missioners as sheep. The prohibitions in a way are connected with the travelers' vulnerability because of which they are like sheep.[16] Those who arrive with purses full of currency and credit cards to circumvent dependence on the host community, with bags capable of containing weapons to overpower the people that welcome, and with sandals that buffer the experience of walking where the people walk are more likely to be wolves in sheep's clothing.

While creatively working though knotty biblical sayings, it may be beneficial to inquire into the intriguing instruction "Greet no one on the road" (Luke 10:4b). In general, from a mindset of Western efficiency this can be interpreted as getting on with the mission that must be accomplished without distractions on the way, but the idea that one can be impolite and insensitive en route to achieving the goals of peace, mutual hospitality, and healing is absurd. Harmonizing of means and ends is an important goal for Christian mission. From my own Indian communitarian cultural backdrop this instruction of Jesus can mean something more attuned to his life and ministry. First, the directive not to greet anyone on the road may indeed be construed as a warning against shallow and superficial communication with strangers when one assumes the commission of going on behalf of Jesus. Thus, while it may have been said by Jesus to discourage fleeting and simulated greetings, it does not forbid deep conversation. Second, the point of this mission is to travel into the depth of human interrelationships. Thus, mission encounters are to pervade the intimate spaces of the family and the community. Notice that Jesus specifies that they will be entering houses (v. 5) and towns (v. 8). It is in the intimate, familiar, and secure locus of the recipients of mission that this cultural and religious exchange ought to take place, and, indeed, this can engender conflict and even hostility.

THE AROMA OF CHRISTIAN MISSION:
SELF-GIVING LOVE AND PEACE THAT CAN BE EXCHANGED

M. K. Gandhi as early as 1931 implored Christian missionaries to reflect the "aroma of Christianity." In a colonial historical context Gandhi lifted up the peaceful and subtle transformation that Christianity could accomplish. "I have a definite feeling that if you want us to feel the aroma of Christianity, you must copy the rose. The rose irresistibly draws people to itself, and the scent remains with it."[17] That the rose is also a widely accepted symbol of love is relevant to this discussion. Though he was explicitly undercutting the vociferous nature of verbal proclamation, Gandhi was also implicitly urging them to exemplify the actions of love.

Thus the energy of self-giving love and explicit exchange of mutual peace are marks that accompany Christian mission. "Every town and place" where Jesus "intended to go" must be entered into by those who go on his behalf with the spirit that he exemplifies and confers on them. The disciples were slow to learn this about the Jesus mission. Jesus had just rebuked his disciples for getting this wrong. They were ready "to command fire to come down from heaven and consume" those who did not receive Jesus (Luke 9:54b). Tannehill uses language of "abuse of power" and "defective disciple" when commenting on this incident: "James and John's suggestion is an abuse of the power that Jesus had given them. . . . It broadens the portrait of defective disciples begun in 9:45–50."[18] This could well have triggered drastic change of mission personnel. Jesus aborted the former mission and started anew by immediately sending out another seventy. Luke 10:1–12 is linked to the former narrative by the phrase "After this the Lord appointed seventy others and sent them on ahead of him" (Luke 10:1). The "after this" clearly refers to the called-off Samaritan mission in Luke 9:51–56. This mission encounter does involve a refusal of the Samaritans to receive Jesus. In this narrative the refusal "is not related to Jesus' racial background. He is rejected simply because he is on his way to Jerusalem."[19]

The difference in the centrality of sacred sites between the Jews and the Samaritans is critical to comprehend this rejection. Mount Gerizim rather than Jerusalem was the center of religious cult for the Samaritans. Thus, they refused to accept Jesus' resolve to journey toward Jerusalem. He was not their Messiah. Jesus' displeasure with the former mission venture did not stem from the Samaritans' refusal to welcome him. After all, every people has a right to say no to the request for hospitality. Rather, the Samaritan mission was abandoned because two of the disciples, James and John, did not grasp the spirit of Jesus' boundary-crossing mission. The "sons of thunder" misread the self-giving love of Jesus that was moving toward emptying his life for the world on the cross. Instead, they wanted to invoke the dramatic effects of the "shock and awe" approach, which wished divine obliteration of those who decided to be religiously different. The rebuke of Jesus in the end is turned upon his own disciples rather than on the Samaritans. They had not grasped the central motif and meaning of Jesus' mission of the reign of God. He tried all over again by commissioning "seventy others."[20]

Just as self-giving love implicitly fuels the Jesus mission, peace is proffered to be its overtly accompanying proposition. Entry into the intimate and protective space of every house ("whatever house you enter" v. 5) is done in the name of peace. Peace is publicly announced as the first word. Peace is also an energy that has the capability of being exchanged between the hosts and the mission guest. In fact, I wish to read the words that follow this peace announcement as suggesting the possibility of mutual sharing of peace. "Anyone who shares in peace" indicates a generic gift. If this peace was specifically brought by the emissaries it would have read "anyone who shares in *your* peace." Thus each party brings the gifts of peace to the intimate and deep cultural and religious encounter. The scattering and the gathering motif that I proposed in explicating the dynamic of the mission of the reign of God is connected with this giving and receiving of peace. The notion that those who accept this peace will receive "your peace . . . but if not it will return to you" may be interpreted negatively to mean that the hosts are left with no peace. However, it can also be construed positively: peace, when exchanged in the sacred interior of intimate relational spaces, always generates more peace.

DEPTH, BREADTH, AND LENGTH COULD BE DIMENSIONS THAT MATTER IN MISSION

Cross-cultural mission encounters are meant to be substantial, entrenched, and perhaps even protracted. There is a difference between excursion and mission. It is noteworthy that the first instruction given by Jesus after the emissaries are told of the possibility that the hosts may not "share in peace" is that they are to "remain in the same house" (Luke 10:7a). This extended time is to be cemented by receiving whatever food and drink is provided by the hosts. The emissaries are expected to be governed by the economic realities and cultural (religious?) patterns of the hosts. In India, as was true in first-century Palestine, such table fellowship is a complex social ritual. Meals semaphore social, economic, and cultural relationships. They mirror socio-economic arrangements, but they also are a canvas on which changes in such relationships can be experimentally initiated. Receiving food and drink from another community was a symbolic act of accepting them as equals. Not receiving such offerings of food and drink symbolized rejection of the hosts. Jesus had his emissaries enter the heart of the public-private and secular-sacred space of the local house and community.

This had radical implications for Jewish missioners since it may well be a forewarning to his emissaries that they will need to break the purity code that kept them apart from Gentiles. "If we see this whole section as prefiguring the Gentile mission, then Luke's Jesus by implication rejects Jewish food laws for later disciples."[21] This is quite consistent with the view that Jesus' table fellowship included sinners, the economically disadvantaged, and social outcasts. Craig Blomberg does a remarkable job of marshalling evidence to establish that Jesus did infringe on certain purity codes to expand God's hospitality to social outcasts.

Germane to our discussion on mission as radical hospitality, Blomberg contends that Jesus practiced something he calls "contagious holiness." Thus, instead of accepting the prevalent view that he would be contaminated by eating and drinking with social outcasts, Jesus believed that his holiness (wholeness or peace) would "rub off on them and change them for the better. Cleanliness, he believe[d], is even more 'catching' than uncleanness; morality more influential than immorality."[22]

S. Kappen highlights the economic implications of such table fellowship advocated by Jesus. While imaginatively reconfiguring the table fellowship promoted by Jesus he states: "Here the products of labor—food and drink—are not commodities but gifts. What is given in freedom mediates the mutual love of the giver and the recipient. As such, it binds the many into one, into one community."[23] Giving and receiving of food and drink in the cause of Christian mission turns transactions of commodities (market economy) into exchanges of gifts (sacramental concord). In the Indian context, where commensality between caste communities and Dalit (untouchable) communities is severely restricted because of the fear of pollution and the need to protect economic distance, this stipulation for table fellowship has prophetic implications. It provides a preview of a transformed community with new patterns of human solidarity that offer a radical social and economic alternative to the present world [dis]order. This is also a challenge for North Americans traveling around the world in the name of Jesus Christ and for the sake of the reign of God. It calls for simplicity of lifestyle, humility to accept hospitality, and willingness to do something about tables without sufficient food and drink in other locations of the world. It is also relevant to notice that such hospitality is sustained and long drawn out. Fly by night, express, incarnation-free, and hit-and-run modes of good news heralding hardly effect organic transformation. Jesus warned against such flighty mission agents: "Remain in the same house . . . do not go from house to house" (Luke 10:7).

COMPLEMENTARITIES OF POWERFUL DEEDS AND EXPECTANT WORDS IN CROSS-CULTURAL MISSION

Cross-cultural exchanges, which have mission objectives and life enhancing prospects, necessarily need to mediate between deeds and word. The spreading out and gathering together of the reign of God in the world of cross-cultural interflow depends upon both peaceful entry by the bearers of good news and a spirit of spontaneous welcome by the receiving host communities. We have seen how this is semaphored in the giving and receiving around table fellowship. Reciprocal food transaction symbolizes the interchange of mutual respect, socio-ethnic honor, economic aspiration, and cultural acceptance. Thus, peaceable entry and wholesome welcome are preconditions for intercultural and interreligious encounters that have transformative effects on the life of the community. Once this reciprocity has been established the emissaries of Jesus are charged to "cure the sick who are there" (Luke 10:9a). Meals partaken and healing mediated under the canopy of peace signal the proximity of God's reign. It is after these gospel performances that the word is proclaimed: "The Kingdom of God has come near to you."

I am struck by the fact that proclamation comes after peaceable reception, mutual hospitality, and complementary healing. It is within this configuration of newness of life—manifested through bringing peace to the household, creating mutual acceptance through table fellowship, and effecting healing of the sick—that the good news of the kingdom's immediacy is announced. The general assertion of Paul Minear that through the whole of Luke "table fellowship interpreted by table talk constitutes the gospel"[24] may have to be changed in this context to conclude that table fellowship and complementary healing precede proclamation of the gospel. The word that is proclaimed seems no more than a statement of what has happened in this profound exchange: God's reign is closer than one expects and imagines. It is interesting that this good news does not eulogize Jesus, nor does it make pious God acclamations. It announces that the reign of God is available here and now through God's gracious gifts sent by Jesus: gifts of gracious peace, mutual acceptance of different persons through table fellowship, generous healing, and proclamation of the reassurance that God is close at hand. One must not get literal about interpreting Jesus' instructions sequentially, but the interrelationship between being sent, arrival, receptivity, humility, hospitality, healing, invitation, and proclamation cannot be missed in Jesus' mission tutorial.

THE CHALLENGE OF INJECTING RECIPROCITY IN CHRISTIAN MISSION

You may already have easily detected my unembarrassed effort to read reciprocity into this interpretation of Christian mission. Let me end this interpretation by stretching this text to do more for this objective, quite aware that I am taking some imaginative leaps. A resource to read reciprocity into this mission episode comes from Koenig's proposal that "Indeed, the goal for Luke on this issue is a cooperative missionary effort characterized by a fluidity in host and guest roles on the part of travelers and residents alike."[25] Of course, he is not suggesting that Luke was envisioning an interreligious sharing of table fellowship and table talk. Yet, this may have to be part of cross-cultural mission when one feels strongly about the possibility of reciprocity of peace, shared fellowship, healing, and proclamation showing that "the kingdom of God has come near." I may even push this further. If cross-cultural emissaries' task includes promoting of peace, "proclaiming the reign of God and healing (10:9), and also, apparently, looking for co-workers to help the harvest"[26] of these fruits, then such resourcing for the approaching kingdom may involve changeability between the role of mission bearers and mission recipients.[27] Recruitment for kingdom mission also takes place among the hosts who have shared peace, participated in ritual acceptance of each other through table fellowship, experienced healing, and testify that the reign of God is near. In a kingdom economy in which "some are last who will be first, and some are first who will be last" (Luke 13:30) surely role reversals between hosts and guests will not only be possible but highly likely.

Rescuing reciprocity will also involve shielding the hosts of mission when they politely refuse to convert to the worldview of the mission guests. Reciprocity in acknowledging disagreement with the other's conviction needs to be guaranteed before, during, and after any cross-cultural mission encounter. Something needs to be done about the less-than-gracious ending of this passage in which those who disagree with the mission emissaries are threatened with destruction. This tilt toward violence seems both out of sync with the thematic progression of peace, hospitality, and healing, and uncharacteristic when one takes seriously the compassion with which Jesus sent his emissaries into the world that he loved so much. The symbolic violence against those who do not welcome them is unmistakable: "Even the dust of your town that clings to our feet, we wipe off in protest against you. . . . I tell you, on that day, it will be more tolerable for Sodom than for that town." As a form of "acted parable against those rejecting them"[28] this anticipates an actual incidence in which Paul and Barnabas "shook the dust off their feet in protest against" those "who stirred up persecution" on account of their ministry (Acts 13:50, 51). How can one retain the graciousness that exemplifies this mission narrative as well as retain elements of a nonviolent God that energized Jesus? From my working in India, where often evangelists and social activists travel barefooted, I can attest that it is not easy to gather enough dust on one's feet. Thus, while one can wipe dust off by using water and/or a towel, one will find it hard to demonstrably shake off dust from one's feet. This may offer us an alternate interpretation. Either the emissaries have to work long and hard enough in the town so as to be able to gather dust on their feet, which in a manner of speaking means infinitely, or when Jesus' emissaries leave a town in frustration they can only take such symbolic action against the inhabitants of the town, which will not become effective since there can never be dust perceptibly shaken off from one's feet. The "on that day . . . for that town" may indeed imply a future continuous sense or may merely be an ironic symbolic charade. My contextual rereading resonates with Tannehill who underscores the notion that, rather than be thought of as "prediction of the future," this use of "forceful language" was "meant to crack the complacency of these [specific] towns."[29]

CONCLUSION

As a conclusion for this seminar on Bible interpretation it may be relevant to offer a couple of brief and sketchy reflective comments on what I take to be the assumptions that drive this essay. The first identifies fragments of a hermeneutic model that may have some value beyond this contextual and imaginative rereading of Luke 10:1–12. Three distinctive factors appear to be operational through my own biblical interpretation: canon sense, culture sense, and common sense. *Canon sense* is a dominant prejudgment I bring to every interaction with Scripture. The deference that I bring to the Bible as worthy of such canon sense is both secure and fragile. It is secure because it is dependent on what I freely bring to my interaction with this library of texts. One can further say that this is not only a personal gift that I offer in biblical interpretation. It is vetted by a diverse cluster of Christian communities and reinforced by the resistance that the Bible puts up to being co-opted. It is fragile because it needs to be established as relevant and true in a concrete world that I inhabit with people who do not give the Bible the same authority. Thus, I feel compelled to transform the notional given of canon sense into concrete demonstrable expressions. Furthermore, how one lets the Bible speak is also determined by which texts are made to speak in what way. It is hardly a self-interpreting book.

Culture sense travels with/within me as an interpreter to determine the manner in which Scripture is comprehended by the specific and local worldview that I also ascribe to, both consciously and unconsciously. It is also a source of knowledge of material and spiritual matters. Culture sense tends to rise in importance when it is attacked or ignored in interpretation. Especially when one's cultural sense has not become part of formation of the canon—in my case because India is not part of biblical history or dominant biblical interpretation, there is a passionate desire to let this form of knowing serve as both interrogator and solution-provider. I will pick this up later in treating a theology of culture.

Common sense is an intercultural and intergenerational sensibility of being human together. This binds us together both with the communities that voice their testimonies through the Bible and the communities that live around the world today. Common sense is more than human reason. It is the mediatory reasoning of the heart, head, and hands and feet. It is rational, passionate, and practical. Sometimes the faith communities through the many generations of their specific religious traditions reflect common sense most fittingly. At other times solidarity between different contemporaneous religious and secular human collectives reflects common sense more compellingly, even if it differs with the forbears of the faith. All three hermeneutical streams (canon sense, culture sense, and common sense) operate simultaneously. They balance each other and inform each other quite aware that in the end all of them come under the authority of God.

The second comment addresses a theological premise that operates through this interpretation. It has to do with where I stand with regard to the relationship between gospel and culture. I disagree with Tillich's initial proposal, which is still in vogue among many theologians, that "religion is the substance of culture, [while] culture is the form of religion."[30] This appears to denote that culture itself, devoid of God, is substanceless and vacuous. More importantly, it is based on the questionable presupposition that substance and form are separable and distinct from each other. Like many Asian theologians empathetic to Hindu and Buddhist worldviews, I too think of gospel and culture as so subtly and integrally meshed that it is impossible to say where one ends and the other begins. That is one reason for my insistence to read reciprocity of peace, love, table solidarity, and kingdom vocation into mission. Christian mission scatters and gathers up fragments of the kingdom strewn by God among guest and host cultures. K. P. Aleaz, an Indian theologian, argues for the possibility of talking of the gospel of Indian culture. For him, this gospel of Indian culture "is the gospel of integral relation between religion and culture, resulting in cultural symbiosis and a composite culture through an ongoing interaction between religions."[31] In a metaphysics that stresses the inextricable intermingling of content and context, substance and form, and essence and structure, it is quite impossible to assert material differentiation between gospel and culture. More so, any theological wedge between substance and form and gospel and culture must break down in the light of an honest acceptance of the implications of the mission of God in the gift of incarnation: the Word became flesh and dwelt among us. In other words, substance fully pervaded form, and Word saturates all creation (words, deeds, and matter). Thus, every dimension of culture is transformed into the arena of divine indwelling: the two became one in Jesus Christ.

ENDNOTES

1. Luke 17:21b, as translated by Raimondo Panikkar, *The Unknown Christ of Hinduism* (rev. ed.; Maryknoll, N.Y.: Orbis, 1981), vii.

2. Hannah Arendt, *Between Past and Future* (New York: Viking, 1968), 4.

3. The idea that "the world is flat" comes from Thomas L. Friedman. Interestingly this phrase originates from his conversation with Nandan Nilekani, a hugely successful business entrepreneur, who is cochair of Infosys Technologies Inc., which is one of the largest software companies in India. Thomas L. Friedman, *The World is Flat: A Brief History of the Twentieth Century* (New York: Farrar, Straus, and Giroux, 2005). For a multiperspective analysis of economic globalization, see Frank J. Lechner and John Boli, ed., *The Globalization Reader* (Malden, Mass.: Blackwell, 2004).

4. John Tomlinson, *Globalization and Culture* (Chicago: University of Chicago Press, 1999), 1. For an excellent introduction to the complex streams that feed into the process of cultural globalization, see Roland Robertson, *Globalization: Social Theory and Global Culture* (London: Sage, 1992).

5. Arjun Appadurai, "Grassroots Globalization and the Research Imagination," in *Globalization* (ed. Arjun Appadurai; Durham, N. C.: Duke University Press, 2000), 5.

6. Ibid., 1–20.

7. Stephen B. Bevans and Roger P. Schroeder, *Constants in Context: A Theology of Mission for Today* (Maryknoll, N. Y.: Orbis, 2004), 396.

8. David J. Bosch, *Transforming Mission: Paradigm Shifts in Theology of Mission* (Maryknoll, N. Y.: Orbis), 390.

9. J. Andrew Kirk, *What is Mission: Theological Exploration* (Minneapolis: Fortress, 2000), 217–218 (emphases in text).

10. The problem of whether Jesus appointed and sent seventy or seventy-two emissaries, both of which have manuscript support, does not seem to concern most Indian Bible scholars. Figuratively this is taken to indicate that a great number more than just twelve disciples were commissioned by Jesus for the Gentile mission: "the Lord appointed seventy [two] others" and sent them to the communities of the "other." In keeping with this symbolic proliferation of mission emissaries I opt for the number seventy. On the one hand, this is an auspicious number that suggests completeness in the mission of Jesus. On the other hand, the number seventy is consistent with the pedagogical intent of highlighting excess that we find in Jesus' teaching on forgiveness: seven times a day (Luke 17:4) or seventy-seven times or seventy times seven (Matt 18:22).

11. The Allelon Missional Schools Project Gathering (February 21–23, Dallas, Tex.) left me more informed and inquisitive and also somewhat dissatisfied and disturbed. However, I was truly enriched by the Bible studies, which involved a collective and dialogical reading of Luke 10:1–12. Some of the ideas that I expand upon in this paper come from my reflective engagement with a host of comments that were made at these inspiring sessions.

12. Warren Carter, "Getting Martha Out of the Kitchen: Luke 10:38–42 Again," in *A Feminist Companion to Luke* (ed. Amy-Jill Levine; London: Continuum, 2002), 228.

13. Herman Hendrickx, *The Third Gospel for the Third World, Volume Three–A, Travel Narrative I: Luke 9:51– 13:21* (Collegeville, Minn.: Liturgical, 2000), 34.

14. John Dominic Crossan, *The Historical Jesus: The Life of a Mediterranean Peasant* (San Francisco: HarperSanFrancisco, 1991), 346. I am aware that Crossan ties the radical nature of this itinerancy to the symbolic enactment of "unbrokered egalitarianism." I am not willing to go this interpretive route when studying this particular passage. One is always left wondering whether the mission objective of spreading radical democratic egalitarianism may well exemplify the mission of the author's historical era (modernity) and geographic location (United States of America) rather than Jesus'. I am much more inclined to talk of mutuality/reciprocity as one of the aspects of this mission initiated by Jesus.

15. Scott Cunningham, *Through Many Tribulations: The Theology of Persecution in Luke–Acts* (JSNTSup 142; Sheffield: Sheffield Academic, 1997), 97–98.

16. Robert C. Tannehill, *Luke* (Nashville: Abingdon, 1996), 174.

17. Robert Ellsberg, ed., *Gandhi on Christianity* (Maryknoll, N. Y.: Orbis, 1991), 45.

18. Tannehill, 170.

19. Cunningham, 95–96.

20. This point is made by James Massey, *Dalit Bible Commentary: The Gospel According to Luke* (New Delhi: ISPCK, 2007), 126.

21. Barbara Shellard, *New Light on Luke: Its Purpose, Sources, and Literary Context* (JSNTSup 215; London: Sheffield Academic, 2002), 94.

22. Craig L. Blomberg, *Contagious Holiness: Jesus' Meals with Sinners* (Downers Grove, Ill.: InterVarsity, 2005), 128.

23. Sebastian Kappen, *Jesus and Society* (New Delhi: ISPCK, 2002), 86.

24. As quoted in John Koenig, *New Testament Hospitality: Partnership with Strangers as Promise and Mission* (Eugene, Oreg.: Wipf and Stock, 2001), 86.

25. Koenig, 119.

26. Sharon H. Ringe, *Luke* (Louisville, Ky.: Westminster John Knox, 1995), 153.

27. While on this matter of reciprocity in cross-cultural mission, one cannot ignore another phrase in this passage. This has to do with a troubling metaphor that introduces the context of cross-cultural mission. To start with we are met with a luscious and delightful agrarian metaphor of "the harvest [that] is plentiful" (Luke 10:2a). I come from a rice-growing country. Thus, when I come across this image I immediately envisage rich, golden, and abundant paddy fields invitingly swaying in the wind. I have known this to be a farmer's ideal scenario during the season of harvest. The problem with this metaphor is that it communicates that mission fields are full of passive humans waiting to be cut, gathered, and stored into mission barns. It ascribes agency only to the missioner who crosses boundaries. It plays into the power dynamic of global cultural traffic that seeks unilaterally to pervade hospitable and porous communities. The asymmetry built into thinking of the hosting [non-Christian] communities as representing the grain harvest and visiting [Christian] missionary communities as representing the human labor leads to an unacceptable hierarchical imbalance. Even if we think of the recipient communities as the 'Lord's harvest' and the missioners as lowly laborers, the unequal relationship symbolized by nonhuman product and human agent cannot be remedied. There comes a time when even scriptural metaphors need to retire gracefully. Perhaps this one needs to die in order for mission to live with more human freedom and Christian reciprocity.

28. Charles H. Talbert, *Reading Luke: A Literary and Theological Commentary on the Third Gospel* (rev. ed.; Macon, Ga.: Smyth & Helwys, 2002), 123.

29. Tannehill, 176.

30. Paul Tillich, *Theology of Culture* (New York: Oxford University Press, 1959), 42.

31. K. P. Aleaz, *The Gospel of Indian Culture* (Calcutta: Punthi Pustak, 1994), 2.

RESPONSE TO CLARKE

SOONG-CHAN RAH

Prof. Clarke's paper is a timely work given the current crisis of overwhelming globalization. The language of "global cultural traffic" presents a starting point for discussion and a handle on how we might interpret globalization through the lens of Scripture. The pace of change evident in our culture has not been met by the pace of adaptation in the culture of the church. This is not to say that the pace of change in the church has to match the pace of change in culture, but the dysfunctional rate of adaptation has led to a noticeable irrelevance. When exploring Christianity's engagement with culture, we are confronted with an increasingly difficult task brought about by the increasing complexity of culture in contrast to the simplistic worldview often held by the church. Prof. Clarke's work calls us to an understanding of the global cultural context and the proper interpretation and application of Scripture, especially Luke 10, in order to further the transforming work of the gospel.

A key concept raised in this paper as it relates to globalization is "the challenge of injecting reciprocity into Christian mission." Globalization without reciprocity is oppressive. A cultural traffic flow that moves only one direction is a new and improved version of colonialism. No longer limited to military or political power, this form of colonialism is expressed through ideas, values, and structures and becomes an expression of cultural imperialism. Reciprocity becomes the corrective in this potentially imbalanced situation. Prof. Clarke identifies asymmetry ("boundary fluidity on one side and border calcification on the other") as a central challenge to reciprocity. Historical and asymmetrical cultural flow and the corresponding lack of reciprocity yields the Western captivity of the church,[1] where the culture of American Christianity more accurately reflects Western culture than scriptural tenets. Consequently, the Western hegemony of theology in the global context produces a global ecclesiological captivity to Western culture.

Prof. Clarke's eye-opening anecdote of a well-intentioned mission team that bullies its way through an evangelistic encounter shows the worst of a Western Christian approach deriving from the Western captivity of the church. An individualized and personalized faith, a consumer mentality of trying to make a sale, and a lack of respect accorded other cultures and people groups are some of the characteristics of the Western captivity of the church that negatively impacts global theological dialogue.

What is interesting, however, about the Western captivity of the church is that some of the best propagators of Western Christianity now reside in non-Western cultures. The Western captivity of the church is an example of one-way cultural traffic flow and globalization at its worst. This raises a question. What does a genuinely reciprocal cultural traffic flow look like if the global Christian culture is already reflective of a Western culture? How can a healthy cultural traffic flow occur in the context of a hegemonic Western Christian culture?

Two examples may illustrate the hegemony of Western culture in the business context as well as in the context of a global Christianity. About a half mile from our campus, on the corner of Pulaski and Lawrence, is an urban shopping center anchored by Staples and Starbucks, two icons of corporate America. The busiest store in this complex is actually the store that has a twelve-foot-tall inflatable chicken straddling its roof. It is a chain restaurant called *Pollo Campero*, which presents an interesting case study of globalization and Western cultural hegemony. Years ago Kentucky Fried Chicken (now known as KFC) opened a franchise in Guatemala. In response, a local businessman started a fast food chicken restaurant called *Pollo Campero*. If you were to close your eyes and taste *Pollo Campero* chicken, you would recognize the taste as a pretty good imitation of KFC chicken. In recent years *Pollo Campero* restaurants have arrived in the United States as the illegitimate grandchild of KFC. Or put another way, Baudrillard's *Simulacra and Simulation* comes to fruition: "It is now impossible to isolate the process of the real, or to prove the real."[2] There *is* a flow of global cultural traffic, but it is a dysfunctional one.

Another example comes from the context of Christian missions. A few years ago our local church made several short-term mission trips to Romania in an attempt to develop a long-term relationship with a church in Severin, a small town in the western part of the country. Unlike the larger cities in Romania, such as Bucharest and Timiswara, larger Western mission agencies do not pay much attention to Severin. Severin is literally a dying community. It is the home to one of only two hard water treatment facilities in all of Europe, the other being Chernobyl. Because of the presence of nuclear radiation, everything is dying in Severin. There is tremendous poverty in this town. The town had once had a flourishing economy based upon agriculture, but because of the presence of nuclear waste in the soil, the fields around the town are barren and trees are withering. There is a very high rate of infertility. One estimate from a local resident was that about one-third of the women in the area were infertile. This estimate was confirmed by a sampling of the rate of infertility of the women in the church.

Furthermore, there was a history of deep racial conflict in Severin. Romania has the highest number of gypsies (*Romas*) in Europe. (The number is disputed and ranges from 500,000 to 2.5 milllion.[3]) The *Romas* are an alienated and persecuted population. Deep-seated animosity and racism is directed towards the *Romas* by the Romanians.

How should the gospel relate to this unique cultural context? There is no easy answer, but here is the reality. The global cultural flow has already occurred even in this remote Romanian town. The larger churches in Timiswara, shaped by mega churches in the United States, have shaped these small churches in Severin so that their main approach to ministry reflects prosperity theology. The teaching of the pastors mimicked the big churches in Timiswara, which mimicked the teaching content of a megawatt smiling pastor of an American mega church. When I visited the churches in Severin, I would often be subjected to health and wealth preaching, while all around me there was overwhelming evidence of the need for a kingdom gospel of justice and reconciliation. In an era of the Western captivity of the church is it possible for there to be mutual, reciprocal global cultural traffic? Or, are we consigned to an asymmetrical global cultural exchange due to the hegemony of Western Christianity?

A second question raised by the paper revolves around the issue of power. As Prof. Clarke points out, ". . . any form of Christian mission that does not interrogate the power dimensions that facilitate the cultural and religious encounter between the self and the other becomes susceptible to covertly furthering colonial objectives." Given the historical asymmetry in missions, Luke 10 needs to be reexamined through the hermeneutic of power and powerlessness. Specifically, how can the act of being sent from one community to another be an expression of an unequal power dynamic? The ability to move from one culture to another and the freedom to move are themselves expressions of power.

The power to choose mobility is real power, particularly from the perspective of American culture. James Jasper in *A Restless Nation*[4] reveals America's obsession with mobility. For example, American-made cars tend to have names associated with movement and the pioneering spirit. Names like the Chevy Trailblazer and Venture and the Ford Explorer, Escape, Mustang, and Bronco all evoke images of movement related to the wild frontier. Often these exotic names belie the reality of minivans and SUVs geared towards usage by suburban soccer moms. Import cars, in contrast, use letters and numbers for their nomenclature. Even the fanciest of sports cars have alpha-numeric designations: Porsche 911, BMW Z4, and Mercedes SLK. Import cars with actual names are serene and calming, such as the Civic and the Accord.

American culture's obsession with mobility reflects the historical association of power with mobility. The power of mobility is reflected in the promise offered in the phrase "Go west, young man." When migration occurs by choice, greater opportunity follows. Immigrant groups who move to the United States by choice to pursue educational and economic opportunities tend to fare better economically. Mobility by choice yields power or the eventual increase of power. On the other hand, forced migration, such as the kidnapping of Africans to the Americas for slave labor and the forced migration and eventual genocide of Native communities, does not yield power.

If we read Luke 10 in the context of Western culture, the idea of mobility and being sent forth can be problematic. There is an imbalance of power in Western culture based upon who has the power of mobility. Therefore, when one is sent out from the dominant Western culture to another culture, the act of movement already reveals an uneven power dynamic. In contrast, the ones being sent out in Luke 10 are coming from a place of powerlessness. They are peasants under the thumb of an imperial power and alienated from all sources of power, whether from the Roman Empire and Hellenistic culture or even from their own people group. When the disciples are sent forth, their only source of power is the power of the Holy Spirit. Lacking political, social, and economic power, the disciples were truly lambs sent out among wolves. But, as Prof. Clarke points out, the lambs going forth may actually be perceived as wolves. How much of a lamb can one be when coming from a nation that is perceived as a ravenous wolf politically, militarily, culturally, economically, and even theologically? How can we incorporate a sense of downward mobility, following the example of our savior:

> Jesus, who, though he was in the form of God, did not count equality with God a thing to be grasped, but emptied himself, taking the form of a servant, being born in the likeness of men. And being found in human form he humbled himself and became obedient unto death, even death on a cross. (Phil 2:6–8)

In our cultural context and our engagement with this contemporary context, how can we better engage the value of powerlessness and an emptying of ourselves, even as we go forth as wolves among lambs?

ENDNOTES

1. The origin of this phrase has its roots in Luther's expression "the Babylonian captivity of the church" (Martin Luther, "The Babylonian Captivity of the Church," in *Three Treatises* [trans. A. T. W. Steinhaeuser; Philadelphia: Muhlenberg, 1947]). In subsequent years phrases such as the "Pelagian captivity of the church" (R. C. Sproul, "The Pelagian Captivity of the Church," in *Modern Reformation* (http://www.modernreformation.org/rc01pelagian.html), the "suburban captivity of the church" (Gibson Winter, *The Suburban Captivity of the Churches* [Garden City: Doubleday, 1961], and the "Constantinian captivity of the church" (Cornel West, *Democracy Matters* [New York: Penguin, 2004], 149) have been used to describe a church's captivity to a particular cultural expression.

2. Jean Baudrillard, *Simulacra and Simulation* (trans. Sheila Faria Glaser; Ann Arbor: University of Michigan Press, 1994), 21.

3. Simona Grigore, "The Roma (Gypsy) Community in Bucharest, Romania," http://www.lausanneworldpulse.com/urban.php/840/10-2007?pg=all.

4. James Jasper, *A Restless Nation* (Chicago: University of Chicago Press, 2000), 69.

THE REASON FOR OUR ENGAGEMENT WITH CULTURE

OSVALDO PADILLA

> I am not ashamed of the gospel, because it is the power of God for the salvation of everyone who believes: first for the Jew, then for the Gentile. For in the gospel a righteousness from God is revealed, a righteousness that is by faith from first to last, just as it is written: "The righteous will live by faith." (Rom 1:16–17)

In order to add depth to our reading of Rom 1:16–17 I think it is necessary to comment on two poles that are encoded in this text. This will allow us to frame the principal question that I wish to address.

The first pole is that of honor. Paul was writing to churches that were located at the center of the Roman Empire. This empire, as has been noted by several historians, was one in which honor played a dominant role. Hence, J. E. Lendon has called it an "Empire of Honour."[1] Honor in the Greco-Roman world, it should be noted, was *ascribed* honor. That is, you gauged your honor, not by what you felt within, but by what *others* said about you. This honor was acquired in several ways. There was the matter of birth: were you born in a respectable *polis*? What was the status of your family background? Were you free or were you born to slaves? There was also the matter of education. Unlike many countries of the modern world there was no centralized educational ministry in the Roman Empire that encouraged and enforced education. Therefore, many were illiterate. Others were able to attend the primary level of education where they learned the alphabet, names of famous Homeric heroes and gods, and learned to sign their names.[2] For the vast majority, this was the highest level of education to be reached. Only the elite were able to proceed to secondary and tertiary education and become the orators, politicians, and philosophers of the *polis*. Needless to say, it was a great honor to have reached the highest educational level. In addition to birth and education, there was the matter of deeds: what had you done for the *polis* lately? Individuals received honor by sponsoring festivals and games, by erecting buildings, and by providing grain for the populace. Their deeds would be inscribed in stones for the rest of the city to view and admire. Lastly, there was the matter of death: in what circumstances and for what cause did the person die? It was honorable to die in battle fighting for one's people. It is in this context that we must read Paul's statements in Rom 1:16–17.

This leads me to the second pole encoded in this text: the matter of the *gospel*. As Paul had stated earlier in chapter one, this gospel had to do with Jesus Christ. But, consider Jesus through the lens of the Roman context of honor. As for his birth, they would have pointed out that he was born in a little, backwater town of Judea. What could one say about his parents? Well, here the matter is difficult. Christians stated that his father was God himself. There were rumors, however, stating that he was an illegitimate child whose real father was unknown. What about his occupation? Mark tells us that he was a carpenter. In the eyes of the elite of the Greco-Roman public, this was demeaning, as manual labor was not viewed as work appropriate to the elite. To depend on a *technē*, a trade, to make one's living was not honorable. As if all these causes for shame were not enough, the circumstances of his death finished the plunge: he was crucified. In the words of a modern author: "In the ancient world crucifixion epitomized shame and humiliation. Death on the cross symbolized all that which was criminal, foreign, servile, and lowly. Those crucified included bandits, prisoners of war, revolutionaries, and murderers."[3]

This leads me to ask the following question: if in the Greco-Roman world this gospel was so shameful, what could have possibly motivated Paul to throw honor to the wind and engage this world with this gospel? What was it about this gospel that led him to the loss of honor, liberty, and eventually death? As we Christians engage our culture today, what is it about this gospel that impels us to risk respectability, belongingness, and even money? Romans 1:16–17 helps to answer this question.

THREE WORDS: POWER, SALVATION, AND RIGHTEOUSNESS

Three words—power, salvation, and righteousness—are key in understanding Paul's thought in this text.

First, "power" is used in connection with the gospel in v. 16. The term is employed in the OT to refer to God's unique power which is exercised to deliver his people. As such, it is used in reference to the exodus when God delivered his people from Egyptian oppression (Exod 9:16; Ps 77:14–15). In LXX Ps 139:8, David addresses the Lord as the power of his salvation (*kyrie, kyrie, dynamis tēs sōtērias mou*). We can speak of the gospel, therefore, as the medium through which God exercises his power in order to deliver his people. Given the connection of the gospel to Jesus as outlined in Romans, our concept of God's power must be grasped through the lens of the revelation of Jesus.

The second term in this text is "salvation." From the syntax of the sentence, we can see that the *telos*, the goal, of God's power is the salvation of all those who believe in Jesus. More than likely, as in "power" above, Paul's concept of salvation stems from the OT. Although used in many senses in the OT, I call attention to the use of *sōtēria* in passages such as Isa 46:13; 49:6; and 52:7. The emphasis of these texts is on God's eschatological salvation of his people. It is difficult to resist the idea that Paul's use of the term in this passage has a sense of subversion attached to it. This could be the case if one keeps in mind the historical context in which Paul is writing. The Roman propagandists had hailed the reign of Augustus as an age of salvation:

> . . . a saviour (σωτήρ) who put an end to war and will restore order everywhere: Caesar, by his appearing has realized the hopes of our ancestors; not only has he surpassed earlier benefactors of humanity, but he leaves no hope to those of the future that they might surpass him. The god's birthday was for the world the beginning of the gospel (*euangelion*) that he brought" (*I. Priene* 105.35).

The Roman churches, more than likely aware of these sorts of propagandists' maneuvers, may have read this passage as a direct challenge to the statements from the emperor.

The third expression of this passage that I would briefly like to examine is the "righteousness of God." Broadly speaking, the expression has been understood in two main ways: 1) as a reference to God's *own* attribute, that is, God as just and upright (*iustitia distributiva*); and 2) as a reference to God's action of putting people into a right relationship with himself. The latter is probably the best understanding, especially in view of the OT subtexts, where "righteousness of God" language is coupled with salvific terms. For example, Isa 46:13 says, "I am bringing my righteousness near, it is not far away; and my salvation will not be delayed. I will grant salvation to Zion, my splendor to Israel." Similarly Isa 51:5 has, "My righteousness draws near speedily, my salvation is on the way, and my arm will bring justice to the nations. The islands will look to me and wait in hope for my arm."

Having briefly examined these three terms, I suggest that Paul's basic thought in this passage is the following: whenever the gospel is preached, God is intervening in human history to bring people back into a right relationship with himself.[4] *This*, I would suggest, is one of the main reasons why Paul is not ashamed of the gospel. He realizes that through the foolishness of preaching and his own weakness God breaks into the human realm to redeem individuals. So it is with us today, whenever we stand up and through our faltering words and imperfect acts of compassion proclaim the gospel, God is unleashing his salvific power. I cannot think of a higher calling in our engagement with culture.

Let me add that although the preaching of the gospel opens up the possibility of salvation, it also introduces the matter of justice. If "righteousness of God" speaks of God bringing all of creation back to himself, there is an implied action on his part. In order to make right, God must also deal with the wrong (i.e., those who violate his laws).[5] The king's salvation is not only displayed by blessing those who are on his side but also by bringing to justice those who have chosen to remain as rebels. Let me thus state that one of the fundamental ways through which we are instruments of justice is precisely by our proclamation of the gospel. In the words of Paul: "For we are to God the aroma of Christ among those who are being saved and those who are perishing. To the one we are the smell of death; to the other, the fragrance of life" (2 Cor 2:15–16).

CONCLUSION

Let me therefore conclude by saying that in a Christian engagement with culture, the gospel must be the foundation of this engagement. In order to be called properly *Christian* engagement with culture, the gospel, in both its proclamatory and incarnational spheres, must be present from beginning to end. To do otherwise is not a *Christian* engagement with culture; it may be religious but not Christian. The result of this particularity will be costly. As in the case of the apostle who penned the words we have examined, this gospel-centered engagement may result in the loss of our social status, our colleagues, our money, our freedom, and even our lives. However, the possibility of being agents of God in history in order to unleash his salvation to the world and bring the oppressors to justice is strong motivation to throw our personal gains to the wind and not be ashamed of the gospel.

ENDNOTES

1. J. E. Lendon, *Empire of Honour: The Art of Government in the Roman World* (Oxford: Clarendon Press, 1997).
2. See Raffaella Cribiore, *Writing, Teachers and Students in Graeco-Roman Egypt* (Atlanta: Scholars, 1996).
3. Peter J. Scaer, *The Lukan Passion and the Praiseworthy Death* (Sheffield: Phoenix, 2005), 1.
4. See in this respect Douglas Moo, *The Epistle to the Romans* (Grand Rapids: Eerdmans, 1996), 70.
5. See Mark Seifrid, "Righteousness Language in the Hebrew Scriptures and Early Judaism," in *Justification and Variegated Nomism* (Vol. 1 of *The Complexities of Second Temple Judaism*; ed. D. A. Carson, Peter T. O'Brien, and Mark A. Seifrid; Tübingen: Mohr-Siebeck, 2001), 415–442.

ANNOTATED BIBLIOGRAPHY ON CHRISTIANITY'S ENGAGEMENT WITH CULTURE*

Anker, Roy M. *Catching Light: Looking for God in the Movies.* Grand Rapids: Eerdmans, 2004. There are numerous books on the market that seek to find God in Hollywood releases. Roy Anker, an English professor at Calvin College, offers a particularly insightful analysis of several classic Academy Award-winning films.

Avis, Paul. *A Church Drawing Near: Spirituality and Mission in a Post-Christian Culture.* London: T. & T. Clark, 2003. Avis provides a British perspective on the work of the church in late modernity. After a cultural analysis he gives what he thinks is the proper Christian response and calls the church to a triple-sided mission of word, sacraments, and pastoral responsibility to restore its trust from the surrounding community and to bring healing to broken people in an increasingly broken society.

Bader-Saye, Scott. *Following Jesus in a Culture of Fear.* Grand Rapids: Baker, 2007. Contemporary Westerners are gripped by fear. Sometimes the fear is legitimate, but more often than not it is used to advance political or economic campaigns. Bader-Saye highlights these concerns and explores how Christians might follow a God and Savior who routinely asks followers to go into uncomfortable and risky situations for the advancement of the kingdom.

Barth, Karl. *Wolfgang Amadeus Mozart.* Grand Rapids: Eerdmans, 1986. Barth, a lifelong Mozart devotee, published this slim book in 1956 in honor of the two-hundredth anniversary of the composer's birth. He celebrates the freedom expressed in Mozart's work. According to John Updike, who contributed the forward to this volume, Barth's appreciation for Mozart says something about what it means to live ordinary life in light of his understanding of God's absolute otherness.

Beckford, Robert. *Jesus Dub: Theology, Music, and Social Change.* London: Routledge, 2006. Dub is a style of African Caribbean music which deconstructs extant songs and reforms them to make various statements, often political. Beckford's treatise gives an example of how Christian theology, particularly liberation theology, may be put into cultural context by applying the dub techniques of tearing down and reshaping to particular areas of theology. This work is technical.

Bediako, Kwame. *Jesus and the Gospel in Africa.* Theology in Africa Series. Maryknoll, N.Y.: Orbis, 2004. Bediako, a Ghanaian, provides an introduction to the contemporary struggle of African appropriation of Jesus and the gospel message. Part one discusses present perspectives and Christologies, part two discusses theology and culture, particularly looking

---

*This bibliography is based on contributions and suggestions made by the participants of the symposium and was augmented, compiled, and annotated by Chris Nelson and Nathanael Putnam, to whom sincere thanks are heartily expressed.

to the early fathers as a model for contextualization, and part three examines Africa's role in the history of Christianity.

———. *Theology and Identity: The Impact of Culture upon Christian Thought in the Second Century and in Modern Africa.* Oxford: Regnum, 1992. According to Bediako theology in any age arises from culturally rooted questions about Christian self-definition. His work sheds light on the modern African theological enterprise by considering the parallel experience of the second-century Church Fathers in their Greco-Roman world.

Begbie, Jeremy S. *Resounding Truth: Christian Wisdom in the World of Music.* Grand Rapids: Baker, 2007. Begbie's core question is, What can Christian theology bring to music? The first two sections of the book are concerned with laying a foundational understanding of music in the Bible and through the history of Western culture, but part three turns to a theology of music within God's creation today.

Berkouwer, G. C. *General Revelation.* Grand Rapids: Eerdmans, 1955. In this classic work Berkouwer develops a theology of general revelation that avoids the dichotomy between the natural and the supernatural. Appealing first of all to the Scriptures, Berkouwer opposes an identification of general revelation with natural theology, interacts with the distinct views of Barth, Brunner, and the Roman Catholic Church, and ultimately views general revelation not in terms of nature but in terms of God's universal activity.

Berry, Wendell. *The Unsettling of America: Culture and Agriculture.* San Francisco: Sierra Club, 1977. Wendell Berry's classic book challenges Americans to consider their history of mechanistic exploitation of the land and how it has led to the modern ecological and agricultural crisis. Berry claims that this is a crisis not just of agriculture but of character and culture as well. Many of the values Berry articulates here in essay form—human dignity and health, meaningful work, and connection with the earth—are also accessible in his widely acclaimed fiction and poetry.

Beuken, Wim, and Seán Freyne, eds. *The Bible as Cultural Heritage.* London: SCM, 1995. This issue of the *Concilium* theological journal, a Roman Catholic publication, contains a variety of articles on the Bible as an inspiration for culture. Articles address cultures in the Bible, culture and Bible translation, and the influence of the Bible on the arts and human values.

Boff, Leonardo. *Sacraments of Life/Life of the Sacraments.* Washington, D.C.: Pastoral, 1987. According to Boff a sacrament is a way of thinking. Over the course of this short volume he develops a sacramental theology that encompasses all of life before returning to the seven sacraments of the Roman Catholic Church.

Bonhoeffer, Dietrich. *The Cost of Discipleship.* 2d ed. New York: Macmillan, 1959. Lutheran theologian, pastor, and martyr under Hitler, Dietrich Bonhoeffer offers a persuasive account of how the authentic Christian life is based in costly grace, not cheap grace. Bonhoeffer dedicates a large portion of the book to a meditation on the Sermon on the Mount. This is a devotional classic on Christ's call on his followers' lives. A new translation based on the German critical edition is entitled *Discipleship* (Dietrich Bonhoeffer Works, vol. 4. Minneapolis: Augsburg Fortress, 2003) and is deemed a more accurate rendering of the original.

———. *Letters and Papers from Prison.* Rev. ed. Edited by Eberhard Bethge. New York: Macmillan, 1967. This collection of letters and meditations stems from the time of Bonhoeffer's arrest to his execution under Hitler. Perhaps most well-known for the controversial phrase "religionless Christianity," this work offers profound insight into the Christian's engagement with modernity and secularism and a window into Bonhoeffer's inner life at a time of profound spiritual and intellectual unrest.

Bosch, David. *Believing in the Future: Toward a Missiology of Western Culture.* Valley Forge, Pa.: Trinity Press International, 1995. This short volume begins by detailing the challenges facing the church in the postmodern age and climaxes in a missiology for today's Western culture. He concludes with five crucial ingredients for this missiology; it must be ecological, countercultural, ecumenical, contextual, and led by the laity.

_____. *Transforming Mission: Paradigm Shifts in Theology of Mission.* Maryknoll, N.Y.: Orbis, 1991. This is the bible of missiology for those taking the subject seriously. Stan Nussbaum's recently published *A Reader's Guide to Transforming Mission* (Maryknoll, N.Y.: Orbis, 2005) makes this volume much more accessible.

_____. *Witness to the World: The Christian Mission in Theological Perspective.* London: Marshall, Morgan & Scott, 1980. This lesser known volume is actually much more user friendly than Bosch's more famous work, *Transforming Mission,* listed above. For students and those interested in a basic theology of mission this is the volume.

Bouma-Prediger, Steven. *For the Beauty of the Earth: A Christian Vision for Creation Care.* Grand Rapids: Baker, 2001. This is a very good evangelical treatment of the relation of Christianity and care of the earth. It is theologically and ecologically informed and pushes the church and its leaders to be much more attentive to care of the earth—for theological reasons.

Breckenridge, James and Lillian. *What Color Is Your God? Multicultural Education in the Church.* Wheaton, Ill.: Victor, 1995. In the United States we may not have to travel more than a few blocks for the opportunity for cross-cultural evangelism and Christian education. James and Lillian Breckenridge call for individuals and churches to seize this opportunity by raising their cultural awareness. Special attention is given to central issues and effective teaching methods for Hispanic-American, Native-American, Asian-American, and African-American cultures.

Brownson, James V., et al. *StormFront: the Good News of God.* The Gospel and Culture Series. Grand Rapids: Eerdmans, 2003. Rather than focusing on how to present a gospel in the present day American context, the four authors focus on what that gospel message should be. They present a message that is alive and moving with purpose and which demands allegiance of its followers and communion with its risen Lord against the powers of evil. This gospel message ends with a call to action for the church.

Budde, Michael L. *The (Magic) Kingdom of God: Christianity and Global Culture Industries.* Boulder, Col.: Westview, 1997. Budde, a Roman Catholic scholar, outlines the decisively negative impact of the "global culture industries" of advertising and media on the vitality and mission of the church. He argues that an emphasis on narrative theology and lifelong Christian formation is essential to counter the paralyzing force of the culture industry.

Budde, Michael L., and Robert W. Brimlow, eds. *The Church as Counterculture.* SUNY Series in Popular Culture and Political Change. Albany: State University of New York Press, 2000. Scholars from a variety of denominations and disciplines provide essays ranging from historical analyses of the church to present reflections on ethics and theology about the relation of church to the culture in which it lives. Contributors include Michael J. Baxter, Walter Brueggemann, and Stanley Hauerwas.

Carson, D. A. *Christ and Culture Revisited.* Grand Rapids: Eerdmans, 2008. In this soon-to-be-released book, Carson provides a biblical-theological approach to the Christ and culture problem. While constructively engaging H. Richard Niebuhr's paradigm, Carson offers his own construal that seeks to do justice to biblical-theological frameworks.

Carter, Craig A. *Rethinking Christ and Culture: A Post-Christendom Perspective.* Grand Rapids: Brazos, 2007. This is one of the strongest arguments against Niebuhr's position. Carter explains that H. Richard Niebuhr's classic *Christ and Culture* was written in a predominantly Christian cultural context. Facing an increasingly post-Christian/post-

Christendom culture, Carter evaluates Niebuhr's model and proposes an alternative typology that he believes is better suited for Christian mission in a post-Christendom world.

Christianson, Eric S., Peter Francis, and William R. Telford, eds. *Cinéma Divinité: Religion, Theology and the Bible in Film*. London: SCM, 2005. This is a collection of scholarly essays on the critical engagement of theology and film. After laying the groundwork with some key concepts in the discussion, the heart of the book is made up of "case studies" in which the writers interact with specific films, filmmakers, and genres. The epilogue records a lively discussion among the contributors about Mel Gibson's *The Passion of the Christ*.

Clapp, Rodney. *A Peculiar People: The Church as Culture in a Post-Christian Society*. Downers Grove, Ill.: InterVarsity, 1996. This book provides a blueprint for what it means to be the church in our post-modern, post-Christian context. Clapp argues that the church is not simply a collection of individuals with a particular philosophy, ideology, or political agenda. Rather, the church is a community that transforms society by modeling a new kind of culture.

Clarke, Anthony J., and Paul S. Fiddes, eds. *Flickering Images: Theology and Film in Dialogue*. Regent's Study Guide 12. Macon, Ga.: Smyth & Helwys, 2005. This collection of essays addresses the subject of film and theology in three main categories. In the first, theology and film is dealt with in theory with a discussion of method. In the second, method is applied to several movies, providing an example of doing theology in film. The final section presents theological discussion of several movies that can be used in local churches.

Clouse, Robert G., Richard V. Pierard, and Edwin M. Yamauchi. *Two Kingdoms: The Church and Culture through the Ages*. Chicago: Moody, 1993. This unique church history focuses not on the history of theology but on the mutual influence of church and culture over the last two thousand years. Special attention is given to the diverse cultural expressions of Christianity in the modern period.

Collier, Jane, and Rafael Esteban. *From Complicity to Encounter: The Church and the Culture of Economism*. Harrisburg, Pa.: Trinity Press International, 1998. Roman Catholics Collier and Esteban argue that the church in the West is deeply enmeshed in the Western culture of Economism. This arrangement has compromised the ability of the church to speak to this culture. The authors show on the basis of the mission theology of the Second Vatican Council that the future of the church's mission lies not in reactionary confrontation but in two-way encounter whereby both culture and church call each other to conversion.

Cornille, Catherine, and Valeer Neckebrouck. *A Universal Faith? Peoples, Cultures, Religions, and the Christ: Essays in Honor of Prof. Dr. Frank De Graeve*. Louvain, Belgium: Peeters; Grand Rapids: Eerdmans, 1992. This volume contains a variety of essays on inculturation and interreligious dialogue. Special attention is given to India, Japan, the Philippines, Muslims of North Africa, and the Oromo people of East Africa.

Cote, Richard G. *Re-Visioning Mission: The Catholic Church and Culture in Postmodern America*. New York: Paulist, 1996. Speaking as an American Catholic, Cote calls for a new sense of mission in the church. He argues for an inculturation of the gospel for America by using the metaphor of marriage to relate faith and culture. To this end he challenges misconceptions about culture and ideology, which he decisively separates, and offers a more positive and redemptive view of culture. This lays the groundwork for his discussion in the final two chapters of mission and spirituality in the postmodern context.

Crowe, Jerome. *From Jerusalem to Antioch: The Gospel across Cultures*. Collegeville, Minn.: Liturgical, 1997. The author describes his book as "a case study of that first example of the transculturation of the gospel." Making use of social and historical information about the Jewish and Hellenistic cultural contexts, Crowe considers how the church adapted as it moved out from Palestine into the Greco-Roman world. The book is quite readable and concludes with implications for missions today.

Cultural Encounters: A Journal for the Theology of Culture. This journal, which appears twice each year, seeks to provide a biblically informed, Christ-centered trinitarian engagement with contemporary culture in its various manifestations.

Daniélou, Jean. *Holy Pagans of the Old Testament*. London: Longmans, Green, 1956. This classic work features a still refreshing look at the important but rarely discussed topic of God working through non-Israelite peoples and cultures in the Bible.

Daugherty, Kevin. "*Missio Dei:* The Trinity and Christian Missions." *Evangelical Review of Theology* 31 (2007): 151–168. Daugherty proposes that it is the doctrine of the Trinity that is the operating theme behind the sending God (*missio Dei*) and that this is the starting point for partnering with God in global mission.

Davis, Ellen F. *Scripture, Culture, and Agriculture: An Agrarian Reading of the Bible*. Cambridge: Cambridge University Press, 2008. This work, which will appear in the fall of 2008, will provide further analysis in line with Davis's paper in this journal.

Dawson, Christopher. *The Historic Reality of Christian Culture: A Way to the Renewal of Human Life*. New York: Harper & Row, 1960. Dawson (1889–1970) wrote prolifically on the subject of religion and culture. This small book stands alongside Niebuhr's *Christ and Culture* as one of the foundational works on the subject. Dawson briefly surveyed the history of Christian culture, but his primary concern was the crisis in the relationship between Christianity, secularism, and Western culture. He remained committed to a Christian transformation of society as a way forward.

Deena, Seodial Frank H., and Karoline Szatek, eds. *From Around the Globe: Secular Authors and Biblical Perspectives*. Lanham, Md.: University Press of America, 2007. The twenty-six essays here seek to find connections between global literature and the Bible. The authors seek to uncover biblical layers and allusions in various genres from different regions of the world, whether they were placed there intentionally or not.

Demarest, Bruce. *General Revelation: Historical Views and Contemporary Issues*. Grand Rapids: Zondervan, 1982. This book provides a historical survey of revelation theology from an Evangelical perspective. Demerest gives an overview of Christian answers to the question "How is God known?" from Augustine, Anselm, and Aquinas to modern indigenous theologies in Africa, Asia, and Latin America. He then concludes with his own biblical theology of general and special revelation that defends the exclusive claims of Jesus Christ.

Detweiler, Craig, and Barry Taylor. *A Matrix of Meanings: Finding God in Popular Culture*. Grand Rapids: Baker, 2003. The authors show through a whirlwind tour of several modern media forms that even the most debased cultural form can carry God's presence.

Dube, Musa. *Postcolonial Feminist Interpretation of the Bible*. Atlanta: Chalice, 2000. Dube, a biblical scholar at the University of Botswana, analyzes the inherent patriarchal and imperialist agendas of ancient, modern, and biblical texts and, through the use of intertextuality and literary-rhetorical study, advocates a method for "decolonizing" biblical literature, which she applies in part three of her book to Matt 15:21–28, the story of the Syro-Phoenician woman.

Duffy, Regis A. *An American Emmaus: Faith and Sacrament in the American Culture*. New York: Crossroad, 1995. Duffy explores the relationship between being Catholic and being American. He asks two basic questions: "To what extent does American culture help or hinder Catholics in their worship of God?" and "What impact does the worship and witness of the church have on American culture?" The significance of the liturgy and sacraments are of primary concern throughout.

Dulles, Avery. *Revelation Theology*. New York: Herder & Herder, 1969. Dulles provides a sweeping view of the history of revelation theology beginning with its biblical roots, proceeding through the bulk of Christian history, and concentrating on the views of key figures in the nineteenth and twentieth centuries. His conclusion highlights the fact that perspectives on revelation and faith are ever-changing, though he identifies three basic streams of revelation theology that have been consistently represented by various theologians throughout history.

Dyrness, William A. *Learning about Theology from the Third World*. Grand Rapids: Zondervan, 1990. This introduction for Westerners to Christian theology outside the West includes broad overviews of theology in Africa, Latin America, and Asia.

Eliot, T. S. *Christianity and Culture: The Idea of a Christian Society and Notes Towards the Definition of Culture*. New York: Harcourt, Brace, 1949. In these two essays, poet and playwright T. S. Eliot shows himself adept at philosophy and theology as well. In "The Idea of a Christian Society," Eliot shows that only two options present themselves for the future of Western society: either to become a pagan society or a Christian society. He ultimately envisions a rapprochement between church and State. The second essay, "Notes towards the Definition of Culture," examines culture more generally, noting several essential attributes and considering its relationship to religion, politics, and education.

Fiddes, Paul S., ed. *Faith in the Centre: Christianity and Culture*. Regent's Study Guides 9. Macon, Ga.: Smyth & Helwys, 2001. The essays gathered in this book all come from the "Centre for the Study of Christianity and Culture," a group based in Regent's Park College at Oxford devoted to the formation of Christian culture. The essays of the first part discuss the theoretical aspects of inculturation, and the essays of the second treat historical examples of inculturation.

Francis, Mark R. *Shape a Circle Ever Wider: Liturgical Inculturation in the United States*. Chicago: Liturgy Training, 2000. This is a strictly Catholic perspective on inculturation and liturgy. The first three sections deal with inculturation on a theoretical level and as it has happened historically in the Catholic Church. The last two chapters offer ideas for inculturation in the contemporary United States.

Frost, Michael. *Exiles: Living Missionally in a Post-Christian Culture*. Peabody, Mass.: Hendrickson, 2006. Frost presents a missiology for the emergent church. After presenting an argument for abandoning a Christendom mentality, he calls believers to a missional discipleship in a postmodern world. Chapter five, "The Exile's Esprit de Corps: We Will Serve a Cause Greater than Ourselves," probably the strongest argument in this book, is where Frost really expands on his concept of *communitas* as the operative norm of the church.

Gaillardetz, Richard R. *Transforming Our Days: Spirituality, Community and Liturgy in a Technical Culture*. New York: Crossroad, 2000. Recognizing the inability to escape a culture drenched with technology, Gaillardetz offers a theological exploration for finding ways to rediscover God in the mundane tasks of life, especially by utilizing Christian liturgy.

Gallagher, Susan VanZanten, ed. *Postcolonial Literature and the Biblical Call for Justice*. Jackson: University of Mississippi Press, 1994. Essayists engage with the works of twelve postcolonial writers from around the world to consider how Christianity has acted as both an oppressing and a liberating force in their lands. Authors interact with biblical texts and theoretical issues related to indigenization, ethics, and justice.

Gorringe, T. J. *Discerning Spirit: A Theology of Revelation*. London: SCM, 1990. Gorringe asserts "when we speak of revelation we are in fact speaking of the Holy Spirit, God's presence in the world." He develops his theology of revelation through an examination of biblical "Spirit" language in the areas of community, sexuality, politics, and art.

Greene, Collin J. D. *Christology in Cultural Perspective: Marking out the Horizons*. Grand Rapids: Eerdmans, 2003. After laying basic ground rules for how Christology is to be done and three basic categories in which it can be done (cosmological, political, and anthropological), Greene shows how Christology was handled in the modern period. Then he offers a critique of post-modernity and suggests possible ways that Christology can be done in its context.

Greinacher, Norbert, and Norbert Mette, eds. *Christianity and Cultures*. London: SCM, 1995. This issue of the Roman Catholic journal *Concilium* contains eleven articles on the topics of multiculturalism and inculturation of the gospel. Part II, "Test Cases," looks at Christianity in context in the Coptic Church, Zaire (now the Democratic Republic of Congo), Pakistan, Latin America, and French Canadian youth culture.

Griffin, Mark, and Theron Walker. *Living on the Borders: What the Church Can Learn from Ethnic Immigrant Cultures*. Grand Rapids: Brazos, 2004. Confronted with the American "melting pot," outside groups seem to have only two choices—assimilate or separate. Griffin and Walker bring to light immigrant communities' struggles to become part of the culture and still keep an identity. They then offer these communities as a model for the church to both keep a distinct identity and be a relevant part of American culture.

Hackett, David G., ed. *Religion and American Culture: A Reader*. New York: Routledge, 1995. This wide-ranging volume touches on the interaction of religion and culture over the course of the last 500 years of American history. It considers not just the traditional narrative of Protestant America but the stories of Native Americans, African Americans, Catholics, Jews, and other groups. This reader is a valuable alternative to traditional textbooks on American religious history.

Hauerwas, Stanley. *After Christendom? How the Church Is to Behave if Freedom, Justice, and a Christian Nation are Bad Ideas*. Nashville: Abingdon, 1991. Hauerwas challenges Christendom's modernist presupposition that Christians believe "what anyone would believe upon reflection." This leads him to make several provocative claims about the mission and identity of the church vis-à-vis liberal democratic culture. Hauerwas calls for the church to become a community of disciplined disciples rather than volunteer individuals, and in the process he challenges widely-held views about salvation, justice, freedom, sex, and education.

Hawn, Michael C. *Gather into One: Praying and Singing Globally*. Grand Rapids: Eerdmans, 2003. One of the more difficult aspects of contextualization is balancing it with the biblical call for unity in the church. Hawn calls for Christians to use liturgy and song more globally by highlighting the contextualized work of hymn and liturgy writers from around the world and showing how their work can enrich the church by providing different perspectives.

Hillman, Eugene. *Toward an African Christianity*. New York: Paulist, 1993. Hillman suggests that the Western colonial models of Christianity are fundamentally at odds with African culture and that for a truly African Christianity to emerge a radically new attitude toward inculturation will be required. Hillman examines Maasai traditional religion as one model of African culture and suggests that a truly African Christianity might include practices such as polygamy and ritual animal sacrifice.

Hipps, Shane. *The Hidden Power of Electronic Culture: How Media Shapes Faith, the Gospel, and Church*. Grand Rapids: Zondervan, 2005. Using his background in advertising, Hipps first tries to uncover the subtle ways an increasingly electronic culture has and is influencing the church and its ministry. He compares this to the effect of the printing press on the modern church. He then explores how community, worship, and leadership might occur in an electronic culture.

Hunsberger, George R., and Craig Van Gelder, eds. *The Church between Gospel and Culture: The Emerging Mission in North America.* Grand Rapids: Eerdmans, 1996. This collection of essays considers the mission of the church to North America and the intersection of gospel, church, and culture. In light of the declining position of the church within society, these authors point neither toward the regaining of lost ground nor toward retreat into a Christian subculture but toward a missionary engagement of gospel and culture.

Irarrázaval, Diego. *Inculturation: New Dawn of the Church in Latin America.* Translated by Phillip Berryman. Faith and Culture Series. Maryknoll, N.Y.: Orbis, 2000. One of the many things to emerge from the liberation theology movement of the 1970s was an interest in the topic of inculturation. This book presents a Catholic perspective on and approach to Latin American inculturation.

Johnston, Robert. *Reel Spirituality.* 2d ed. Grand Rapids: Baker Academic, 2006. This expanded and revised edition includes discussion of visual, aural, and literary criticism in film and discussion of theological ethics. Johnston's book provides a comprehensive and accessible survey of the conversation between film and theology.

_____, ed. *Reframing Theology and Film.* Grand Rapids: Baker Academic, 2007. The study of film is still a developing discipline, and this collection of essays seeks to broaden the discussion of film and theology in six areas: moving beyond a strictly literary view of film, broadening the selection of films to study, expanding the body of conversation partners, accounting for viewer response, reconsidering "normative" film criticism, and redefining theology's role as it relates to film.

Kabasele Lumbala, Francois. *Celebrating Jesus Christ in Africa: Liturgy and Inculturation.* Maryknoll, N.Y.: Orbis, 1998. Part of the Orbis *Faith and Culture Series*, which explores global Christianity after Western hegemony. Kabasele Lumbala offers accounts of uniquely African celebrations of baptism, Eucharist, marriage, blessings, and other liturgies among African Roman Catholics.

Kaplan, Steven, ed. *Indigenous Responses to Western Christianity.* New York: New York University Press, 1995. Contributors to this volume examine the responses of seven broadly-defined cultures to their early encounters with Christian missionary activity. Peoples in Africa, Thailand, South America, Japan, India, China, and Mexico are considered for what elements of Christianity and accompanying Western culture they chose to adopt or reject and how Christianity was indigenized in their context.

Kraft, Charles. *Christianity in Culture: A Study in Dynamic Biblical Theologizing in Cross-Cultural Perspective.* Maryknoll, N.Y.: Orbis, 1979. Kraft presents several models of culture which help expand upon Niebuhr and take a more missiological position. A helpful volume with provocative statements.

_____. *Appropriate Christianity.* Pasadena, Calif.: William Carey Library, 2005. A collection of articles illustrating several ways in which Christianity has been reinterpreted and contextualized in a number of distinct cultural contexts.

Küng, Hans. *Mozart: Traces of Transcendence.* Grand Rapids: Eerdmans, 1993. While much has been written on Mozart and his music, very little has explored its religions underpinnings. In the first part of his book Küng discusses Mozart's formation in a Catholic background, and in the second part he critiques Mozart's "Coronation Mass" against its contemporary setting of growing religious tension.

Küster, Volker. *The Many Faces of Jesus Christ*. Maryknoll, N.Y.: Orbis, 2001. Küster's book provides a good introduction to Christologies from Asia, Latin America, and Africa. In addition to giving sketches of each region's christological image, he explores the differences and similarities between them and the implications for ecumenical learning.

Legrand, Lucien. *The Bible on Culture*. Maryknoll, N.Y.: Orbis, 2000. Legrand's thesis that the people of God are called to live in an acute tension between intercultural dependence and countercultural witness is supported by careful and thorough biblical study in the OT, the life of Christ, and the ministry of Paul.

Long, D. Stephen. *Theology and Culture: A Guide to the Discussion*. Eugene, Oreg.: Wipf and Stock, 2008. This work analyzes the various ways in which "culture" is used in contemporary theological discourse.

Lynch, Gordon. *Understanding Theology and Popular Culture*. Malden, Mass.: Blackwell, 2005. This is a useful text for defining the term "popular culture" and for viewing popular culture theologically through case studies.

McDonald, H. D. *Theories of Revelation: An Historical Study 1700–1960*. Grand Rapids: Baker, 1979. *Theories of Revelation* is a combination of two previous books by McDonald covering the periods from 1700 to 1860 and 1860 to 1960. The two works form a cohesive whole that explores in depth the historical emergence and progression of conflicting views regarding biblical inerrancy, inspiration, and authority since the Enlightenment.

Magesa, Laurenti. *Anatomy of Inculturation: Transforming the Church in Africa*. Maryknoll, N.Y.: Orbis, 2004. Magesa's study of inculturation in the Catholic Church of East Africa (Kenya, Tanzania, and Uganda) comes in three parts. The first surveys the present conditions of the church in each country, the second provides a biblical basis and precedents for inculturation, and the third provides suggestions for future inculturation in East Africa.

Menuge, Angus J. L., ed. *Christ and Culture in Dialogue: Constructive Themes and Practical Applications*. St. Louis: Concordia, 1999. This collection of essays is centered on a Lutheran "two kingdoms" perspective on Christ and culture, or in Neibuhr's words, "Christ and Culture in Paradox." The volume contains interaction with Neibuhr's work, application toward concrete social issues, and discussion of the tensions between Christ and culture in worship, evangelism, and Christian education.

Metzger, Paul Louis. *The Word of Christ and the World of Culture: Sacred and Secular Through the Theology of Karl Barth*. Grand Rapids: Eerdmans, 2003. This is a constructive synthesis of Christ and culture through recourse to Karl Barth's christological categories. The work focuses on how Barth's unique doctrine of the word enabled him to relate Christ to culture in inseparable terms while yet maintaining a distinction between them. It also traces the way Barth framed culture within his theological model even while he continued to champion the secular domain.

Middleman, Udo. *The Market Driven Church: The Worldly Influence of Modern Culture on the Church in America*. Wheaton, Ill.: Crossway, 2004. Middleman, who is Swiss, provides a negative example of contextualization by offering an outsider's critique of the American church's tendency to get swept away in a consumerist mindset. He calls for the church to return to a more historic Christianity.

Mitchell, Jolyon, and Sophia Marriage, eds. *Mediating Religion: Conversations in Media, Religion and Culture*. London: T. & T. Clark, 2003. This collection of essays stems from a 1999 international conference on media, religion, and culture and treats the relationships between these three topics. Essays are divided into several categories including identity, conflict, popular piety in media and religion, and the relations of media literacy, media ethics, and film to religion.

Moltmann, Jürgen. *The Spirit of Life: A Universal Affirmation.* Minneapolis: Fortress, 1992. In this third volume of Moltmann's systematic theology, which he describes as 'a holistic pneumatology,' he takes a broad view of the Holy Spirit as the Spirit of Life which we experience in the everyday, thereby closing the gap between divine revelation and human experience. Moltmann makes use of and interacts with liberation, feminist, ecological, and charismatic theologies.

Moore, T. M. *Culture Matters: A Call for Consensus on Christian Cultural Engagement.* Grand Rapids: Brazos, 2007. Interacting with Niebuhr, Moore reviews the many ways in which Christians have chosen to interact with culture. He works historically from Augustine to present-day figures like Chuck Colson and builds a case for a Christian consensus on engagement with culture. Moore concludes with several guidelines for individuals and Christian communities to consider regarding a positive interaction with culture. Each of the six chapters includes questions for group discussion.

_____. *Redeeming Pop Culture: A Kingdom Approach.* Phillipsburg, N.J.: Presbyterian and Reformed, 2003. Instead of focusing on modernism or post-modernist categories, Moore embraces the larger category of American pop culture in this book. He provides a "biblical critique," which analyzes pop culture, judges both its good and bad aspects, and seeks a place for mission of the gospel to occur within it.

Mouw, Richard J. *He Shines in All That's Fair: Culture and Common Grace.* Grand Rapids: Eerdmans, 2001. Originally a lecture given at Calvin College, this book provides a decidedly Calvinist perspective on the relation of church and culture. Mouw revisits the debates over common grace and points to the doctrine's importance for understanding how the church should relate to the world around it.

Newbigin, Lesslie. *The Gospel in a Pluralist Society.* Grand Rapids: Eerdmans, 1989. Reflecting on his pastoral experience, Newbigin offers his thoughts on how the gospel and an increasingly relativistic and pluralist society come together. The book is not a systematic exploration but an introduction to the topic from a pastoral point of view.

Ng, David, ed. *People on the Way: Asian North Americans Discovering Christ, Culture, and Community.* Valley Forge, Pa.: Judson, 1996. Each chapter in this book raises an issue regarding East Asian culture in a North American context (e.g., community, worship, identity, women's roles). Short stories of personal experience are told around this theme followed by questions and analysis from a Christian perspective. This is an excellent resource for group discussion.

Niebuhr, H. Richard. *Christ and Culture.* New York: Harper & Brothers, 1951. In this classic work Niebuhr surveys and evaluates Christians' engagement with culture through the centuries. Niebuhr sets forth five basic categories or types: "Christ against culture," "Christ of culture," "Christ above culture," "Christ and culture in paradox," and "Christ the transformer of culture." This book has defined the terms of discussion for Christianity's relation to culture and Christian ethics for over five decades.

_____. *The Meaning of Revelation.* New York: Macmillan, 1941. Another classic by Niebuhr, this book situates revelation within the historical perspective of the believer's experience. He offers an existential view of revelation which is not dependent on historical objectivity.

Norman, Edward. *Secularisation: New Century Theology.* London: Continuum, 2002. Norman provides an "insider's" diagnosis of the decline of the Anglican Church in contemporary Britain.

Oduyoye, Mercy Amba, and Hendrik M. Vroom. *One Gospel—Many Cultures.* Amsterdam: World Alliance of Reformed Churches, 2003. Perhaps one of the best international collections on the subject of Christianity's engagement with a wide variety of the world's cultures. Culture and gender diversity are represented well by the contributors.

The Other Journal: An Intersection of Theology and Culture. Available online at http://www.theotherjournal.com. This journal describes itself as "an online quarterly publication that promotes vibrant discourse at the intersections of theology and culture."

Peck, M. Scott. *A World Waiting to Be Born: Civility Rediscovered.* New York: Bantam, 1993. Following Peck's earlier work on community, this work uses the term "civility" as a paradigm for what is missing in Western dominant culture. His startling conclusions regarding the church's negative reaction towards building true community are found at the end of the last chapter.

Peelman, Achiel. *Christ is a Native American.* Ottawa, Canada: Novalis-Saint Paul University; Maryknoll, N.Y.: Orbis, 1995. Peelman writes that there can be no truly Native American church until we can envision a Native American Christ. After reviewing the complex interactions between Native American peoples and Christianity over the years, he turns to a deductive approach built on "local theologies" gathered from conversations with Native American Christians across Canada. His research lays the groundwork for a Native American Christology.

Pelikan, Jaroslav. *Jesus Through the Centuries: His Place in the History of Culture.* New Haven: Yale University Press, 1999. Distinguished church historian Jaroslav Pelikan traces how each era has represented Christ in accordance with its own defining characteristic traits. The work analyzes the significance of Jesus for Western culture over the past two millennia. Predominant images include Jesus as rabbi, monk, poet, and liberator. This is an important work for anyone interested in studying Jesus' impact on culture and culture's impact on our understanding of Jesus.

Percy, Martyn. *Engaging with Contemporary Culture: Christianity, Theology and the Concrete Church.* Explorations in Practical, Pastoral and Empirical Theology Series. Aldershot: Ashgate, 2005. By pointing out that churches themselves are cultures, Percy rejects the notion that theology can stay "opposed to culture." Instead, he calls for a "practical theology" which both engages surrounding cultures and values past traditions. Written from an Anglican/Catholic background, the book shows how secular tools such as sociology can be used to create a "concrete church" that is grounded in reality and can relate better to a largely secular population.

Phan, Peter C. *In Our Own Tongues: Perspectives from Asia on Mission and Inculturation.* Maryknoll, N.Y.: Orbis, 2003. Phan presents a collection of his former essays dealing with Asian missions and inculturation from a Catholic perspective. They are grouped into three categories: missions and the church, both in theory and as practiced in Asia, Asian popular religion, worship, and prayer, and finally theology done in the Asian context.

Pittman, Don A., Ruben L. F. Habito, and Terry C. Muck, eds. *Ministry and Theology in Global Perspective: Contemporary Challenges for the Church.* Grand Rapids: Eerdmans, 1996. Edited by a mainline Protestant, a Roman Catholic, and an Evangelical, this volume brings together contributions from diverse time periods, diverse Christian perspectives, diverse people groups, and diverse faiths to treat the mission of the church in a global context. Over sixty readings compiled from various sources cover topics ranging from Christian views of other faiths to mission and dialogue with peoples and religions around the world.

Pullapilly, Cyriac K. et al, eds. *Christianity and Native Cultures: Perspectives from Different Regions of the World*. Notre Dame: Cross Cultural, 2004. The essays in this collection are the product of a 2002 conference on Christianity and native culture held at St. Mary's College. Scholars from diverse backgrounds present essays grouped by geographic region on concrete examples of contextualization from all around the world.

Regan, Hilary D., and Alan J. Torrance, eds. *Christ and Context: The Confrontation between Gospel and Culture*. Edinburgh: T. & T. Clark, 1993. The papers and responses collected here were presented at an international theological symposium hosted by New Zealand's University of Otago. Issues raised include the complexity of defining truth in the midst of diverse cultural perspectives, the contributions of liberation and feminist theology, the Christian transformation of culture, and Christology that bears on the ecological crisis. Among the contributors are Gustavo Gutiérrez, Jürgen Moltmann, John De Gruchy, Johann Metz, and Elisabeth Moltmann-Wendel.

Roberts, Bob Jr. *Glocalization: How Followers of Jesus Engage the New Flat World*. Grand Rapids: Zondervan, 2007. Roberts sees the growing trend of "glocalization" (connectedness through technology, travel, commerce, and other factors) as the newest and most important horizon for Christians. His book offers a how-to manual for the church to seize this important moment in history.

Robertson, Roland. *Globalization: Social Theory and Global Culture*. London: Sage, 1992. This is an excellent introduction to the complex streams that feed into the process of cultural globalization.

Romanowski, William D. *Eyes Wide Open: Looking for God in Popular Culture*. Grand Rapids: Brazos, 2001. Romanowski calls for an appreciation of God's presence in the arts (particularly film media) as well as an appeal to Christian artists to produce God-honoring quality work that presents the realities of our struggles as human beings.

Sample, Tex. *The Spectacle of Worship in a Wired World*. Nashville: Abingdon, 1998. This is a helpful text for understanding the ways post-World War II generations are *wired* in an age that has moved beyond both oral and literate culture to "electronic culture." Sample examines the importance of moving from words to images, understanding sound in terms of beat, and accounting for visualization in an age dominated by the screen, and he applies a convergence of these practices to Christian worship in our "wired world."

Sanneh, Lamin. *Disciples of All Nations: Pillars of World Christianity*. Oxford: Oxford University Press, 2008. Sanneh celebrates the rise of global Christianity in the post-colonial world. His work takes a historical perspective, beginning with the emergence of Christianity as a *world* religion in imperial Rome and moving through European Christianity's engagement with Islam in the Middle Ages to the colonial period. Sanneh then considers Christianity's radical shift from Europe and North America to Asia, Africa, and Latin America, and the impact post-colonial Christianity has had on those continents and will have on cultural innovation and change for the church. He draws attention to several themes or "pillars" that undergird world Christianity.

_____. *Whose Religion is Christianity?* Grand Rapids: Eerdmans, 2003. Sanneh employs a question and answer format to introduce his views of post-colonial world Christianity, particularly in his native Africa. The final section of the book is concerned with the promises and challenges of vernacular translation of the Bible.

Sarna, Jonathan D., ed. *Minority Faiths and the American Protestant Mainstream*. Urbana: University of Illinois Press, 1998. The chapters of this book, written by scholars of various perspectives, focus on the critical period in the history of American religion from 1860 to

1920 in which minority faiths such as Judaism, Catholicism, and Mormonism found themselves in a world dominated by the Protestant mainstream. The first half of the book describes these minorities' survival strategies while the second half explores areas of conflict between minority and majority faiths.

Schultze, Quentin. *Televangelism and American Culture: The Business of Popular Religion.* Eugene: Wipf & Stock, 2003. Quentin Schultze examines how the marketing culture espoused by televangelism has impacted popular religion and the church. He critiques our faith in the saving power of technology, effective marketing, and cults of personality.

Smith, Efrem, and Phil Jackson. *The Hip-Hop Church: Connecting with the Movement Shaping Our Culture.* Downers Grove, Ill.: InterVarsity, 2005. Smith and Jackson present a practical example of how contextualization of Christ can occur by showing both in theory and personal experience how Christ can use hip-hop to reach an entire generation. First they dissect the hip-hop culture, which is often thought of as averse to Christianity, and then show how it can be and has been used by the church as a tool for Christ.

Smith, James K. A. *Who's Afraid of Postmodernism? Taking Derrida, Lyotard, and Foucault to Church (The Church and Postmodern Culture).* Grand Rapids: Baker, 2006. This book is intended as an introduction to cultural postmodernism for pastors, youth pastors, and others engaged in ministry in our culture. This is a readable guide to the philosophical background, illustrated with reference to recent well-known films and with clear discussion of the implications for ministry. Smith tells us that the way forward involves a return to ancient practices of the church.

Spina, Frank Anthony. *The Faith of the Outsider.* Grand Rapids: Eerdmans, 2005. Spina shows how God's election of Israel moves toward the inclusion of the outsider in the stories of seven biblical figures: Esau, Tamar, Rahab, Naaman, Jonah, Ruth, and the woman at the well.

Stassen, Glen H., D. M. Yeager, and John Howard Yoder. *Authentic Transformation: A New Vision of Christ and Culture.* Nashville: Abingdon, 1996. This work is dedicated to advancing ethical reflection beyond H. Richard Niebuhr's influential work *Christ and Culture*. This set of essays offers a critical analysis of Niebuhr's five classic types of Christ's relation to culture and seeks to show how the church itself must be the central agent in the transformation of culture. Concrete Christian practices receive special attention as necessary instruments for this transformation process whereby the church maintains faithful witness to Christ in the surrounding culture.

Stott, John R. W. *The Message of the Sermon on the Mount—Matthew 5–7: Christian Counter-Culture.* Downers Grove, Ill.: InterVarsity, 1978. Eminent evangelical Anglican preacher and teacher John R. W. Stott here argues that the Sermon on the Mount is the most thorough account of the Christian counter-culture set forth in the NT. Stott interprets the text with keen insight and relates it to contemporary life.

Sugden, Chris. *Gospel, Culture and Transformation.* Regnum Studies in Mission. Oxford: Regnum, 2000. Sugden provides a critique of the work of the late Indian Canon Dr. Vinay Samuel as well as providing a reprint of some of Dr. Samuel's own work on the subject of missions in India.

Sugirtharajah, R. S. *The Bible and the Third World: Precolonial, Colonial and Postcolonial Encounters.* Cambridge: Cambridge University Press, 2001. Sugirtharajah sweeps through the history of India, China, and Africa, examining the relationships of these cultures to the Bible during these three periods. During the colonial period the Bible is considered for its role in the hands of both the colonizer and the colonized while postcolonial topics include indigenization, vernacular hermeneutics, and liberation readings.

Sweet, Leonard, ed. *The Church in Emerging Culture*. Grand Rapids: Zondervan, 2003. This book is the product of a conference of Emerging Church leaders. Instead of a mere collection of essays, it represents actual discussion of the ideas and questions in individual presentations about the church's mission in post-modernity. The participants are Andy Crouch, Michael Horton, Fredrica Mathews-Green, Brian D. McLaren, and Erwin Raphael McManus.

Takenaka, Masao. *God is Rice: Asian Culture and Christian Faith*. Geneva: World Council of Churches, 1986. This volume includes four lectures that reflect on Christian faith in the light of Japanese culture. Takenaka interacts especially with ideals and forms of Japanese art. He was well known as an ecumenical leader in Asia and helped found the Asian Christian Art Association in 1978.

Tanner, Kathryn. *Theories of Culture: A New Agenda for Theology*. Minneapolis: Fortress, 1997. This is a helpful work that lays out major contemporary culture theories and views Christianity as the rituals of others "made odd."

Tarr, Del. *Double Image: Biblical Insights from African Parables*. New York: Paulist, 1994. Stories and parables from West Africa are collected in this volume to shed light on the similarly agrarian world of Jesus and the Gospels. This book illustrates how different world views affect interpretation of Scripture and offers a perspective vastly different from a Western industrial reading. Highly recommended for pastors, teachers, and those who want to deepen their understanding of scriptural imagery.

Theissen, Gerd. *The Bible and Contemporary Culture*. Minneapolis: Fortress, 2007. The title of the first major section of this book, "Why Any Educated Person Should Know the Bible," makes its intentions clear. Theissen argues that understanding the core themes and essentials of the Bible is required for understanding our own culture and for engaging other cultures and religious perspectives in a pluralistic world. It provides a compelling argument for the significance of the Bible for those outside a community of faith and those within one.

Tillich, Paul. *Theology of Culture*. Edited by Robert C. Kimball. Oxford: Oxford University Press, 1959. Often recognized as *the* theologian of culture in his day, Paul Tillich's collection of essays in this volume reflects his theological and philosophical paradigm's bearing on a variety of cultural concerns.

Tomlinson, John. *Globalization and Culture*. Chicago: University of Chicago Press, 1999. This book analyzes the cultural, social, and moral aspects of globalization. The author discusses time and space concerns, cultural imperialism, "deterritorialization," and communication technologies and urges greater respect for cultural differences and a deeper sense of commitment outside our own borders.

Turner, Victor. *The Ritual Process: Structure and Anti-Structure*. Chicago: Aldine, 1969. Turner's classic work on ritual introduces the topics of liminality and *communitas* from an anthropological perspective.

Tutu, Desmond. *An African Prayer Book*. New York: Doubleday, 1995. Prayers of adoration, contrition, thanksgiving, supplication, and daily life from across the continent and the African diaspora.

Twiss, Richard. *One Church, Many Nations*. Ventura, Calif.: Regal, 2000. After briefly providing an account of Christianity among native peoples in America, Twiss shares his vision for a church of "first nations," in which people can fully express themselves outside a Western paradigm and can also evangelize the rest of the world.

Van Gelder, Craig, ed. *Confident Witness—Changing World*. Grand Rapids, Eerdmans, 1999. Twenty-two scholars and ministers from diverse Christian backgrounds wrestle with the mission of the church in North America, where cultural shifts have left churches marginalized. The contributors to this volume emphasize opportunities for applied mission in our postmodern context.

Vanhoozer, Kevin, Charles A. Anderson, and Michael J. Sleasman, eds. *Everyday Theology: How to Read Cultural Texts and Interpret Trends.* Grand Rapids: Baker, 2007. *Everyday Theology* intends to help Christians with cultural exegesis, bringing theology to bear on their surroundings in a way that is culturally sensitive. This is the first book in the Cultural Exegesis series.

Vrame, Anton C., and Cory Dixon, eds. *Essays on Faith and Culture.* Berkley, Calif.: InterOrthodox, 2003. Four essays present an Eastern Orthodox perspective on contextualization and deal with both historical and contemporary topics. Historical topics include how the Eastern Fathers dealt with Christ and culture and how inculturation took place in Russia during its conversion. Contemporary topics treat the difficulty of translating Greek liturgies into English and the struggle of women in today's Orthodox Church.

Wainwright, Geoffrey. "Types of Spirituality," in *The Study of Spirituality.* Edited by Cheslyn Jones, Geoffrey Wainwright, and Edward Yarnold. New York: Oxford University Press, 1986. In this essay Duke theologian Geoffrey Wainwright borrows H. Richard Niebuhr's categories for Christ's relationship to culture to describe various views of Christian spirituality through the centuries. Not only does the essay shed light on various spiritual traditions within the church, but it also illumines Niebuhr's own classic study *Christ and Culture.*

Ward, Graham. *Christ and Culture.* Challenges in Contemporary Theology Series. Oxford: Blackwell, 2005. Instead of offering a systematic approach to contextualized theology, Ward presents a collection of former essays which represent his thoughts on the notion of incarnation and its inherent nature as contextualized in several different arenas. He offers theories on contextualization in the abstract more than specific examples of how contextualization might occur. It is a technical read.

Webber, Robert. *The Secular Saint: A Case for Evangelical Social Responsibility.* Eugene: Wipf & Stock Publishers, 2004. Webber analyzes the age-old tension of Christ and culture from a biblical and historical perspective. The biblical discussion assists the reader in making sense of Judeo-Christian cultural concerns, while the historical material assists the reader in grasping the various ways in which the church through the ages has responded to the surrounding culture. Webber provides the reader with biblical and historical principles and patterns so as to address contemporary issues meaningfully.

Winter, Bruce W. *Seek the Welfare of the City: Christians as Benefactors and Citizens.* Grand Rapids: Eerdmans, 1994. Winter challenges the perception that early Christians in the Roman Empire sought to withdraw from society. He interacts with the NT, Greco-Roman primary sources, and recent socio-historical research to show that first-century Christians participated as citizens and benefactors in the public sphere.

Wirzba, Norman, ed. *The Essential Agrarian Reader: The Future of Culture, Community, and the Land.* Lexington: University Press of Kentucky, 2003. An excellent collection of essays from agrarian writers of two generations which shows the current scope of the discussion.

Wright, Christopher. *The Mission of God: Unlocking the Bible's Grand Narrative.* Downers Grove, Ill.: InterVarsity, 2006. This masterful work follows the theme of *missio Dei* in detail through both Testaments.

NORTH PARK THEOLOGICAL SEMINARY

SYMPOSIUM ON THE THEOLOGICAL INTERPRETATION OF SCRIPTURE

SEPTEMBER 27–29, 2007

CHRISTIANITY'S ENGAGEMENT WITH CULTURE

THE PRESENTERS

SATHIANATHAN CLARKE
   Wesley Theological Seminary, Theology

ELLEN DAVIS
   Duke Divinity School, Old Testament

PAUL DE NEUI
   North Park Theological Seminary, Missions

BOAZ JOHNSON
   North Park University, Old Testament

ROB JOHNSTON
   Fuller Theological Seminary, Theology and Culture

ANDREW MBUVI
   Shaw University Divinity School, New Testament

PAUL METZGER
   Multnomah Biblical Seminary, Theology and Culture

OSVALDO PADILLA
   Trinity Evangelical Divinity School, New Testament

DAVID TIEDE
   Augsburg College, New Testament

THE RESPONDENTS

G. SUJIN PAK
    Garrett-Evangelical Theological Seminary, Church History

JIM DEKKER
    North Park University, Youth Ministry

VELDA LOVE
    North Park University, Justice Center

AMANDA BECKENSTEIN MBUVI
    Duke Divinity School, Ph.D. Student

OSVALDO PADILLA
    Trinity Evangelical Divinity School, New Testament

SOONG-CHAN RAH
    North Park Theological Seminary, Church Growth and Evangelism

LUIS R. RIVERA
    McCormick Theological Seminary, New Testament

FRANK M. YAMADA
    Seabury-Western Theological Seminary, Old Testament

EX AUDITU

Volumes Available

Ex Auditu Vol. 1 (1985) consists of selected articles presenting the issues inherent in the theological interpretation of Scripture.

Ex Auditu Vol. 2 (1986) discusses the theme: "Church and State Relationship." In addition there are two lead articles, one by Peter Stuhlmacher on "EX AUDITU and the Theological Interpretation of Holy Scripture," and the second by Ben F. Meyer on "The Primacy of Consent and the Uses of Suspicion."

Ex Auditu Vol. 3	(1987)	"Creation."
Ex Auditu Vol. 4	(1988)	"The Church and Israel (Romans 9-11)."
Ex Auditu Vol. 5	(1989)	"What is Salvation?"
Ex Auditu Vol. 6	(1990)	"Prophetic and/or Apocalyptic Eschatology."
Ex Auditu Vol. 7	(1991)	"Christology and Incarnation"
Ex Auditu Vol. 8	(1992)	"Worship."
Ex Auditu Vol. 9	(1993)	"Resurrection."
Ex Auditu Vol. 10	(1994)	"The Church."
Ex Auditu Vol. 11	(1995)	"Biblical Law and Liberty."
Ex Auditu Vol. 12	(1996)	"Holy Spirit."
Ex Auditu Vol. 13	(1997)	"What is a Human?"
Ex Auditu Vol. 14	(1998)	"The Theological Significance of the Earthly Jesus."
Ex Auditu Vol. 15	(1999)	"Idolatry and the Understanding of God."
Ex Auditu Vol. 16	(2000)	"The Task of Interpreting Scripture Theologically."
Ex Auditu Vol. 17	(2001)	"Biblical Ethics."
Ex Auditu Vol. 18	(2002)	"Spiritual Formation."
Ex Auditu Vol. 19	(2003)	"The Authority and Function of Scripture."
Ex Auditu Vol. 20	(2004)	"Judgment."
Ex Auditu Vol. 21	(2005)	"Health and Healing."
Ex Auditu Vol. 22	(2006)	"Justice."
Ex Auditu Vol. 23	(2007)	"Christianity's Engagement with Culture."

Pickwick Publications
An imprint of Wipf & Stock Publishers
199 West 8th Avenue, Ste. 3
Eugene OR 97401

www.ingramcontent.com/pod-product-compliance
Lightning Source LLC
Chambersburg PA
CBHW081351230426
43667CB00017B/2795